INTERNATIONAL MONETARY AND FINANCIAL ISSUES FOR THE 1990s

Research papers for the Group of Twenty-Four

VOLUME XI

UNITED NATIONS
New York and Geneva, 1999

Note

Symbols of United Nations documents are composed of capital letters combined with figures. Mention of such a symbol indicates a reference to a United Nations document.

*

* *

The views expressed in this compendium are those of the authors and do not necessarily reflect the views of the UNCTAD secretariat. The designations employed and the presentation of the material do not imply the expression of any opinion whatsoever on the part of the Secretariat of the United Nations concerning the legal status of any country, territory, city or area, or of its authorities, or concerning the delimitation of its frontiers or boundaries.

*

* *

Material in this publication may be freely quoted; acknowledgement, however, is requested (including reference to the document number). It would be appreciated if a copy of the publication containing the quotation were sent to the Editorial Assistant, UNCTAD, Division on Globalization and Development Strategies, Palais des Nations, CH-1211 Geneva 10.

UNCTAD/GDS/MDPB/6

UNITED NATIONS PUBLICATION
Sales No. E.99.II.D.25
ISBN 92-1-112465-4 ISSN 1020-329X
Copyright © United Nations, 1999 All rights reserved

Editorial note

This volume concludes the series *International Monetary and Financial Issues for the 1990s*, published in the context of the UNCTAD project on technical support to the Intergovernmental Group of Twenty-Four on International Monetary Affairs. From the year 2000 onwards the studies prepared under this project will be individually published, jointly by UNCTAD and Harvard University, in a new series entitled *G-24 Papers on International Monetary and Financial Issues*.

Contents

ADEQUACY OF INTERNATIONAL LIQUIDITY IN THE CURRENT FINANCIAL ENVIRONMENT

Aziz Ali Mohammed 51

ORDERLY WORKOUTS FOR CROSS-BORDER PRIVATE DEBT

Steven Radelet 61

SOCIAL FUNDS IN STABILIZATION AND ADJUSTMENT PROGRAMMES

STRENGTHENING DEVELOPING COUNTRIES IN THE WTO

Abbreviations

AfDB	African Development Bank
AMF	Asian Monetary Fund
APEC	Asia-Pacific Economic Cooperation
ASEAN	Association of South-East Asian Nations
BCBS	Basle Committee on Banking Supervision
BIS	Bank for International Settlements
BIT	bilateral investment treaty
BWIs	Bretton Woods institutions
CFA	Communauté financière africaine
CPSS	Committee on Payment and Settlement Systems
DAC	Development Assistance Committee (of OECD)
DFI	development finance institution
EC	European Commission
ECSC	Euro-currency Standing Committee
EDG	Employment Guarantee Scheme
EFM	Emergency Financing Mechanism
EIB	European Investment Bank
EMTs	economic management teams
EMU	European Monetary Union
EPU	European Payments Union
ERM	European Exchange Rate Mechanism
ESAF	Enhanced Structural Adjustment Facility
ESAL	Emergency Structural Adjustment Lending
EU	European Union
FDI	foreign direct investment
FFIEC	Federal Financial Institutions Examination Council
FICORCA	Fideicomiso Para la Cobertura de los Riesgos Cambiaros
FSA	Financial Supervisory Authority
FY	fiscal year
GAB	General Arrangement to Borrow
GATS	General Agreement on Trade in Services
GATT	General Agreement on Tariffs and Trade
GCI	General Capital Increase
GDP	gross domestic product
GNP	gross national product
HIPCs	heavily indebted poor countries
HLIs	highly leveraged institutions
IAIS	International Association of Insurance Supervisors
IBRD	International Bank for Reconstruction and Development
ICSID	International Centre for Settlement of Investment Disputes
IDA	International Development Association
IFDI	inward foreign direct investment
IFI	international financial institutions
IIF	Institute of International Finance
IMF	International Monetary Fund
IOSCO	International Organization of Securities Commissions
IPRs	intellectual property rights

LBRP	Labour-Based Relief Programme
LDCs	least developed countries
LLR	lender of last resort
MEGS	Maharastra Employment Guarantee Scheme (India)
MERCOSUR	Southern Cone Common Market
MFI	Multilateral Framework on Investment
MFN	most favoured nation
MIGA	Multilateral Investment Guarantee Agency
MTNs	multilateral trade negotiations
NAB	New Arrangements to Borrow
NAFTA	North American Free Trade Agreement
NGO	non-governmental organization
NIE	newly industrializing economy
ODA	official development assistance
ODI	Overseas Development Institute
OECD	Organization for Economic Co-operation and Development
OPEC	Organization of Petroleum Exporting Countries
OSFI	Office of the Superintendent of Financial Institutions
PEM	Minimum Employment Programme
PFP	Policy Framework Paper
PINs	Public Information Notices
R&D	research and development
S&D	special and differential (treatment)
S&L	Saving and Loan
SAF	Structural Adjustment Facility
SAL	structural adjustment loan
SAP	Structural Adjustment Programme
SDR	Special Drawing Right
SE	social expenditure
SEC	Securities and Exchange Commission
SECALs	Sector Adjustment Loans
SEFs	Social Emergency Funds
SFs	Social Funds
SIF	Social Investment Fund
SILICs	severely indebted low-income countries
SoAP	Social Action Programme
SORP	Statement of Recommended Accounting Practice
SRF	Supplemental Reserve Facility
SSA	sub-Saharan Africa
TNC	transnational corporation
TRIM	Trade-Related Investment Measure
TRIP	Trade-Related Intellectual Property Right
UDROP	universal debt roll-over option with a penalty
UNDP	United Nations Development Programme
WDR	World Development Report
WTO	World Trade Organization

The authors

- **Montek S. Ahluwalia**, Member of the Planning Commission in the Government of India

- **Kwesi Botchwey**, Director, Africa Programs and Research, Harvard Institute for International Development, Cambridge, MA

- **Andrew Cornford**, Economic Adviser to the Division on Globalization and Development Strategies, UNCTAD, Geneva

- **Giovanni Andrea Cornia**, Director, United Nations University/World Institute for Development Economics Research, Helsinki

- **Bhagirath Lal Das**, formerly Director of International Trade Programmes in UNCTAD, and former Ambassador and Permanent Representative of India to the GATT

- **Stephany Griffith-Jones**, Institute of Development Studies, University of Sussex, Brighton, United Kingdom

- **Jenny Kimmis**, Institute of Development Studies, University of Sussex, Brighton, United Kingdom

- **Steven Radelet**, Harvard Institute for International Development, Harvard University, Cambridge, MA

- **William Milberg**, Department of Economics, New School for Social Research, New York

- **Aziz Ali Mohammed**, G-24 Liaison Office, Washington, DC

Preface

The Intergovernmental Group of Twenty-Four on International Monetary Affairs (G-24) was established in November 1971 to increase the negotiating strength of the developing countries in discussions that were going on at that time in the International Monetary Fund on reform of the international monetary system. Developing countries felt that they should play a meaningful role in decisions about the system, and that the effectiveness of that role would be enhanced if they were to meet regularly as a group, as the developed countries had been doing for some time in the Group of Ten (G-10).

It soon became apparent that the G-24 was in need of technical support and analysis relating to the issues arising for discussion in the Fund and Bank, including the Interim and Development Committees. In response to representations by the Chairman of the G-24 to the Secretary-General of the United Nations Conference on Trade and Development (UNCTAD), and following discussions between UNCTAD and the United Nations Development Programme (UNDP), the latter agreed in 1975 to establish a project to provide the technical support that the G-24 had requested. This was to take the form, principally, of analytical papers prepared by competent experts on issues currently under consideration in the fields of international money and finance.

Mr. Sidney Dell, a former Director in UNCTAD's Money, Finance and Development Division and subsequently Assistant Administrator of UNDP headed the project from its establishment until 1990. During this period, some 60 research papers were prepared by the Group of Twenty-Four. The high quality of this work was recognized by the Deputies and Ministers of the Group and the reports were given wide currency, some being published in five volumes by North-Holland Press and others by the United Nations.

The project work was resumed in 1990 under the direction of Gerry K. Helleiner, Professor of Economics, University of Toronto, Canada. The UNCTAD secretariat provides both substantive and administrative backstopping to the project. Funding is currently being provided by the G-24 countries themselves, the International Development Research Centre of Canada and the Governments of Denmark and the Netherlands. As a result, it has been possible to continue to provide the Group of Twenty-Four with timely and challenging analyses. These studies are being reissued periodically in compendia. This is the eleventh volume to be published.

THE IMF AND THE WORLD BANK IN THE NEW FINANCIAL ARCHITECTURE

Montek S. Ahluwalia*

Abstract

The frequency of crises in recent years has drawn attention to the weaknesses in the international financial system and rekindled interest in its reform. At first, the crisis in East Asia, followed by the collapse in the Russian Federation, with spillover effects on Wall Street, created a widespread perception that the existing system was hopelessly inadequate and a radical reform was needed. This was the spirit of Prime Minister Blair's impassioned call for "building a Bretton Woods for the new millennium", which raised expectations of a major institutional restructuring. More recently, as financial markets have stabilized, the initial enthusiasm for radical reform has subsided and the ongoing discussions on the new financial architecture have a more limited scope. They focus on ways of improving surveillance in international financial markets, strengthening the financial system in developing countries, and increasing transparency and the flow of information to private markets to allow them to function better. Talk of restructuring the Bretton Woods institutions for the new millennium has given way to a more modest objective of strengthening cooperation between the International Monetary Fund and the World Bank to increase their effectiveness in crisis prevention and crisis management.

The Fund and the Bank have a long history of cooperation, and one can certainly build on this tradition to improve their capacity to meet future challenges. However, the nature of cooperation in the future need not be a simple extrapolation of the past. The challenges facing the international financial system today are quite different from those of the past, and it is precisely because of these differences that there is a need for a new financial architecture. The purpose of this paper is to evaluate the impact of developments on the relative roles of the Fund and the Bank in the future. The paper is divided into four sections. Section I provides a brief overview of the changing roles of the Fund and the Bank in the past which led to a considerable overlap in their activities in the 1980s. Section II summarizes why the crises of the 1990s are fundamentally different from earlier episodes of balance-of-payments difficulties and therefore call for very different responses. Section III discusses some of the main elements which have been proposed as part of the new financial architecture and examines their implications for the roles of the Fund and the Bank. Section IV presents a summary assessment of various proposals for improving coordination between the Fund and the Bank currently under consideration and evaluates their relevance in the light of the larger reforms needed in the system.

* The views expressed are those of author and do not necessarily reflect the views of the Government of India. Acknowledgements are due to Yilmaz Akyüz, Gerry Helleiner, Deena Khatkhate, Sarwar Latif and Narendra Jadhav for useful comments on an earlier draft.

I.   Evolution of the overlap between the Fund and the Bank

The Fund and the Bank were originally established as part of the international financial architecture created at Bretton Woods, based on the system of "fixed but adjustable par values". Under this system countries undertook two critical commitments: (i) to maintain their exchange rates within a very narrow range of the declared par values, to be changed only with the prior approval of the Fund; and (ii) to eschew restrictions on current payments. These commitments reflected the determination of participating countries at the time to avoid the debilitating experience of the inter-war years when competitive devaluations and exchange restrictions produced a downward spiral in world trade. Restrictions on current payments were seen to be antithetical to the expansion of trade and were therefore to be avoided, but the system did not seek to eliminate or even regulate restrictions on capital account transactions which were in place in most countries and were expected to continue.

A.   *The first phase: distinct identities*

The Bretton Woods architecture envisaged very different roles for the International Monetary Fund and the World Bank. The Fund was established to be the guardian of the par value system and was expected to oversee its operation, ensuring that countries complied with the commitments undertaken by them. It also stood ready to provide short-term finance, subject to appropriate macroeconomic conditionality, to help countries deal with temporary balance-of-payments problems in a manner which would not be "destructive of national and international prosperity". As supervisor of the system as well as a financier, the Fund dealt with both industrialized and developing countries and its approach to managing balance-of-payments problems was very similar in both cases.

The World Bank's original function was the financing of reconstruction in war-torn countries and development in developing countries. The former was quickly taken over by Marshall Aid and the Bank settled down at a very early stage to the task of financing projects in developing countries. It was expected to finance projects which were economically viable but which otherwise might not be financed because of the scarcity of domestic resources and the difficulty in obtaining external finance since international capital markets were relatively undeveloped at the time. Bank financing was generally accompanied by project-level conditionality which occasionally also extended to sector-level policies, but it did not involve macroeconomic conditionality. The Bank did make regular assessments of development policies and prospects of individual borrowing countries, but this was primarily to establish the creditworthiness of the borrower and not with a view to specifying conditionalities for its lending.[1] Unlike in the case of the Fund, the Bank's membership was asymmetric, distinguishing between borrowing and non-borrowing members, with the Bank lending only to the former.

The two institutions functioned with very little overlap for the first 25 years of their existence, as each provided finance which was for different purposes and was linked to very different types of policy conditionality. However, development finance can never be completely divorced from macroeconomic policy and there were some jurisdictional overlaps in the early years.[2] Recognition of the possibility of overlapping activities led to the issuance in 1966 of formal guidelines for Fund-Bank collaboration, demarcating areas of primary responsibility for each institution. The Fund was assigned primary responsibility for "exchange rates and restrictive systems, for adjustment of temporary balance-of-payments disequilibria, and for evaluating and assisting members to work out stabilization programmes as a sound basis for economic advance". The Bank was assigned primary responsibility for "the composition and appropriateness of development programmes and project evaluation including development priorities".

The 1966 guidelines recognized that between these two "clear cut areas of responsibility" there were other areas of interest to both institutions, e.g. the structure and functioning of financial institutions, the adequacy of money and capital markets, the capacity to generate domestic savings, external financing and external debt, and that in these areas each institution would form its own view and differences were implicitly accepted. However, in the event of a conflict of views in an area within the primary responsibility of one institution, the view of that institution would prevail over that of the other. These issues could be discussed between the two institutions, but the guidelines explicitly ruled out any critical review by one institution with a member country on issues within the primary responsibility of the other institution, except with the latters' prior consent.

B. The overlap in the 1980s

Changes in the world economy in the 1970s forced both the Fund and the Bank to reorient their activities in a manner which considerably increased the overlap between the two institutions in the 1980s. The role of the Fund changed dramatically after the collapse of the par value system in 1973. The shift by major currencies to floating rates, combined with the growth of capital markets, made the Fund irrelevant as a source of finance for industrialized countries. No major industrialized country borrowed from the Fund after 1976 and its financing role thereafter focused only on developing countries, with countries in transition being added in due course. The Fund responded to the needs of its exclusively developing country clientele by introducing several new facilities tailored to their special requirements, which had the effect of moving Fund financing closer to development financing of the type provided by the Bank.

The critical factor driving the change was the recognition that the balance-of-payments problems of many developing countries were of a structural nature and therefore very different from the traditional Fund conception in which balance-of-payments deficits were seen as a reflection of excess aggregate demand. Deficits caused by excess demand were obviously best handled by demand restraint, supplemented by exchange rate changes whenever it was felt necessary to stimulate the production of tradeables relative to non-tradeables. Adjustment was expected to be accomplished in a relatively short period of time, which is why IMF standby arrangements typically provided finance for a period of between one year and 18 months, to be repaid between three to five years after each drawing. This approach was inappropriate for developing countries suffering from structural constraints which limited their capacity to expand the production of tradeable goods. Reducing aggregate demand to reduce the current account deficit in this situation often led to underutilization of capacity and unemployment, which could not be countered by depreciating the exchange rate to stimulate the production of tradeables. Expanded production of tradeable goods could be achieved only by removing structural bottlenecks, which often required a period of increased investment, a process which would take time. This meant that current account deficits had to be financed over a longer period and the period of repayment also had to be extended. These considerations led to the establishment of the Extended Fund Facility (EFF) in 1974, which enabled developing countries to receive assistance over a three-year period (and therefore also

in a larger total amount) and extended the repayment period to between four and eight years, which was later extended to between four and 10 years.

Fund financing also moved closer to Bank financing because of the introduction of concessionality for low-income countries. In 1976 the Trust Fund was established, financed by profits on the sale of a part of the Fund's gold, to make medium-term loans (repayable over a period of between five and 10 years) to low-income countries at near zero interest rates and with weak conditionality.[3] Ten years later another concessional facility was introduced responding to the problems of low-income countries in Africa suffering from persistent economic stagnation after the oil shocks of the 1970s. It was recognized that revival of growth in these countries was possible only if larger balance-of-payments deficits could be financed, and that the financing had to be on concessional terms because their debt-servicing capacity was severely constrained. In 1986 the Fund established the Structural Adjustment Facility (SAF) to make loans to IDA-eligible countries at 0.5 per cent interest repayable between the fifth and tenth year after each drawing. This was followed a year later by the Enhanced Structural Adjustment Facility (ESAF), designed to provide a larger volume of resources on the same terms, but with more stringent conditions.[4]

The Bank also moved closer to Fund-type activity by shifting from its earlier exclusive focus on project financing to providing balance-of-payments support. Most developing countries experienced a mounting burden of debt following the oil crisis which created serious macroeconomic imbalances and led to a slowdown in growth by the end of the 1970s. The Bank's management came to the conclusion that it could make little impact on development in this situation if it continued to focus only on project lending. Weaknesses in macroeconomic and sectoral policies in the developing countries were seen to be at the root of their poor performance and unless these policy weaknesses were corrected it was felt that continued project lending could make little difference.[5] The Bank therefore introduced Structural Adjustment Loans (SALs) in 1980 to provide non-project tied assistance in support of wide-ranging policy reforms aimed at increasing the efficiency of resource use. The package of reforms typically covered tax policy, price decontrol, trade policy, privatization of public enterprises and reforms in the financial sector. In 1982 Sector Adjustment Loans (SECALs) were introduced with policy conditionality being more narrowly focused on a particular sector.

Since adjustment lending resembled balance-of-payments financing it created an obvious overlap with the Fund, with the possibility of conflict between the two institutions. To avoid conflict, it was clarified that SALs would deal with policy issues other than fiscal policy and exchange rates, which were the core areas of the Fund. Since fiscal and exchange rate issues could not be entirely avoided in formulating SALs, the Bank undertook to coordinate with the Fund on these issues in order to ensure that adjustment lending did not become a means of sustaining an unviable macroeconomic position. In fact, the expectation was that in practice SALs would generally be used in cases where a Fund programme was already in place.

For its part, the Fund recognized that its ESAF programmes for low income countries had to be firmly grounded in appropriate structural policies which could bring about sustainable growth. ESAF programmes were therefore preceded by consideration by the Board of a Policy Framework Paper (PFP), prepared jointly by country authorities and the staffs of the Bank and the Fund, which was expected to lay out the medium-term policy agenda to be followed by the country. Joint preparation of the PFP was intended to ensure full coordination with the Bank and also to ensure "ownership" by the country. In practice, it did achieve coordination between the two institutions, but for a variety of reasons, including the lack of capacity in many low-income countries, the success achieved as regards ownership is questionable.

Adjustment lending proved to be a useful innovation partly because it responded to developing country demands for more flexible conditionality than that usually associated with Fund programmes. Fund conditionality was typically limited to a few (at most 10) key macroeconomic policy variables and focused heavily on fiscal discipline and restraint on domestic credit expansion. Targets for each performance variable were precisely quantified by specifying particular levels of domestic credit, credit to the government, or reserves to be met at the end of each quarter, and failure to meet any one target could lead to drawings being interrupted. SAL conditionality was much broader, often covering as many as 30-50 policy actions in different areas![6] Instead of fixing specific compliance dates for policy action, SALs were tranched so that disbursement under each tranche could be effected once the agreed set of policy actions relating to that tranche had been taken. The Bank was generally also more flexible in determining compliance, relying on a broad assessment of whether the programme was on track. SECALs added a new dimension of flexibility since developing countries were able to obtain financing based on reforms in only one sector, where they might be more easily acceptable for domestic reasons. Adjustment lending increased rapidly, reaching about 25 per cent of Bank lending in the second half of the 1980s; and this is a measure of the extent of overlap between the two institutions.

A by-product of the overlap was the emergence of the so-called Washington Consensus, which sought to integrate the approaches of the Fund and the Bank. Sound development policy was sought to be defined as a combination of (i) macroeconomic balance (basically a low fiscal deficit), which was the traditional concern of the Fund, and was viewed as an essential precondition for growth, and (ii) efficiency-enhancing reforms (e.g. decontrolling private sector activity, opening the economy to trade and foreign investment, and privatizing the public sector as much as possible), which was the focus of the structural reform effort spearheaded by the Bank. The consensus was modified over time in response to criticism on some important points, e.g. the possibly negative effect of fiscal discipline, and sometimes also market-oriented reforms, on the poor. This led to a redefinition of the consensus to recognize that structural reforms must be supplemented by direct efforts at poverty alleviation by protecting certain types of government expenditure, e.g. in the social sectors, which were especially important for the poor and also by increasing expenditure on poverty alleviation programmes.

Developing countries were particularly concerned that a consensus on broad directions of policy should not degenerate into a "one size fits all" approach, and they consistently emphasized the need to tailor programmes to suit the circumstances and constraints of individual countries. Differences across countries could arise on issues of pace and sequencing, and also on the strategic importance of concentrating on particular areas. The Fund and the Bank also differed on these issues. The Fund typically placed much greater emphasis on fiscal balance, calling for relatively quick reductions in the fiscal deficit irrespective of how they were achieved, while the Bank focused much more on efficiency-enhancing reforms some of which could involve trade-offs with deficit reduction. The emphasis to be placed on tariff reduction as a structural reform measure at a time of fiscal stringency is an obvious example where the Bank was often in favour of a faster reduction in tariffs to reduce trade distortions even at the cost of a higher fiscal deficit, while the Fund tended to be much more concerned about the impact of such reductions on fiscal balance.

Conflict over Argentina and the Concordat of 1989

Despite the overlap there was no overt conflict between the Fund and the Bank until the celebrated case of Argentina in 1988, when the Bank decided to go ahead with adjustment lending even though negotiations with the IMF for an Extended Fund Facility had recently collapsed. In the Bank's view, the Fund was insisting on too strong a fiscal correction because of its traditional focus on aggregate demand, whereas the Bank, being more concerned about structural reforms, was willing to accept a less ambitious fiscal target. It is well known that the Bank's management was under pressure from the United States Treasury to go ahead with the loan.[7] In the event, the Fund's judgement was vindicated when it became clear, shortly after the approval of the adjustment loans by the Bank's Board, that Argentina would not be able to meet the expected criteria of fiscal performance and disbursements had to be interrupted.

The Argentina fiasco, as it has been described by Polak (1997), generated concern in several quarters. It was the first case where the Bank proceeded with adjustment lending despite a clear finding of macroeconomic unsustainability by the Fund staff. The Fund was understandably concerned that it might create a precedent which would encourage countries in difficulty to postpone or avoid taking necessary corrective steps, and seek support from the Bank as an easier alternative. This would undermine the credibility of the Fund as the established arbiter of what was needed to achieve macroeconomic stabilization and devalue its good housekeeping seal of approval. Also, the G-10 deputies were concerned about lack of coordination between the two institutions leading to the possibility of conflicting policy advice to the country concerned.

Intensive consultations ensued between the two institutions to resolve these problems and culminated in the so-called Bank-Fund Concordat of 1989, which superseded the earlier guidelines on Bank-Fund collaboration. The main features of the Concordat are summarized in box 1. It is significant that the Concordat did not seek to eliminate, or even reduce, the overlap between the Bank and the Fund. On the contrary, the overlap was accepted as a natural development given the changed circumstances of the world economy and the difficulties being experienced by so many developing countries. The Concordat focused instead on the limited objective of improving coordination between the Bank and the Fund and avoiding conflicting advice if possible, while preserving the independence of action of each institution.

In the event of a disagreement, the Concordat prescribed an extensive process of consultation but the final decision was left to be taken by the Executive Board of the institution concerned after hearing the view of the other institution. What this meant was that the management of one institution could not be vetoed by the management of the other, even if it differed on issues within the primary responsibility of the other institution. In such cases the Executive Board of the lending institution would have the right, after having heard the view of the other institution, to act independently.

II. The crises of the 1990s: new sources of fragility

Issues of coordination between the Fund and the Bank surfaced again at the time of the East Asian crisis as both institutions worked together to help crisis-hit countries. Each institution also introduced innovations in its lending policies to respond to the new situation. At first glance this can be viewed as a logical continuation of the overlap which had developed over the 1980s. However, there are significant differences between the crises of the 1990s and earlier payments problems suffered by developing countries, and these differences have important implications for the role of the two institutions in the future. A brief digression on the distinctive features of the new type of crisis is therefore appropriate.

A. Crises of confidence

Each of the major crises in the 1990s – Mexico in 1994, East Asia in 1997, the Russian Federation in 1998 and Brazil in 1999 – had features peculiar to itself, but they all shared an important common characteristic. They were crises of confidence originating in the capital account and therefore very different from earlier episodes of payments problems in developing countries which typically arose in the current account.[8] The vulnerability of developing countries to such crises has increased in the 1990s because many countries have liberalized restrictions on capital

Box 1

THE CONCORDAT OF 1989

The Concordat of 1989 defined each institution's area of "primary responsibility" more elaborately than in the 1966 guidelines.

• The Fund's areas of primary responsibility were "the aggregate aspects of macroeconomic policies and their related instruments – including public sector spending and revenues, aggregate wage and price policies, money and credit, interest rates and the exchange rate".

• The Bank's areas of primary responsibility were development strategies, sector and project investments, structural adjustment problems, policies dealing with the efficient allocation of resources, priorities in government expenditure, reforms of the administrative system, the production trade and financial sectors, the restructuring of state enterprises and issues related to creditworthiness. The mandate of the Bank specifically excluded the aggregate aspects of economic policies, which were the exclusive preserve of the Fund.

• It was recognized that both the Fund and the Bank had legitimate concerns with regard to macroeconomic and structural issues, and that each institution would need to undertake independent analysis of these issues and take the results into account in their policy advice and lending operations.

• Elaborate procedures were laid down to enhance coordination between the Bank and the Fund through periodic meetings at various official levels, including sharing of information between the two institutions. These procedures were designed to keep each institution aware of the views of the other on a more continuous basis. The Bank was expected to ascertain the view of the Fund on the adequacy of macroeconomic policies, before formulating its own opinion, even in cases where there was no Fund programme. Similar obligations were imposed on the Fund vis-à-vis the Bank with regard to developmental and structural policies.

• In the event of irreconcilable differences on a matter within the primary responsibility of one institution, the Concordat stipulated that "the institution which does not have primary responsibility would, except in 'exceptional circumstances', yield to the judgement of the other institution". Polak (1997) reports that the original draft prepared by the Fund had made it mandatory to yield in such cases but this was not acceptable to the Bank, and the present version with the exception clause was finally agreed. Exceptional circumstances were "expected to be rare", but when they did arise the managements were expected to consult their respective executive boards before proceeding.

• Each institution was also allowed to lend to a member in arrears to the other institution subject to appropriate consultation. The key consideration was that each institution would consider whether the arrears to the other were an indication that its own resources would not be safeguarded.

---

movements in order to integrate more fully into global financial markets and improve their access to international capital flows. While access has definitely improved, this has been achieved at the risk of greater volatility and instability. Financial markets have long been known to suffer from euphoria and panics which can create boom-bust cycles, and this applies to the international capital market also. Inflows can exceed the level warranted by underlying fundamentals when perceptions are favourable, as was clearly the case in East Asia before the crisis, but outflows can also be disproportionately large when perceptions change and there is a loss of confidence.

It is important to appreciate that the risks faced by developing countries integrating with global financial markets are substantially greater than for industrialized countries. One reason for this is that developing countries are objectively more vulnerable to changes in external economic circumstances and this is bound to be reflected in greater instability in investor perceptions. However, this "objectively justifiable" instability is magnified by information deficiencies. Investors, especially portfolio investors, typically have much less information about conditions in developing countries than in industrialized countries and this can exaggerate the response to negative developments, leading to greater volatility. Lack of information also increases the likelihood of herd behaviour and the risk of contagion, both of which intensify volatility. Developing countries not only face greater volatility, but they are also more vulnerable to any given level of volatility because of the thinness of their markets compared with the size of resources that can be moved by global investors. The same degree of volatility in capital flows therefore has a much greater impact on prices in developing country markets (both forex and equities) than in industrialized countries.

Instability is heightened by the fact that it is not easy to predict what can cause a crisis of confidence in a particular situation. One can be fairly sure that economies that are fundamentally strong on all counts are unlikely to become victims of panic behaviour. At the opposite end of the spectrum, economies that are visibly weak will invariably have problems, though such economies are more likely to suffer from chronic external payments difficulties rather than the danger of a sudden crisis. Between these extremes, however, there will be many countries where an otherwise strong economic performance may be suddenly clouded by the emergence of some weaknesses. If investor perceptions always changed as a continuous response to changes in economic fundamentals, inflows would dry up gradually as weaknesses emerged, giving clear warning signals and ample time to take corrective action. However, investor perceptions often change in a discontinuous fashion. A build-up of negative factors may be ignored for some time by investors in the belief that it is either temporary or will be corrected by appropriate policies, but if this does not happen perceptions can change suddenly, triggering a sudden reversal of capital flows. This can easily turn into a self-fulfilling panic in which the financial markets may fail to play a stabilizing role. Instead, the system is pushed from an initial equilibrium to another equilibrium which is much less favourable and from which recovery is not easy.[9]

What triggers a panic will vary from situation to situation. In Mexico, for example, vulnerability had built up over time with a steady deterioration in the current account, reaching 8 per cent of GDP in 1994, and a substantial real appreciation in the peso in the years preceding the crisis. The large current account deficit was not seen to be a problem at the time because it was financed by strong private inflows.[10] Perceptions changed in the course of the year because of a series of negative developments including a shift to a more expansionary macroeconomic policy, the assassination of a presidential candidate and the rebellion in the Chiappas region. Lack of transparency in disclosing the extent of reserve use in the course of the year intensified the strength of the negative investor reaction, which led to a large withdrawal of funds towards the end of the year.

East Asia's vulnerability arose from what we now know was a pervasive weakness in the financial sector, though this was completely missed by Fund surveillance and also by the World Bank, which had an extensive involvement in Indonesia and some involvement in Thailand. It was also missed by the international credit rating agencies which are an important source of information for financial markets. The only warning signals spotted by Fund surveillance in 1996 were the size of the current account deficit in Thailand and the real appreciation of the baht, and these were discussed by the Fund with the Thai authorities.[11] However, the depth of the crisis in Thailand and its spread to other countries as investors concluded that similar weaknesses were endemic, was certainly not anticipated.

The major factors which contributed to fragility in East Asia varied across countries and are summarized in box 2. They are clearly linked to weaknesses in the financial sector in the sense that a stronger financial system would have avoided many of the problems. Banks would not have lent so extensively to highly leveraged corporations, especially those with large volumes of unhedged foreign debt. They would also have avoided large unhedged exposure to foreign borrowing on their own account. This would have moderated foreign inflows in the earlier years by creating a more realistic perception of the returns on investment and the risks involved. It would also have avoided the very large build-up of short-term loans from international commercial banks which was an important source of vulnerability in all the affected countries.

Box 2

FACTORS UNDERLYING EAST ASIAN CRISIS

Many of the factors which contributed to the currency crisis in East Asia reflect weaknesses in the financial sectors of the countries of the region. There were variations from country to country, but the following factors were relevant over most of the region.

- Large private inflows, attracted by favourable investor perceptions, were channelled into unproductive domestic investments by banks and other financial intermediaries which were either too weak to undertake proper credit appraisal or were knowingly engaged in cronyism, or both.

- The financial system tolerated high debt-equity ratios which made corporations, and also the banks lending to them, highly vulnerable in the event of a downturn.

- Exchange risk was underestimated by both banks and corporations, possibly because of the experience of nominal exchange rate stability. This encouraged an excessive unhedged exposure to foreign borrowing, often short term.

- Total external debt was not high (except perhaps in Indonesia) but the ratio of short-term debt to foreign exchange reserves increased sharply in the years preceding the crisis. Banks in the Republic of Korea were actually encouraged to borrow short term as this segment was liberalized, while longer-term borrowing remained restricted. The offshore banking facilities in Thailand had the same effect. The build up of short-term debt added to vulnerability in the event of non-renewal of such loans.

- Lack of transparency also made surveillance ineffective and may have delayed adjustment. Thailand's intervention in forward exchange markets pre-committed much of Thailand's available reserves without this being known to the market. Similarly, the Republic of Korea's foreign exchange reserves were not effectively available because they had been lent to branches of the country's banks abroad to meet their short-term obligations. Earlier public disclosure of these actions would have led markets to change perception earlier, in which case the change may have been more gradual.

- Foreign banks lent excessively to East Asian banks possibly because of the perception that governments would ultimately guarantee these loans. Critics have argued that the Fund's Mexico bailout contributed to the perception that such loans were effectively government-guaranteed.

B.　*Managing the new type of crises*

Managing the new type of crisis poses special problems. A loss of confidence, whatever its cause, can be highly destabilizing because of the possibility of a large reversal of capital flows. Net positive inflows on which a country depended in order to finance the current account deficit may cease altogether, as new lending is held back. It may also become negative as short-term loans are not rolled over. The open capital account also makes it easier for domestic capital to flow out in anticipation of exchange rate depreciation.[12] Unlike the traditional balance-of-payments crises originating in the current account, in which pressure typically built up gradually, crises originating in the capital account can explode quite suddenly, creating a sudden need for financing with very little time to negotiate a programme. The volume of finance needed is much larger than earlier, and most of the financing is also generally needed up front if confidence is to be restored. If credible corrective policies are quickly put in place and enough financing is made available to calm markets, it may be possible to restore confidence relatively quickly, in which case capital flows may return relatively quickly to normal levels. In such

Table 1

FISCAL BALANCE TARGETS IN FUND PROGRAMMES

	Actual 1997	*Initial package*	*First revision*	*Second revision*	*Third revision*
Indonesia	0.2	1.0	-1.0	-3.0	-8.5
Malaysia	2.6	2.5	0.5	-3.5	--
Philippines	-0.9	0.0	-1.0	-3.0	--
Republic of Korea	0.3	0-0.3	--	-0.8	-1.8
Thailand	-0.9	1.0	1.0	-1.6	-2.4

Source: World Bank (1999).

situations it may not be necessary for the financing package mobilized to be fully disbursed and, even if it is, repayments can be made very rapidly from the restoration of normal capital flows. Unlike in the case of structural balance-of-payments problems, the financing needed for a crisis of confidence does not have to be long term and, in any case, certainly not concessional.

Restoration of confidence must obviously be the prime objective of policy in such crises, but it is often not clear what is needed to achieve this objective. In Mexico in 1994 the crisis was quickly contained and Mexico made a relatively quick recovery. East Asia, on the other hand, was very different. The Fund was able to put together rescue packages for Thailand, Indonesia and the Republic of Korea in a commendably short time, and it received full cooperation from the World Bank and the Asian Development Bank, both of which contributed to the rescue packages in the form of structural adjustment loans to supplement Fund financing. However, unlike in the case in Mexico, the Fund's East Asia programmes did not succeed in stabilizing the situation; in fact, the currency collapse actually intensified after the programmes were put in place and all three countries suffered an exceptionally sharp economic contraction. Growth forecasts for the programme countries were revised downwards on several occasions in quick succession, giving rise to criticism in some quarters that the Fund's programmes were not only inadequate but also may have actually worsened the situation. These developments clearly eroded the credibility of the Fund as a crisis manager.[13]

The East Asian experience illustrates the ineffectiveness of traditional stabilization programmes, with their reliance on fiscal restraint and interest rate policy in the face of crises originating in the capital account. The Fund has been widely criticized for insisting on a traditional dose of fiscal restraint in East Asia even though none of the East Asian countries suffered from fiscal imbalances at the time of the crisis. It has argued that even if a fiscal imbalance was not the cause of the problem, some fiscal restraint had to be part of the solution because an increase in government savings was necessary in order to bring about the improvement needed in the current account to ensure external balance. However, this argument ignores the special nature of the East Asian situation where capital outflows had precipitated excessive currency depreciation, which had strongly negative balance-sheet effects on banks and corporations, which in turn depressed domestic demand. Fiscal tightening is normally part of a traditional Fund adjustment package, especially one involving depreciation of the exchange rate, because depreciation is normally expected to have a stimulating effect on the demand for tradeables and aggregate demand restraint is needed to maintain macroeconomic balance while allowing the current account to improve. In East Asia, however, any demand-stimulating effects of currency depreciation, working through the relative price of tradeables, were completely swamped by the negative balance-sheet effects of the large currency depreciation. This negative effect was not taken into account in the Fund's programmes, perhaps because the extent of the depreciation was not anticipated. The initially tight fiscal targets were of course loosened very considerably when it became evident that the economies were undergoing an exceptionally sharp economic contraction (see table 1). Nevertheless, the initial tightness calls into question the appropriateness of the macroeconomic policy design.

The Fund also relied heavily on interest rate policy in its East Asian programmes, and again in Brazil, but this policy failed to prevent an exchange rate collapse in all these cases while imposing severe economic costs in the short run. The World Bank (1999) has implicitly criticized the Fund's approach by arguing that the empirical evidence that high interest rates help restrain currency depreciation is inconclusive, whereas there is strong evidence that they damage economic growth. The limitations of interest rate policy in handling a currency crisis originating from the capital account certainly need to be studied carefully, especially because the financial community tends to regard high interest rates as an essential element in any stabilization package.

One can be reasonably certain that high interest rates will succeed in reducing pressure on the currency when this pressure arises from a widening of the current account deficit in a situation of excess aggregate demand. In such a situation high interest rates help to reduce aggregate demand, which automatically moderates the pressure on the exchange rate. However, where exchange rate depreciation is being driven by capital outflows, higher interest rates are presumably expected to help by increasing the return on domestic assets and encouraging an inflow of capital. This relationship may not work quite as expected. The interest rate level needed to offset the perception of an imminent depreciation is very high and such high rates, if maintained for any length of time, can depress the real economy. Stiglitz and Furman (1998) point out that if the disruptive effect of raising interest rates on the real economy leads to a sufficient increase in the default risk it could theoretically counter the incentive effect of high interest rates on capital flows and thus actually worsen the situation. East Asia was particularly vulnerable to the negative effects of high interest rates because corporations were highly leveraged and commercial banks were also extensively exposed to the property sector against collateral of real estate, the value of which is highly sensitive to interest rates.

Critics of the Fund have argued that lower interest rates would have avoided some financial distress without necessarily worsening the extent of exchange rate depreciation, and might even have helped achieve an earlier recovery because the real economy would have performed better, encouraging an earlier return of confidence. Fund spokesmen point to the gradual recovery in exchange rates which has since taken place in the Republic of Korea and Thailand, with a parallel decline in interest rates in those countries, as evidence that the policy was basically sound

though painful in the short run.[14] This is clearly an area where further research is necessary.

III. The new financial architecture: some key elements

The new type of crisis witnessed in the 1990s has important implications for the functioning of the Fund and the Bank in the future. These institutions had evolved mechanisms for cooperating in handling the older types of payments problems, but the crises of the 1990s pose new challenges and possibly also call for somewhat different policy responses. In this section we focus on some of the key elements currently being discussed in the context of the new international financial architecture to help deal with these problems. These are:

- Strengthening the financial sector in developing countries;

- Improving bilateral and multilateral surveillance;

- Making the Fund a genuine lender of last resort;

- Introducing mechanisms for orderly negotiations with private creditors;

- Managing the social consequences of crisis;

- Creating an internationally agreed regime for restrictions on the capital account.

The future role of the IMF and the World Bank should be defined in the light of decisions made on these issues.

A.   *Strengthening the financial sector*

The most commonly discussed lesson from East Asia is that it is necessary to strengthen the financial sector in developing countries, especially for countries integrating with international financial markets. This is ultimately a process of institutional development which can be achieved only over several years, but the first step is to improve the regulatory framework governing various parts of the financial sector. The discussions on the new financial architecture have outlined the action needed on several fronts. Reforms in the banking system must obviously have top priority, given the special importance of banks in the financial system. This calls for improvement in the prudential norms and standards applied to commercial banks and also in the supervisory system for monitoring and enforcing them. Regulatory reform is also needed in the operation of securities markets and the functioning of the insurance sector. These reforms need to be underpinned by reform of the substructure. Accounting practices and standards need to be upgraded in most developing countries as an essential precondition for improving the allocative efficiency of both the banking system and the capital market. Also, experience in East Asia has shown that domestic bankruptcy laws are often inadequate for private creditors and domestic banks wishing to take legal action to recover loans. Finally, improvements in corporate governance are also needed.

It is also recognized that the need for reforms is not limited to developing countries and that improvements are needed as well in financial markets in industrialized countries. The international operations of institutions such as hedge funds and other investment institutions operating from offshore banking systems are inadequately regulated at present. Leveraged trading in particular needs better regulation, at least in terms of disclosure, so that lending institutions can be better informed about the risks involved.[15] Some features of bank regulation in industrialized countries actually encourage short-term flows to developing countries by ascribing lower risk weights to short-term loans, thus creating a regulatory incentive for short-run lending which increases the potential volatility of flows to developing countries.

The broad coverage of the reforms needed for the new financial architecture reflects the fact that financial markets are highly interconnected and regulation of one segment of the market will not serve the purpose. It is necessary to take an integrated view of the functioning of the international financial system and all its sub-sectors instead of the present segmented approach in which regulatory issues relating to individual sectors are discussed in separate organizations, e.g. banking issues are discussed in the Basle Committee while issues related to the functioning of the securities markets are discussed in the International Organization of Securities Commissions (IOSCO).

The United Nations Committee on Development Planning suggested the creation of a World Financial Organization as a sort of supranational body exercising supervisory powers over the financial sector as a whole.[16] The G-7 countries have opted for a more modest alternative of bringing together national authorities of the G-7 countries and the major international institutions and other concerned international bodies in a Financial Stability Forum which will act as a consultative group rather than a supranational supervisor. The forum consists of two representatives from the IMF, the World Bank, the Basle Committee, the Bank for International Settlements (BIS), IOSCO and the International Association of Insurance Supervisors (IAIS) respectively, and three representatives from each of the G-7 countries. The 33-member forum will be chaired by the General Manager of the BIS for a three-year period and will be serviced by a small secretariat based in the BIS. No developing countries are included in the forum at present, although it has been reported that it may be expanded to include some emerging market countries "at a later stage". Inclusion of major developing countries in this forum is surely essential to ensure even a minimal degree of participation and representation.

It is important to recognize that there are practical problems in establishing international regulatory standards for various parts of the financial sector. It is necessary to distinguish between those areas where standards already exist, which have gained wide acceptability among industrialized countries, and other areas where this has yet to be achieved. Examples of the former are the standards relating to prudential norms and supervision of banks evolved by the Basle Committee, the standards relating to the operation of securities markets evolved by IOSCO and standards for regulating insurance evolved by IAIS. Considerable homogenization of standards has taken place across industrialized countries, but there are important differences. Prudential standards applied in the Japanese banking system, for example, did not fully meet international expectations.

A practical problem in applying international standards of financial regulation to developing countries is that these standards may require some modifications to take account of developing country characteristics. For example, the Basle Committee standards for prudential norms and supervision of commercial banks were designed for banks operating in industrialized countries with fully developed financial markets and very efficient legal systems, and could pose problems if applied in countries which do not have similar well-developed financial markets. For example, mark-to-market practices for valuing securities can present problems when securities markets are illiquid. Similar problems will arise in other areas where standards already exist, such as in the operation of securities markets and in insurance. The existing standard-setting bodies are dominated by industrialized countries and are not likely to identify modifications of international standards for developing countries. There is an area where the Fund and the Bank could play a useful role by defining modifications appropriate for developing countries and also by determining phased transition paths for achieving full compliance with international standards. Transition paths defined by the Fund and the Bank are more likely to acquire international respectability and will provide developing countries with operational guidance in moving to higher standards. Progress by individual countries could be monitored by the Fund in the course of bilateral surveillance. In addition, the Fund and the Bank could offer technical assistance to countries needing such assistance to achieve compliance in individual areas.

Establishing common standards in some of the other areas will be much more difficult. Accountancy standards, for example, are much stricter in the United States than in Europe and although the International Accounting Standards Committee is working to evolve common standards, it is not clear whether the United States would accept any dilution of the Generally Accepted Accounting Principles. Corporate governance is a relatively new concern even in industrialized countries and there are considerable differences in corporate governance practices, depending on whether the country follows the Anglo-Saxon model, the German model or the Japanese model. The OECD is currently working on an international standard for corporate governance, but it is unlikely to go much beyond stating some very broad principles, the practical application of which would be very different in different countries. Common standards for bankruptcy laws are perhaps furthest in the future. Here again, practice varies considerably across industrialized countries, with the balance between debtor and creditor interest being struck differently from country to country.

To summarize, the effort to upgrade regulatory and supervisory systems in different parts of the financial system in developing countries will certainly increase the transparency of, and flow of information from, emerging country markets, and this should help financial markets to function more effectively vis-à-vis these countries. However, some caveats are important. First, the introduction of regulatory structures is no guarantee against a financial crisis – there are numerous examples of crises occurring in regulated financial markets in developed countries. The effectiveness of regulation depends on how the system is implemented in practice, and this depends heavily on the quality of supervision. It will take several years for supervisory institutions in developing countries to build the supervisory skills needed. Another caveat relates to the nature of regulation itself. There is a growing body of opinion that the focus of supervision in banking should move away from enforcement of standard norms relating to capital adequacy, asset classification by risk category, provisioning etc. to a comprehensive assessment of the risk management system in each bank. Supervision would then focus on assessing the adequacy of the risk management system in each bank and checking whether the system is actually being followed. It is obviously impossible to define common international standards in this type of approach. Nor would it be appropriate for developing countries to be judged by adherence to traditional mechanical norms while industrialized country institutions switch to more sophisticated systems of risk assessment, which give their financial institutions much greater flexibility.

All this underscores the fact that conventional wisdom on financial regulation is itself evolving and it is important for the developing country constraints and perspectives to be taken into account in evolving standards in future. The expansion of the Financial Stability Forum to include developing countries and the role of the Fund and the Bank as spokesmen for the developing countries are particularly important in this context.

B. *Improved surveillance*

Surveillance is a core activity of the Fund, which conducts bilateral surveillance of individual countries through its annual Article IV consultations and multilateral surveillance through periodic reviews of the international economic situation in the form of the *World Economic Outlook*. Both types of surveillance need to be strengthened so that vulnerabilities are identified at an earlier stage in future.

Bilateral surveillance needs to be strengthened to address the various information deficiencies which contribute to instability in financial markets facing developing countries. Timely availability of information and transparency are critical in this context. The establishment of the IMF's Special Data Dissemination Standard in 1996 is an important advance. For its part, the Fund has published a Code of Good Practices on Fiscal Transparency and is currently working on a Code of Conduct on Monetary and Financial Policy. Implementation of these codes will help present a much more reliable picture of the fiscal and monetary conditions in member countries on a comparable basis.

Particular attention will have to be paid to financial sector weaknesses, especially in developing countries which are more integrated with global financial markets. Since both the Fund and the Bank are actively involved in work on the financial sector there is scope for greater cooperation between the two, and we will return to this subject in section IV. However, effective surveillance requires the Fund to cooperate not only with the World Bank but also with other important players, including in particular BIS and IOSCO. The recently established Financial Stability Forum will help the Fund in this context.

In the past, surveillance was designed primarily to keep the Fund and member governments informed of developments in individual countries. In future it must play a much larger role in feeding information to financial markets to improve market efficiency. This raises problems because of the constraints of confidentiality associated with Article IV consultations. The Fund has recently introduced the practice of releasing Public Information Notices (PINs) summarizing the outcome of Board discussions of Article IV consultation reports, where the country under review requests such release. This is clearly a step in the right direction. However, out of 138 Article IV consultations concluded in 1997/98 countries chose to have PINs released in only 77 cases, a fact which indicates that many countries wish to retain confidentiality. This may be partly because countries which do not have and are not seeking substantial access to international financial markets do not see any advantage in releasing PINs. However, countries seeking access to financial markets are likely to take a different stand and in any case will be pushed towards greater disclosure by market pressure.

If surveillance is expected to improve the functioning of financial markets it must also pay greater attention to market perceptions than is done at present. It is not easy for the Fund to incorporate market perceptions in formal surveillance activity since governments can always downplay such assessments as being subjective. But greater use of market sources can often add useful information. For example, the build-up of non-performing assets in some of the East Asian banking systems was not documented in official circles but was definitely suspected by market circles, which routinely discounted the low officially reported figures (Khatkhate and Dalla, 1995).

Multilateral surveillance also needs to be improved. It must focus more sharply on developments which could add to instability in the external environment facing developing countries. The impact of industrialized countries' policies on developing countries through their impact on world trade has been the focus of attention for some time. Their impact on capital flows to developing countries is equally important. For example, low interest rates in industrialized countries created conditions which favoured a heavy flow of capital to developing countries and also made them vulnerable to a reversal, but this vulnerability was not sufficiently highlighted in multilateral surveillance. These linkages need more attention in future. Multilateral surveillance does not of course imply an ability to achieve policy correction. The Fund has not played a significant role in policy coordination among the G-7 countries in the past and this situation is unlikely to change.[17] However, it could try to become a more vocal spokesman for developing countries, which are not represented in G-7 deliberations at all, and yet are highly vulnerable to G-7 policy decisions.

The Bank can play an independent supplementary role in multilateral surveillance by highlighting longer-term problems of particular interest to developing countries. The recent practice of issuing an anual publication on global economic prospects for developing countries is a useful step in this direction; it is not necessary to achieve close coordination between this publication and the *World Economic Outlook*. Differences in perspective between the Fund and the Bank can legitimately exist in view of the Bank's special focus on development issues, and transparency requires that these differences be fully aired.

C. The Fund as lender of last resort

A major issue in the discussions on the new financial architecture is whether there should be an international lender of last resort to deal with situations where otherwise well-managed economies are hit by panic outflows of capital. The analogy is drawn with the domestic banking system, where the central bank acts as a lender of last resort to prevent a solvent bank from falling victim to a run on deposits. Since countries with open capital accounts are potentially vulnerable in the same way to a loss of confidence which may not reflect any weakness in fundamentals, it is argued that the new financial architecture should include an international lender of last resort to help countries deal with such situations. There are several practical problems which have to be resolved before this idea can be put into practice.

One set of problems relates to the availability of resources on the scale required. The Supplemental Reserve Facility (SRF) introduced by the Fund in December 1997, is an important new instrument which allows the Fund to provide short-term finance without limit in the event of exceptional balance-of-payments difficulties attributable to a sudden and disruptive loss of market confidence.[18] However, the Fund's total resources are not sufficient, even after the implementation of the last quota increase and the activation of the New Arrangements to Borrow (NAB), to enable it to meet all the financing needs that could arise in this context. Keynes' original vision of a Fund empowered to create its own liquidity without limit is too radical to be accepted. A less radical but feasible alternative would be to amend the Articles to allow the Fund to issue SDRs to itself for use in lender-of-last-resort operations, subject to a cumulative limit on the total volume of SDRs that could be created by the Fund for this purpose. The limit could be determined by an 85 per cent majority, as is the case for a general allocation of SDRs. Within this limit the Fund should be empowered to issue SDRs to itself to finance lender-of-last-resort operations approved by the Board. SDRs created for this purpose should be extinguished on repurchase by the borrowing country, to be reactivated again only in similar circumstances. This arrangement has several advantages. It would not amount to a permanent increase in unconditional liquidity as in the case of a general allocation of SDRs. The additional liquidity would be activated only in the context of lender-of-last-resort programmes and would be linked with appropriate conditionality and subject to majority support in the Board, which in practice requires substantial support from the G-7 countries. The liquidity created would be only for the duration of the crisis since the SDRs would be extinguished on repurchase.

In the absence of such an arrangement, the only alternative is the one proposed by Fischer (1999), who argues that while an international lender of last resort is definitely needed it is not necessary that it must be able to create its own liquidity. That function could be just as effectively performed by the Fund "arranging" finance from different sources. The credibility of this alternative obviously depends on the ability of the Fund to mobilize resources on a sufficient scale when needed. The East Asian experience is not encouraging in this context. The Fund was able to mobilize a total of $117 billion for Indo-nesia, the Republic of Korea and Thailand, consisting of its own resources and contributions from the World Bank and the Asian Development Bank and from bilateral sources (see table 2). However, the bilateral contributions for Indonesia and the Republic of Korea, which were almost half of the total package for these countries, were only a "second stage back-up" with considerable uncertainty about the circumstances under which they would become available.[19] The programmes of Indonesia and the Republic of Korea were clearly inferior to the Mexican programme in 1995, in which there was a large bilateral United States contribution ($21 billion). If the bilateral contributions for Indonesia and the Republic of Korea are excluded, the total volume of resources mobilized for East Asia was only $76 billion compared with $49 billion for Mexico, whereas a comparable figure for the three East Asian countries, using GDP as the scaling factor, would be close to $200 billion! The inadequacy of the financing provided in East Asia has been identified by the World Bank (1999) as one of the reasons why the Fund programmes did not succeed in stabilizing the situation in the initial stages.[20]

We also need to consider whether it is desirable to draw on the resources of the World Bank and the relevant regional development bank to meet the needs of crisis financing. This may have been unavoidable in the East Asian case because there was no other source from which resources could have been mobilized, but the discussions on the new financial architecture should consider whether this is an ideal arrangement. As pointed out earlier, the financing needed to deal with crises of confidence is quite different from that normally provided by multilateral development banks, and this would suggest that the appropriate longer-term response is to strengthen the capacity of the Fund to meet all the requirements. Direct involvement of the World Bank and the relevant regional development bank in crisis lending operations only distracts these organizations from their primary function, which is to provide long-term development finance, a distraction which is particularly undesirable in an environment where the flow of such lending has been declining in real terms over the past decade. The Bank should of course be free to negotiate adjustment lending separately for crisis-hit countries, and such lending may well be needed as part of structural reforms in the post-crisis phase, but this should be a separate activity with no compulsion to complete the process in time to include resources as part of the total financing package. Structural adjustment lending requires time in order to design an appropriate policy framework, and this

Table 2

COMPOSITION OF RECENT RESCUE PACKAGES [a]

($ billion)

	IMF	World Bank	Regional dev. bank	Bilateral	Total
Brazil, 1998	18.1	4.5	4.5	14.5 [b]	41.6
Indonesia, 1997	11.2	5.5	4.5	21.1	42.3
Mexico, 1995	17.7	--	--	31.1 [c]	48.8
Republic of Korea, 1997	21.1	10.0	4.2	23.1	58.4
Russian Federation, 1998 [d]	15.1	6.0	--	1.5	22.6
Thailand, 1997	4.0	1.5	1.2	10.5	17.2

Source:

   a The rescue packages for each country represent resources available over different periods for each case.

   b From industrial countries, including direct assistance from Japan and from others through BIS.

   c Comprises $20 billion from the United States, $1.1 billion from Canada and a $10 billion credit line from the BIS.

   d Conditional commitments to the end of 1999. Of these, $1.5 billion shown under "bilateral" consists of Japanese support co-financing the World Bank.

process should not be hurried to fit within the time-frame in which a crisis management package has to be finalized.

These considerations suggest that there is a need to strengthen the Fund's ability to provide finance in crisis situations. One way of doing this is through a greater expansion of quotas. Industrialized countries have been reluctant to agree to large quota increases in the past on the ground that such increases are not necessary because creditworthy countries have ample access to liquidity under normal conditions in global capital markets. However, crises originating in the capital account exemplify cases of market failure and since these cases can multiply rapidly because of contagion, there may be a need for Fund financing on a large scale in such situations. It can still be argued that a large increase in Fund quotas is not the best way of empowering the Fund to deal with crisis situations since quotas increase the general financing capability of the Fund. This concern can be met by giving the Fund access to special borrowing facilities available only for lender-of-last-resort programmes. The General Arrangements to Borrow (GAB) and the NAB provide such backup, but the availability of these resources is subject to the specific consent of the contributing countries for each call, in effect giving each contributing country a veto on the use of its resources for each particular pur-pose. What is needed are pre-arranged lines of credit from the major central banks, which could be coordinated through the BIS and be available automatically for use by the Fund in lender-of-last-resort programmes approved by the Fund's Board. The major developing countries, which are members of the BIS, could join in contributing to these lines of credit on an appropriate-burden sharing basis. If becomes necessary to access resources from the World Bank or the relevant regional development bank, this should be in the form of bridge finance to the Fund, which can be repaid by the Fund in a short time.

The conditionality to be attached to last-resort financing also poses formidable problems. One view is that such a facility must be very different from the present arrangement whereby countries negotiate programmes with the Fund after a crisis has arisen and access to resources therefore depends on the outcome of negotiations undertaken in situations where the country is in a weak position and can be pressured into accepting unnecessarily tough conditionality.[21] Since central banks acting as lenders of last resort lend freely (i.e. in large amounts) to solvent banks facing liquidity problems, with no conditions except a penal interest rate, it is sometimes argued that countries facing panic outflows should have similar access to large volumes of finance to calm markets without having to negotiate on conditionality at that time (see, for example, Griffith-Jones, 1999). This ignores the fact that central banks provide last-resort financing only to banks which face liquidity problems but are otherwise solvent and that central banks are particularly well placed to judge the solvency of banks in distress because of intensive supervision. The existence of supervision reduces the moral hazard that could otherwise arise with last-resort financing. Since similar intrusive supervision does not exist for countries, automatic extension of low-conditionality financing would attract the charge of moral hazard. Conditionality in this situation becomes the only basis for ensuring solvency.

One way out of the dilemma would be establish a precautionary or contingency financing arrangement under which a country could pre-qualify for future assistance by complying with performance conditions agreed with the Fund before there is any crisis, in exchange for which it would obtain assured access to short-term financing on a large scale in the event of a crisis. The knowledge that such an arrangement is in place can be expected to calm markets and reduce the likelihood of a panic-induced crisis. A proposal of this type was considered by the IMF at the time of the Mexican crisis but was not found practical. It is being considered again in the wake of the East Asian crisis. There is considerable support for such an arrangement, but designing a precautionary facility poses several problems.

The major difficulty with a contingency financing facility is that performance criteria thought to be appropriate prior to a crisis cannot continue to be the only performance requirements if a crisis does occur. This is because crises rarely take the form of a purely irrational panic arising in an otherwise completely normal situation. What is much more likely is that countries face a crisis because they are suddenly perceived to have become vulnerable because of some adverse external or internal development, or because of belated recognition of a weakness which existed earlier but was not known to the market. In such situations there is a need for some adjustment in policy to reflect the new development.[22] A partial solution lies in treating pre-qualification as a basis for releasing at least a first tranche of the crisis package, with relatively minimal conditionality, while simultaneously initiating negotiations to determine appropriate conditionality for additional support. Such an arrangement could help to stabilize markets if pre-qualification is seen to increase the probability that Fund resources will be made available in the event of a crisis.[23]

Pre-qualification could also pose some difficult problems in the pre-crisis period. Any departure from agreed performance criteria would either require prompt corrective action or withdrawal of cover. Since the effectiveness of the pre-qualification safety net depends upon its availability being publicly known, any withdrawal of cover would also have to be made public, and this could generate controversy because the withdrawal of cover could itself precipitate a loss of confidence. Performance requirements in the pre-crisis period could also change as a result of a change in external circumstances which in the view of the Fund might warrant intensification of policy parameters for continued eligibility for cover. If the required change in those parameters is not accepted by the country, the Fund may have to withdraw cover, which again is bound to attract controversy.

D.   *Orderly debt restructuring*

A lacuna in the existing system, which makes it difficult to handle crises of confidence, is that creditors have an incentive to exit at the first sign of trouble in the hope of escaping before the crisis gets out of hand, which in turn intensifies the crisis. It is argued that the system would be more stable if countries facing panic outflows could have recourse to an internationally sanctioned mechanism for invoking a temporary standstill during which the government could initiate discussions with major private creditors, inform them of measures being taken to deal with the crisis and, where relevant, of the extent of Fund support available, and negotiate a restructuring of payment obligations so that the country could meet them without a disruptive depreciation of the currency.[24] Such an arrangement would ensure that the burden of adjustment is shared more fairly between lenders and the debtor country and would avoid the moral hazard in the present system whereby Fund resources are used to repay private creditors who get away scot free.[25] It could also be used to encourage new private sector lending if new flows could be given seniority over pre-crisis debt, thus creating incentives to "bail in" the private sector.

Debt negotiations with private creditors have taken place in the past, but they have had no formal legal sanction and creditors have been technically free to treat suspensions of payment as a default. In practice, the outcome has depended upon the degree of support a country can mobilize from official quarters. In the 1980s the Managing Director of the Fund took the initiative to persuade the New York banks to provide a fresh infusion of funds as a condition for Fund financing of debt-burdened Latin American countries. More recently in the Republic of Korea, the United States Treasury Secretary is reported to have intervened personally to encourage the New York banks to cooperate in restructuring the short-term obligations of banks from the Republic of Korea. However, these cases involve a high degree of non-transparency and it is doubtful whether similar support would be extended to other countries, especially those which do not pose systemic risk. Establishing an internationally agreed procedure whereby countries could introduce a temporary standstill with IMF approval, and perhaps also involve the IMF in the restructuring negotiations, would make the process more transparent and even-handed.[26]

Several practical problems have to be resolved before debt restructuring can be implemented. First, there is the problem of determining which debts should be covered by the standstill and the subsequent restructuring negotiations. Clearly, trade credit should be completely excluded to avoid disruption in current payments. Other debts can be categorized into (a) sovereign debt owed to government or other official sources; (b) sovereign or semi-sovereign debt owed to private creditors, i.e. banks or bondholders; (c) commercial bank debt owed to other banks or bondholders; and (d) private sector debt. Attempting to restructure debt in all these categories is impractical and it is therefore necessary to focus on some important categories. Sovereign debt owed to governments is covered by the Paris Club. Private sector debt is best left to normal market forces and bankruptcy procedures. Debts in (a) and (c) above are perhaps the most suitable for negotiated restructuring. Since the context in which the restructuring may be considered is a crisis of confidence, the focus of the negotiation must be on short-term debt in these categories. This could be defined as debt with original or residual maturity of one year to 18 months, leaving other debts in these categories outside the restructuring. Even if debt restructuring is limited to some categories, it is relevant to consider whether the standstill provisions should be applied to all categories pending the outcome of negotiations.

More generally, it is necessary to consider whether the standstill should extend beyond debt-related payments to cover other capital outflows as well. It is difficult to justify unilaterally freezing payments due to foreign creditors while an open capital account allows domestic capital to exit freely and intensify the crisis, which could lead to demands for more drastic debt restructuring to ensure viability.

Special problems arise where foreign residents hold bonds denominated in domestic currency. It is not practical to seek to restructure repayment obligations to foreign holders of domestic bonds but not to others. If payments are allowed in domestic currency but it is sought to block repatriation, this becomes a restriction on repatriation of capital. Should such repatriation be restricted while other repatriation (e.g. by direct foreign investors) is not? There is no consensus as yet on these issues.

Another set of issues relates to the practical problem of conducting negotiations with a large number of creditors. In the Latin American debt crisis of the 1980s, most of the debt was sovereign debt owed to a handful of commercial banks and it was easy to identify and negotiate with few major creditors. Today, commercial bank debt is much less concentrated than it was earlier, and so the number of commercial banks involved is much larger. This creates a possible free-rider problem in which smaller banks have an incentive to act as free-riders, refusing to accept restructuring. It is not clear how this can be eliminated. The proportion of debt in the form of bonds has also increased substantially, and it is impossible to negotiate with large numbers of bondholders in the absence of legal provisions in bond contracts providing for collective representation and specifying the extent of majority consent needed to apply the restructuring terms to all bondholders.

Perhaps the most difficult issue is the extent to which the IMF should be directly involved in providing some sort of official sanction to the standstill and possibly also assisting the country concerned in debt negotiations. Involvement of the IMF has advantages because it would help to evolve uniform practices which can be followed in all cases. It could also link the availability of additional Fund support to an agreement on restructuring, incentivizing both the debtor and the creditor to come to a reasonable agreement, and also ensuring effective burden-sharing. However, there is resistance to getting the IMF directly involved in sanctioning departures from debt contracts and in determining the terms of renegotiation.

The current state of the consensus on debt restructuring in official circles is perhaps best reflected in the report of the G-22 Working Group on Financial Crises. The report emphasizes the high cost of even a temporary suspension of payments and therefore urges the need "to make the strongest possible efforts to meet the terms and conditions of all debt contracts in full and on time". It recognizes that a temporary suspension may become unavoidable in certain circumstances, but it stipulates that this option should be considered only when it is clear, from consultations with the Fund and other international financial institutions, that even with appropriately strong policy adjustments the country will experience an exceptionally severe financial and balance-of-payments crisis. The report specifically warns against "disruptive unilateral action" – an implicit criticism of the Russian unilateral repudiation in 1998 – and recommends trying to achieve a cooperative solution. The report goes on to recommend facilitative measures which would make it legally possible to renegotiate with creditors should this become necessary, such as the inclusion of various types of collective representation clauses in bond contracts.

To summarize, the G-22 Working Group stops short of endorsing an internationally approved process for invoking a standstill with IMF approval. The requirement of prior consultation with the Fund and examination of alternative policy options implies that debt restructuring is not a "first resort" instrument in crisis containment and that countries must first try to stabilize the situation through conventional methods. In practice, this means that there could be a period during which the system will be under pressure and outflows could continue to occur. In the absence of financing of the lender-of-last-resort type, efforts to contain these outflows may not be very successful and may force resort to restrictive high interest rate policies which may have very high short-term economic costs. This illustrates the basic dilemma with debt restructuring proposals. There are strong moral hazard grounds for discouraging debt restructuring except as a last-resort option. However, if debt restructuring can be resorted to only after conventional means have been exhausted, there is a danger that it will be used only after most of the damage has been done, and not to forestall damage as its proponents would like.

E. Managing the social consequences of crises

An important feature of recent crises is that the impact on the poor can be very severe. Estimates provided for Indonesia, Mexico, the Republic of Korea and Thailand by the World Bank (1999) show a sharp decline in real wages and an increase in unemployment rates between the pre-crisis year and the post-crisis year in all these cases. Estimates of changes in poverty in East Asia are more tentative because they depend on the change in income distribution, which is not easy to predict, but large increases in poverty are expected in all the crisis-affected countries.

Crisis management strategies must therefore try to ensure that the negative impact on the poor is minimized. Although fiscal discipline may require a reduction in total real government expenditure, this should be achieved while protecting those expenditures which are of particular importance for the poor. For example, a reduction in total subsidies may be unavoidable but the focus should be on cutting subsidies which are not effectively targeted, of which there are usually many, while preserving those subsidies which are effectively targeted at the poor. There may even be a case for increasing targeted subsidies in certain circumstances. Similarly, it is necessary to protect expenditure on social services, especially health and education, which are crucial inputs into the welfare and human capital of the poor. These expenditures often suffer during periods of fiscal tightening and this is typically at the expense of the poor. The effort to preserve or perhaps even increase pro-poor expenditures while reducing total expenditure can succeed only if other expenditures can be subjected to even deeper cuts. This is not easy, but that only reveals the nature of the difficult choices involved in achieving adjustment with a human face.

Special efforts can also be made to provide social safety nets which would help to maintain income levels of the poor and those affected by unemployment. Special public works programmes for providing wage employment could be introduced, or expanded where they already exist. The cost-effectiveness of these programmes, however, depends critically on the extent of leakage to non-target groups and also on the productivity of the resulting assets created. International experience suggests that leakages to non-target groups can be very large unless programmes are very carefully designed and monitored. Efforts to achieve quick results will lead only to projects which have high public visibility but low efficiency.

This is clearly an important area for Fund-Bank collaboration. The Bank can help in formulating appropriate performance criteria for Fund programmes which would ensure that the pro-poor components of expenditures in the government budget are not reduced. The Bank can also directly finance social safety net programmes which can be very useful in the post-crisis phase, provided that they are designed in a manner which maximizes effectiveness. However, as pointed out earlier, these programmes should be separate from financing provided in the context of crisis management which should ideally be sourced from the Fund.

F. Capital account liberalization

Prior to the East Asian crisis, industrialized countries were pressing for broadening the mandate of the Fund to include liberalization of capital movements, and this was reflected in the Interim Committee's statement in Hong Kong (China) in October 1997 calling for consideration of an amendment to the Fund's Articles to make liberalization of capital movements one of the purposes of the Fund. Although many developing countries have liberalized the capital account to varying degrees, most still retain substantial capital controls and many developing countries have reservations about giving the Fund an expanded mandate in this area for fear that it might create pressure to liberalize capital account transactions at a faster pace. The crises in East Asia and Brazil have highlighted the problems which can arise if the capital account is liberalized prematurely and the pressure for rapid movement in this area has therefore diminished, but the issue remains on the agenda of the Fund's Board and will have to be addressed as part of the new architecture for the global financial system.

Given the increased importance of capital flows in the global economy, and the fact that many developing countries are progressively integrating with the global financial market, it is somewhat incongruous that the Fund has no mandate at all in this area. If the Fund is to function effectively as the principal international overseer of the international financial system, it can be argued that it must have some mandate for monitoring, and perhaps even regulating, restrictions on capital account transactions. It is important that this should not become an instrument for pushing developing countries prematurely into liberalization of the capital account, denying them the flexibility to impose controls on capital flows if they feel these are needed for macroeconomic management. One way of giving the Fund a limited mandate would be to abandon the approach of including the liberalization of capital movements as one of the purposes of the Fund and focus instead on the limited objective of enabling the Fund to supervise capital restrictions with a view to creating more orderly conditions in international capital markets.

The only obligation on members should be to inform the Fund of the restrictions they impose on capital account transactions and also any changes made therein. Countries would then be free to adopt any regime they liked, and also change it at will, but the subject would become a legitimate issue for discussion by the Fund, and countries would be under some pressure to justify their actions in the course of surveillance.[27]

A regime of this sort could also evolve into one whereby developing countries may, of their own volition, accept binding obligations to avoid imposing restrictions on certain types of capital transactions except in consultation with the Fund. Restrictions imposed in emergency conditions could be made subject to review, with a presumption of return to normal conditions within a predetermined period. This would give the Fund a role in supervising obligations accepted by developing countries of their own volition and help to increase transparency and investor confidence in emerging markets. The incentive for developing countries to accept obligations voluntarily would depend on whether financial markets viewed such discipline with favour as reflected in credit ratings and yield spreads.

From the perspective of developing countries there will be the lurking suspicion that even a limited mandate is likely to generate pressure on them to liberalize their capital account at a faster pace and could also be reflected in Fund conditionalities at times when Fund financing is needed. This is a legitimate concern which cannot be lightly dismissed. To some extent it can be addressed by suitable drafting of the mandate. More substantively, developing countries could insist that such arrangements should only be considered as part of a package where the Fund's ability to act as a lender of last resort is strengthened, and it is also given some authority to provide legal sanction to restrictions on capital payments which may have to be imposed in an emergency. Industrialized countries have so far shown little inclination to support proposals which increase the financing available to the Fund or put the Fund in a position where it may legitimize new restrictions imposed on capital movements by a developing country. However, a one-sided use of the Fund to push for liberalization of capital markets, without also strengthening it in ways that would help contain volatility and instability is clearly unbalanced. Progress in this aspect of the new financial architecture may require balanced movement on both fronts.

IV. The Fund and the Bank in the new architecture

In this section we examine various proposals relating to the future role of the IMF and the World Bank which are being considered as part of the discussions on the new financial architecture. These proposals reflect the state of the current consensus on architecture issues, which emphasizes the need to make financial markets work more effectively rather than supplant them. The role envisaged for the Fund and the Bank in this framework is one of improving surveillance and contributing to strengthening the financial sector in developing countries to prevent crises from occurring. It also envisages strengthening the capacity of these institutions to deal with crises if they occur, and this is to be achieved not by radical restructuring but by improvements in their existing capacities and better cooperation.

The existing arrangements for cooperation between the two institutions have been reviewed on the basis of the experience in handling the East Asian crisis. Both institutions have concluded that the Concordat of 1989 continues to provide an acceptable framework for Fund-Bank cooperation, but additional arrangements for cooperation are needed in some areas.

A. Cooperation in financial sector work

There is general agreement that Fund-Bank cooperation needs to be greatly enhanced in work related to the financial sector. Strengthening the financial sector in developing countries is necessary both from the point of view of macroeconomic stability and from the point of view of allocative efficiency. Both institutions therefore have a strong interest in this area with somewhat different emphases. The Fund is concerned with financial sector issues which affect macroeconomic balance, are relevant for the effectiveness of macroeconomic policy instruments, or concern problems which can generate systemic risk. The Bank is concerned with developing and implementing strategies for the medium-term development of the financial sector, including restructuring of banks and financial institutions, improving systems of prudential regulations and supervision, and related capacity-building. This broad division of responsibilities necessarily leaves a substantial area of overlap.

The United Kingdom recommended the establishment of a common department for financial sector issues to service both institutions. This has not found favour and instead each institution plans to strengthen its own capability with elaborate arrangements for consultations at various levels, including field-level coordination in financial sector work, participation in each other's missions and even joint missions. A Financial Sector Liaison Committee has been established comprising senior staff of the Monetary Affairs and Exchange and the Policy Development and Review Departments of the Fund and of the Financial Sector Board and the Poverty Reduction and Economic Management Network of the Bank. The committee will help coordinate the work of the two institutions in this area and delineate respective roles for the two institutions reflecting their mandates and comparative strengths.

The effectiveness of these arrangements can only be judged on the basis of actual experience in the future. However, it is important to emphasize that while mechanisms for consultation aimed at eliminating disagreements to the extent possible are desirable, the achievement of a common Bank Fund position on all financial sector policy issues should not be viewed as an overriding objective. Financial sector development in developing countries in an environment of global financial integration is a complex process in which perceptions of best practice are still evolving. There may be room for different views on many points and it is more important for the Fund and the Bank to remain open to ideas from outside in this area, including the views of market participants and national regulators, than to reach common positions on all issues.

An important area where the Fund and the Bank can cooperate is in ensuring that the concerns of developing countries are appropriately taken into account in the development of international regulatory standards for the financial sector. As participants in the G-7 Financial Stability Forum, they can help shape the evolution of an international consensus on the application of standards in different areas to developing country situations. Once standards are agreed in the relevant international forum they can help to evolve guidelines for applying these standards in developing countries, including the determination of appropriate transition paths which take account of country-specific constraints. They can also provide technical assistance to developing countries seeking assistance in attempting to comply with agreed standards. Finally, the two institutions can cooperate to enhance the effectiveness of Fund surveillance in monitoring implementation of these standards in individual developing countries.

B. *Coordination in crisis management operations*

While existing mechanisms for coordination between the two institutions for their normal lending operations are broadly acceptable, they are not adequate in crisis situations, as the East Asian experience shows. The suddenness with which the crisis broke in East Asia left very little time for consultation and, as it happened, the Bank differed from the Fund on many aspects of crisis management. Some of these differences relate to differences on structural policies which are within the domain of the Bank. For example, the Fund programme involved closure of 16 insolvent banks. Because of the severe time constraints within which the Indonesian programme was formulated, the Bank was not adequately consulted. We now know that the Bank had reservations about the Fund's approach. The closure of the banks was announced in a manner which created uncertainty about the security of deposits in the other banks, leading to a run on deposits and a flight of capital which worsened the currency collapse. The Bank also appears to have had a different view on the extent of fiscal restraint and the interest rate policies advocated by the Fund, both of which are within the Fund's area of primary responsibility. However, this division of responsibility should not make the Bank's views irrelevant. Since short-term stabilization measures can disrupt the development process, or conflict with longer-term structural policy objectives, it is necessary for the Bank's views to be adequately reflected in formulating crisis management programmes.

Recognizing these difficulties, the two institutions have reached agreement on new procedures to ensure effective coordination between them in future crisis management operations. The responsibility for the overall stabilization programme, including the adoption of urgent structural measures which may have to be taken in the initial stage of stabilization, rests squarely with the Fund. However, in future the Bank will be fully involved in programme formulation in the early stages through participation by Bank staff in Fund missions or through parallel missions. The Bank's involvement is obviously especially necessary in order to deal with structural issues where it has primary responsibility, and where it may later even engage in direct lending. The proposed procedure will also allow the Bank to contribute to the formulation of other parts of the programme as well. If the Bank was not in a position to make firm recommendations on structural issues within the time-frame in which the crisis management package has to be finalized, the Fund would take the necessary decisions, on the basis of preliminary understandings with Bank staff, to be modified later on the basis of more in-depth work. The introduction of *ex post* flexibility in this way is a definite improvement. Follow-up activity on the structural side would be undertaken by the Bank, with Fund staff participating in Bank-led missions.

The Bank's contribution to programme formulation would obviously be most useful in situations where it has an ongoing involvement in the crisis-hit country, but this cannot be taken for granted. The Fund and the Bank therefore propose to identify a group of key emerging countries where significant financial sector reforms are under way, or are likely to be required, and to assist the authorities in evolving appropriately sequenced plans for financial sector reform. By focusing Fund surveillance and Bank sector work on structural issues in the financial sector in these countries in this way, both institutions expect to develop an improved understanding of the financial system and to identify possible problems for corrective action, which will help in formulating crisis management programmes should this become necessary.

The current consensus on Fund-Bank cooperation also appears to favour direct financing by the Bank to supplement Fund financing at times of crisis. The Emergency Structural Adjustment Lending (ESAL) procedure recently approved by the Bank is designed to enable the Bank to play this role.[28] The approach adopted in this paper is different. We have argued that Bank financing should not be part of the crisis management package, although the Bank may well involve itself in adjustment lending as part of post-crisis restructuring.

In addition, the Bank could play an even more important role in the post-crisis recovery phase by helping countries regain access to international capital markets. Given the information asymmetries from which developing countries suffer, and the market failures associated with contagion, it is quite possible that crisis-hit developing countries may find it difficult to access commercial markets even though policy correctives have been put in place which justify fresh access. The World Bank could play a market-compatible role, bringing developing country borrowers back to the market earlier rather than later through the use of its guarantee facility. Since market access is likely to be needed by the private sector, the Bank's insistence upon a government counter-guarantee is not an ideal arrangement. Diluting this requirement will require legal changes in the Bank's Articles, but it is time that the Bank considered such changes to allow it to use suitably priced guarantees to help private sector borrowers to re-enter international capital markets in the post-crisis phase.

C. Should the Fund be merged with the Bank?

An issue which needs to be addressed is whether, in view of the perceived need for cooperation and coordination between the Fund and the Bank in so many areas, there is a case for merging the two institutions. Proposals for merger have surfaced in the past because the overlap between the two institutions made it difficult to distinguish the Fund's activities from those of the Bank and merger was seen as a logical way of avoiding duplication of work and possible conflicting advice (see Crook, 1991). The suggestion for a merger has been advanced again – in the aftermath of East Asia – by former Secretary of the Treasury, George Schultz.[29]

A merger would be logical only if one were to conclude that there is no distinctive role for the Fund in the new financial architecture which cannot be performed just as efficiently by the Bank. This is clearly not the case. On the contrary, the distinctive features of latter-day crises imply that the Fund's role, both in surveillance and as a financing institution, has become more distinct from that of the Bank. Surveillance in future must focus much more on market perceptions and short-term factors which could affect confidence, and these areas are outside the special expertise of the Bank. Surveillance by the Fund in future must therefore involve more extensive consultation between the Fund and many other participants in the international financial system in addition to the Bank. The financing requirements for handling latter-day crises are also very different from what they used to be. The Fund has to be able to provide large volumes of finance to support programmes aimed at restoring confidence, but unlike in 1980s such financing does not have to be long-term and certainly not concessional.

These developments suggest that instead of a merger of the two institutions the role of the Fund in

the future should actually become more distinct from that of the Bank. The Fund should focus more sharply on sources of instability in the international financial system and on handling balance-of-payments problems which are either short-term or systemic in nature. It could even be argued that financing operations related to chronic balance-of-payments problems of low-income countries, e.g. the ESAF and the Heavily Indebted Poor Countries (HIPC) Initiative, are much closer to structural adjustment lending where corrective policies focus heavily on extensive structural reform, and should perhaps be shifted to the Bank, with cooperation from the Fund being made available on technical matters. The problem of transferring the resources involved, which are currently located in the Fund, will present legal difficulties, but this problem could be overcome provided that the principle is accepted.

D. Reform of the Interim and Development Committees

A common complaint about the present system is the lack of a high-level political forum which takes a unified look at interrelated issues such as the functioning of the international financial system, macroeconomic stability and policy coordination in the major industrialized countries, special problems of vulnerability of emerging market economies, and the impact of international trends on the development process. The Fund-Bank annual meeting of Governors is largely ceremonial, and given its size it cannot be anything else.

The Interim Committee and the Development Committee are more compact political-level bodies which meet twice a year. Though they have a substantially overlapping membership, they function as separate committees with Fund-related issues being dealt with in the Interim Committee and Bank issues in the Development Committee. Their functioning leaves a great deal to be desired. Until recently, both committees operated with procedures in which most of the time was devoted to prepared speeches with little opportunity for substantive interaction between Ministers. The procedure has been greatly improved in this respect in recent years, but the objective of creating a forum capable of taking an integrated view of the interrelated issues of international finance, trade and development, with substantive discussions at a high political level, has yet to be achieved.

The principal reason why the two committees have not served as forums for substantive discussions is simply that the industrialized countries have not found it necessary to use them for this purpose. They engage in fairly extensive interaction among themselves in the G-7, based on detailed preparatory work at the official level by deputies from capitals, and positions arrived at through this process are often presented in the meetings of the two committees more or less as faits accomplis. Industrialized countries do not perceive the need for a substantive discussion with developing countries at a political level before formulating their own position, because the consent of the developing countries is not actually needed in order to push policy in the Fund and the Bank in the direction they want. On rare occasions developing countries have used their voting power to block an initiative by industrialized countries, as happened in Madrid in 1994, when the industrialized countries had a strong interest in pushing through a special allocation of SDRs in favour of transition countries but were unwilling to concede a significant general increase. Since the decision required an 85 per cent majority, the developing countries were in a position to block the proposal, which they did, but they did not succeed in extracting agreement on a general increase.

The need to consult developing countries was seen to be more compelling in the wake of the East Asian crisis in order to secure agreement on the broad outline of the new financial architecture. However, the United States, which took the initiative on this issue, bypassed the Interim Committee and invited an ad hoc collection of 22 countries (the G-22, which has since been expanded to G-33) to discuss the issue. The group included a number of emerging market economies which were judged to be "systemically" important, many of which would not have been included if the discussions had taken place in the Interim Committee, which reflects the constituency structure of the IMF Board. It is more representative of the diversity of developing countries, but it does not include all the economically significant emerging market economies, and involvement of significant "stakeholders" was obviously felt to be necessary.

Various proposals for reform of the Interim and Development Committees have been made in the recent past. A long-standing proposal to convert the Interim Committee into a council with decision making powers, which was provided for in the Second Amendment, was recently considered by the IMF Board but did not meet with approval. Two proposals for restructuring the Interim and Development Committees are currently under consideration.

(i) The first is to retain the present two-committee structure but make the committees more symmetric by making the Bank a full partner in the Interim Committee and enforcing a clear delineation of responsibilities between the two committees to avoid overlaps. In this case, global economic issues, including their implications for development, would be discussed only in the Interim Committee while the Development Committee would focus on specific development-related initiatives, including those in which they Fund is involved such as ESAF and HIPC.

(ii) The second alternative involves the creation of a single overarching group at Ministerial level to address global economic issues, with the Interim Committee and the Development Committee continuing to address specific Fund and Bank issues as at present. The Fund and the Bank would be full partners in the new group, while other institutions such as the WTO, UNCTAD, BIS and IOSCO could be permanent observers and could be involved in the preparatory work for agenda items in these areas. The group could meet twice a year as the Interim and Development Committees do at present, with a plenary session in the morning for the overarching group followed by separate Interim and Development Committee meetings as at present. The new group could also meet on other occasions if circumstances warranted without being linked to meetings of the two committees.

The first alternative clearly reflects a minimalist approach and is unlikely to achieve any significant improvement on present practice other than giving the Bank a more elevated position in the Interim Committee in the event that the committee is not converted into a council. The second alternative is clearly more ambitious and involves a substantive change in the present arrangements. Its main advantage is that it would create a new international forum at which major industrialized countries and developing countries, including all the emerging market countries, could interact with each other and also with the major players in the global financial system, such as the BIS, UNCTAD, IOSCO and WTO, in order to evolve a consensus on critical issues facing the global economy from the perspective of both industrialized and developing countries.

The country composition of the new forum could be made wider than that of the Interim Committee by including the top 10 industrialized countries by size of quota in the Fund, plus the top 10 among the other members, which include oil-exporting countries, transition countries and developing countries, plus all those countries not already covered by this criterion but which represent their constituencies on the IMF Board.[30] This formula is likely to produce a group of around 30 countries which would include all the major "stakeholders" defined in terms of economic potential, and would ensure a degree of representativeness based on objective selection criteria.

This would create a credible international forum which could take an integrated view of the functioning of the global economic system in which operational issues related to the Fund and the Bank would be only part of the agenda. The forum would include some of the major non-government participants in the international financial system, which is necessary given the enormously increased role of private markets. The proposal also has the advantage of continuing the Interim and Development Committees in more or less their present forms, which is useful for providing operational guidance for the Fund and the Bank respectively. A potential problem in this proposal will be the pressure to expand the new international forum to include various international agencies connected with one or other aspect of development. Too broad a definition of development will widen the net too much and dilute the effectiveness of the forum if it is ever established. This should obviously be avoided.

Notes

1   Both the quality of its project portfolio and the creditworthiness of its borrowers were important considerations for an organization dependent on the markets for its funds.

2   In the 1960s, for example, the Bank adopted a "programme of projects" approach in some Latin American countries, linking disbursements for a group of projects to the pursuit of macroeconomic policies to control inflation. In the mid-1960s the Bank also engaged in non-project lending for India to provide much needed balance-of-payments support (see Kapur et al., 1997).

3   The Trust Fund was included in the package at the time of the Second Amendment to the Articles in 1976 in order to obtain the consent of the developing countries to the amendment. These countries had participated in the discussions on international monetary reforms in the Committee of Twenty in the hope of securing some link between the provision of liquidity through SDRs and the expansion of development assistance. No such link was accepted, however, and the Trust Fund was offered instead as a sop.

4   ESAF interest rates were subsidized by grants from the aid budgets of some aid donors. This introduced an overlap (admittedly very small) on the resources side between the Fund and the Bank/IDA, since interest subsidies came from the same pool of resources from which IDA contributions were made.

5   Fiscal problems in borrowing countries also made it difficult for many developing countries to maintain a pipeline of new projects, because they could not always find the counterpart domestic resources needed to add to the projects already under way.

6   Many of these policy initiatives involved regulatory, legal and institutional changes which could not be reduced to precise quantitative targeting. Some of the multitude of actions were in the nature of consequential action within the same areas to bring about institutional reform.

7   It is relevant to note that the Bank's Vice President for Development Policy at the time, Stanley Fischer, who is now First Deputy Managing Director of the Fund, had expressed reservations on proceeding with the Argentine loan in view of the fiscal problems identified by the Fund (see Kapur et al., 1997).

8   Balance-of-payments problems in the past typically arose from a deterioration in the current account caused either by domestic policy misalignments or a change in external circumstances or, in the case of developing countries, by structural constraints on the supply side. The structural nature of balance-of-payments problems in developing countries has long been recognized and it calls for a longer period of adjustment, and therefore a larger cumulative amount of financing, but the annual financing need in such cases is still defined by the degree of pressure on the current account.

9   The theoretical literature on panics and bank runs treats such cases as examples of multiple equilibria (see, for example, Diamond and Dybvig, 1983).

10 The conventional wisdom at the time was that if a current account deficit was not a reflection of public sector deficits, and was being financed by private flows, the market had clearly judged it to be sustainable and there was no cause to worry. This obviously ignored the potential instability in private flows, a lesson which has been learned since then.

11 The Thai current account deficit had reached 8 per cent of GDP, the same level as in Mexico before the crisis, and there was also a real appreciation of the baht, though not as much as in the case of the peso. Fund surveillance clearly picked up signals which had preceded the crisis in Mexico, but it did not pick up financial sector weakness which had not been identified as a cause of crises earlier.

12 This is not to deny that capital flight can take place even without capital account liberalization. However, while a regulated system has leakages, the speed at which outflows can take place in the face of restrictions is obviously much lower.

13 See, for example, Radelet and Sachs (1998). The failure of the Fund's programmes in the Russian Federation and Brazil was less damaging to the Fund's credibility, because in those cases the failure was due to non-performance of the requirements under the programme. This is most glaring in the case of the Russian Federation, but it was also true in Brazil, where fiscal commitments under the programme were called into question in the legislature, thus creating doubts about the government's ability to implement the programme.

14 A Fund Staff study (Lane et al., 1999) has defended the high interest rate policy followed in East Asia by arguing that it was not associated with an excessive contraction in money supply. Real growth in money supply and domestic

15 Disclosure alone may not be much help because the complexity of many derivative instruments makes it very difficult to determine the net exposure to risk of institutions extensively involved in derivatives trading. The whole issue of the management of risks associated with derivatives is one which needs greater attention from regulators not only in developing countries but also in industrialized countries.

16 The relationship between such a body and the national regulators was never clarified, although it is clearly an important issue which cannot be avoided.

17 The marginalization of the Fund in substantive policy coordination among G-7 countries was most evident at the time of the Plaza Accord and the Lourre Accord.

18 SRF resources are made available over a period of one year and carry an interest rate 300 basis points above the normal Fund charges. They are expected to be repaid between one and one and a half years after withdrawal, but the repayment period can be extended by a year. In the latter case the interest spread increases to 500 basis points.

19 It was relatively clear that the bilateral package for Thailand was to be disbursed *pari passu* with Fund financing. No part of the bilateral package for Indonesia or the Republic of Korea was disbursed.

20 The Fund staff study of the East Asian experience (Lane et al., 1999) admits that the resources made available under the programmes were deemed to be sufficient only on the assumption that the programmes would lead to a quick restoration of confidence reversing the capital outflow. This did not happen, however.

21 The recent Brazilian package is an example of a Fund arrangement negotiated in anticipation of a crisis, but even that negotiation was carried out at a stage when the crisis was looming and conditionality was therefore fairly stiff.

22 If all possible types of adverse developments could be fully anticipated, the appropriate policy response in each hypothetical case could also be defined and agreed in advance, and financing could be extended automatically in the event of a crisis, subject to the pre-agreed policy corrections being adopted. However, it is clearly impossible to anticipate all the circumstances in which a crisis would be triggered and agreement, reached in advance on the corrective action needed. In the absence of such agreement, some negotiation of suitable conditionality after the crisis occurs appears unavoidable.

23 Since pre-qualification implies a substantial convergence of perceptions between the government and the Fund before the crisis, it could be argued that it increases the probability that a mutually acceptable adjustment programme to deal with the crisis will be negotiated.

24 This process is mutually beneficial for both debtors and creditors just as domestic bankruptcy laws are designed to prevent creditors from engaging in a "grab race" for assets, which would only push the debtor into liquidating. Since the value of the firm as a going concern is generally greater than the value of its assets in liquidation, bankruptcy laws provide opportunities for firms to bring in fresh capital and restructure their debts in a mutually beneficial manner for both debtors and creditors.

25 Exiting creditors would not be seen to benefit if Fund programmes actually succeeded in stabilizing exchange rates. However, when these fail to do so, as in East Asia,

the Russian Federation and Brazil, creditors able to exit because of Fund financing do benefit. The benefit is evident where the debt is denominated in domestic currency and the exit enables them to avoid the loss of confidence, but it is also present where the debt is denominated in foreign currency, since exiting creditors avoid the increase in default risk associated with an exchange crisis.

26 This is not to suggest that it would ensure identical terms of debt restructuring. That would necessarily depend on the circumstances of each case.

27 This is effectively the formula that was used for exchange rate regimes in the Second Amendment after the collapse of the Bretton Woods system. Members can choose whatever regime they wish, but they must inform the Fund of their choice.

28 SALs are specifically designed to allow the Bank to lend in conjunction with a Fund programme to countries facing a crisis where there is a presumption that the country will need structural adjustment lending in the post-crisis phase. ESALs have a much shorter repayment period (between three and five years) and carry an interest rate at least 400 basis points higher than the Bank's normal lending rate.

29 Schultz, writing jointly with William Simon and Walter Wriston (Schultz et al., 1998), first criticized the Fund for imprudent lending and adding to moral hazard in East Asia, and argued that it should be abolished. Subsequently, he suggested the alternative of merging it with the World Bank (Schultz, 1998).

30 The 20 countries that would qualify on this basis in the first two categories are the United States, Germany, Japan, France, the United Kingdom, Italy, Canada, Belgium, the Netherlands and Switzerland among the industrialized countries, and Saudi Arabia, the Russian Federation, China, India, Brazil, Venezuela, Mexico, Argentina, Indonesia and South Africa among the others. All the G-22 participants would be included except Australia, Hong Kong (China), the Republic of Korea, Malaysia, Poland and Thailand. Some of these, e.g. Australia, would be likely to be included as constituency representatives.

References

BRETTON WOODS COMMISSION (1994), *Bretton Woods: Looking to its Future* (Washington, DC: BWC), July.

CROOK, C. (1991), "The IMF and the World Bank", *The Economist*, 12 October.

DIAMOND, D. and P. DYBVIG (1983), "Bank runs, deposit insurance, and liquidity", *Journal of Political Economy*, Vol. 3, No. 3, June, pp. 401–419.

FISCHER, S. (1999), "On the need for an international lender of last resort", paper presented at a joint luncheon of the American Economic Association and the American Finance Association, New York, 3 January 1999.

GRIFFITH-JONES, S. with J. KIMMIS (1999), "Capital flows: How to curb their volatility", background paper for the 1999 *Human Development Report* (New York: United Nations Development Programme).

JAMES, H. (1996), *International Monetary Co-operation since Bretton Woods* (Oxford: Oxford University Press).

KAPUR, D., J.P. LEWIS, and R. WEBB (1997), *The World Bank in its First Half Century*, Vols. I and II (Washington, DC: Brookings Institutions).

KENEN, P.B. (1994), *Managing the World Economy, Fifty Years after Bretton Woods* (Washington, DC: Institute for International Economy).

KHATKHATE, D.R., and I. DALLA (1995), "Regulated deregulation of the financial system in Korea", Economic Discussion Papers (Washington, DC: World Bank).

KRUEGER, A. (1998), "Whither the World Bank and the IMF", Working Paper No. 23 (Stanford, CA: Stanford University, Center for Research on Economic Development and Policy Reform).

LANE, T., A.R. GHOSH, J. HAMMAN, S. PHILLIPS, M. SCHULTZ-GHATTAS, and T. TSIKATA (1999), "IMF-supported programmes in Indonesia, Korea and Thailand: A preliminary assessment", not published (Washington, DC: International Monetary Fund); available on the Internet at www.imf.org.

POLAK, J. (1997), "The World Bank and the IMF: A changing relationship", in D. Kapur et al. (eds.), *The World Bank in* *its First Half Century,* Vol. II (Washington, DC: Brookings Institutions).

RADELET, S. and J.D. SACHS (1998), *The East Asian Financial Crises: Diagnosis, Remedies, Prospect* (Cambridge, MA: Harvard Institute for International Development), 20 April.

SCHULTZ, G. (1998), "Merge the IMF and World Bank", *The International Economy*, Vol. 12, No. 1, January, pp. 14–16.

SCHULTZ, G., W.E. SIMON, and W.B. WRISTON (1998), "Who needs the IMF", *Wall Street Journal*, 3 February.

SOROS, G. (1998), "To avert the next crisis", *Financial Times*, 4 June.

WORLD BANK (1999), *Global Economic Prospects and the Developing Countries 1998-99: Beyond Financial Crisis* (Washington, DC).

THE BIS AND ITS ROLE IN INTERNATIONAL FINANCIAL GOVERNANCE

Stephany Griffith-Jones
with Jenny Kimmis*

Abstract

There is growing consensus concerning the need to improve international mechanisms for the prevention and management of financial crises. The Bank for International Settlements (BIS) has a mandate to promote international cooperation on monetary and financial issues with the objective to contribute to international financial stability. Initially, BIS's activity focused very much on financial stability in the major industrial countries, but it has increasingly widened its activities to include developing countries, for which international financial stability and greater efficiency in financial markets worldwide is essential for sustaining economic stability and growth.

BIS and the Basle Committees[1] – which are part of the so-called "Basle process" – do not operate as supranational or multinational entities; there is no international law that provides a basis for their global activities. Rather, collective agreements among members of BIS and the Committees are implemented on the basis of national legislation or regulation of each of the countries involved in the process. Frequently such agreements are also adopted by countries not participating in the Basle process, the most prominent case being the capital adequacy standards adopted by the Basle Committee on Banking Supervision (BCBS), which have been accepted by bank regulators worldwide as effective global standards.

An important question for the future role of BIS is whether this procedure continues to be appropriate as financial globalization deepens and as the role of developing countries increases. Another important challenge is the growing need to include in the Basle process more participants from developing countries, which are playing an ever more important role in international finance and which suffer most from the effects of financial instability and currency crises.

This paper first reviews the main functions of BIS and the features of the Basle process. It examines the work for promoting financial stability and preventing crises carried out by the key BIS Committees and the role of BIS in crisis management, and discusses the issue of membership and management of BIS, in particular the growing but still very limited role of developing countries. The paper also makes some suggestions on how BIS's work should be deepened and broadened, especially with regard to the particular concerns of the developing countries. Specifically, it recommends that BIS and the Committees be developed into a body of global prudential regulation, promoting financial stability globally and in individual countries; that the role of BIS in official lending be extended to supplement the recently created the IMF Contingency Credit Line; that the participation of developing countries in BIS and the Committees be further increased; and that BIS provide more information on capital and banking markets, especially for policy makers.

---

* We should like to thank Gerry Helleiner for commissioning this interesting study and for his valuable and detailed suggestions. We are very grateful to many BIS colleagues for their perceptive insights and for all the information and material provided during a visit to BIS. We are also grateful to Yilmaz Akyüz and John Toye at UNCTAD for their interesting suggestions. As always, the responsibility for any mistakes is our own.

I. Introduction

Over the last two decades, financial crises have tended to occur with increasing frequency. Many of these crises have affected developing countries, often with devastating effects on their growth and development. The crisis which started in mid-1997 in East Asia, and then spread to several parts of the developing world as well as affecting also the developed economies, has illustrated the seriousness of the effects of these crises and the urgent need to improve international mechanisms for both crisis prevention and management.

As a consequence, financial stability – both domestically and internationally – emerges as a key objective of economic policy. BIS had a mandate to promote international cooperation on monetary and financial issues, with the pursuit of international financial stability at the heart of its activities. Initially, its activities focused very much on financial stability in the major industrial countries, but it has increasingly widened its activities to include developing countries. BIS is not just an international organization but also a bank; as such, it offers banking services to virtually all central banks.

From the perspective of developing countries, it seems particularly important that BIS – and the Committees that constitute the Basle process – achieve the two following objectives that are of great importance to developing countries: (i) to contribute as much and as effectively as possible to greater international financial stability and to greater efficiency in financial markets worldwide – efficiency particularly in the sense of helping to sustain long-term growth and development; the pursuit of this objective also implies crisis prevention and better crisis management to make financial crises less likely and less costly if they unfortunately do occur; (ii) to increase the participation of developing countries in the management and activities of BIS itself and in the different Committees, as these constitute an important part of the process of global financial governance. This is desirable with a view to ensuring that developing countries' concerns are addressed and their interests sufficiently well represented, and also to improving the effectiveness of BIS's work related to developing countries.

BIS was created under international law with a specific mandate to promote central bank cooperation for the purpose of maintaining global financial stability and providing additional facilities for international financial operations (Giovanoli, 1989; Helleiner, 1994). International cooperation at BIS is based firmly on the principle of national (home) country control (Kapstein, 1994). This starts from a diagnosis that sovereignty still resides at the level of the nation-state and that parliaments, particularly of large countries, are often unwilling to cede power to international bodies, even though financial systems and capital flows are becoming ever more globalized. Thus, the BIS Committees do not operate as a supranational or multinational entity. Indeed, there is no international law that provides a basis for all their global activities. Instead, national central bankers and regulators meet regularly in the BIS context to negotiate – each pursuing national objectives and perceptions – and to reach compromise consensus agreements. These collective agreements are subsequently implemented using national legislation or regulation.

Furthermore, countries not participating in these discussions, e.g. developing economies, often also adopt the agreements reached through the Basle process. This is well illustrated by the capital adequacy standards adopted by the BCBS, which have been accepted by bank regulators worldwide. The fact that agreements reached via this very ad hoc process are accepted by national legislators and regulators worldwide is seen by senior BIS officials to testify to the perceived legitimacy of the process itself (White, 1998). It could of course be argued that as central banks worldwide become more independent, they become less accountable to their national democratically elected institutions; to the extent that this weakens the legitimacy of central banks at a national level (which has as yet not emerged as a major issue but which may do so, especially where central banks are seen as excessively concerned with inflation and not with growth), BIS could indirectly see its legitimacy weakened. In this respect, it may be desirable for BIS – or its member central banks – to report on a regular basis to national parliaments on its activities to ensure transparency.

More broadly, an important question for the future role of BIS is whether this process of "bottom up" global regulation or "global governance on the quiet" continues to be appropriate as financial globalization deepens and as the role of developing countries increases. If this is so, then the Basle ad hoc methods of global governance need to be deepened and expanded to include, for example, closer collaboration between different regulatory bodies (e.g. the BCBS, the International Organization of Securities Commissions [IOSCO] and the Insurance

Regulators). A very important step along this path was taken by the G-7 finance ministers and central bank governors in February 1999, when they created the Financial Stability Forum with the purpose of ensuring more effective coordination between national and international authorities, relevant supervisory bodies, as well as to reduce systemic risk. The Forum will be chaired for the first three years by Andrew Crockett, General Manager of BIS. It will be supported by a small secretariat located in Basle. If, however, this approach becomes increasingly insufficient to deal with the difficult and complex challenges of financial globalization, a transition towards a more supranational approach may in the medium term be required, along the line of proposals made for a World Financial Authority (Eatwell and Taylor, 1998), although this will probably require more complex international negotiations and an international law or treaty.

Another important challenge, if the path chosen is a continuation and deepening of the BIS ad hoc international governance, as the creation of the Financial Stability Forum indicates, is the growing need to include more participants from developing countries, which are playing an increasingly important role in international financial matters, and which suffer most from the effects of financial instability and currency crises. It may be difficult to make compatible an expansion of BIS membership with maintaining the intimate club-like *modus operandi*, which reportedly facilitates agreement and consensus decision-making. From the perspective of developing countries, the issue is, however, how they can become as integrated as possible into BIS and its surrounding Committees, in ways that assure that their interests are sufficiently represented. This issue has also become particularly relevant for the Forum for Financial Stability, as no developing countries that are recipients of capital flows and prone to currency crises have as yet been invited to participate.

In section II of this paper, the main features and functions of BIS as well as of the Basle process will be examined. Section III will then focus on the work for promoting financial stability and preventing crises, mainly carried out by the key BIS Committees, and examine the role of BIS in crisis management, particularly its contribution to the international financing packages put together for developing countries in crises. Section IV will discuss the issue of membership and management of BIS, and in particular the limited, though growing, role of developing countries. Section V will look at how BIS's

work should continue to be deepened and broadened, particularly in relation to including developing countries and their interests in BIS activities, but also in relation to integrating the regulatory activities of non-banking financial sectors more closely into the activities of BIS and the Committees. Finally, the paper will provide some policy recommendations.

II. Main features and functions of BIS and the Basle process

A. The BIS

The Bank's predominant tasks are summed up most succinctly in part of Article 3 of its original Statutes: they are "to promote the cooperation of central banks and to provide additional facilities for international financial operations". An important aim of this increasing central bank cooperation has been to promote international financial stability. With rapidly integrating financial markets in the world and with the risk of crises also spreading globally, international central bank cooperation is becoming even more essential. Naturally, central bank coordination at BIS has also focused on improved coherence of monetary policies in particular, and macroeconomic policies in general – important subjects which go beyond the scope of this paper. Thus, BIS is an important forum for international monetary and financial cooperation between central bankers and, increasingly, between other regulators and supervisors. As BIS (1998) itself put it, "the stability of the international monetary and financial systems has long been a central concern of the central bankers' meetings at the BIS".

BIS was founded in 1930. It is the oldest international organization in the field of international monetary cooperation. In 1944, on the occasion of the Bretton Woods Conference, it was recommended that BIS be liquidated, following the founding of IMF. In the event, BIS experienced a great expansion after World War II, and began collaboration with IMF. It played a key role in both the creation and operation of various intra-European payments arrangements in the post-World War II era. The Basle governors' meetings generated initiatives which attempted to fight successive waves of speculation against different developed countries between 1960 and 1971. BIS was also the forum for the creation of the General Arrangements to Borrow (GAB), under which the G-10, as well as Switzerland, make resources available to the International Monetary Fund, outside their quotas.

The Governors of the G-10 Central Banks meet regularly on the occasion of the Basle monthly meetings. These G-10 meetings have become an important forum in which much wider activities – including setting up the key Basle Committees – have been put in motion by the G-10 Central Banks in the pursuit of international financial stability, for example in the fields of financial market monitoring, banking supervision, payment and settlements systems. While these meetings and activities traditionally focused on events in the G-10 countries, a growing number of meetings now focus on developments in emerging markets as well, or on the world economy. However, even when emerging-market countries are the focus of discussions, still too often the perspective from which developments in them are analysed is that of the G-10 countries. Indeed, some of the important meetings at which developing economies are discussed are still reportedly only attended by G-10 country representatives, though governors of the major central banks of developing countries (particularly Asian and Latin American), as well as of the Russian Federation, are increasingly invited to attend.

Although much of the focus of the work done by BIS (and of this paper) is on the financial system, it is also important to underline the role of BIS and its meetings in international coordination of monetary policy, as well as technical work and research on the conduct of monetary policy. Between 1964 and the end of 1993, BIS hosted the Secretariat of the Committee of Governors of the Central Banks of the Member States of the European Economic Community. In this context, the secretariat of the European Committee of Governors – based at BIS – performed a number of key functions for the growing European integration, both of an operational nature – BIS acted as Agent for the European Monetary Cooperation Fund – and in the context of preparation for the European Exchange Rate Mechanism (ERM) and European Monetary Union (EMU). Indeed, the Committee of European Governors and the European Monetary Cooperation Fund, both serviced by the secretariat based at BIS, were the bodies for monetary cooperation in the European Community. These tasks were then taken over first by the European Monetary Institute (in January 1994), and then by the European Central Bank. This development has reportedly been an important incentive in encouraging BIS to "fill this gap" by increasing its activities in relation to developing countries since 1994. At

the same time, the need for a greater role for BIS vis-à-vis developing countries increased sharply, particularly owing to the Mexican peso crisis and the East Asian crisis.

Though the direct role of BIS in European monetary integration has diminished, the influence of European countries in BIS (particularly amongst its staff) may be somewhat higher than in IMF. This may be one important factor why BIS has always tended to be more pragmatic on issues such as capital account and financial liberalization in developing countries, tending to stress both costs and benefits, and always emphasizing issues of timing and preconditions for successful liberalization.

B.   *The process of achieving agreements*

The process of achieving agreements – on matters such as international standards for regulation of the financial sector in different countries – is a difficult one, as each country starts off with different traditions, accounting systems and domestic regulations. Domestic firms press for minimizing the extent and costs of any changes arising from international agreements. BIS and, in particular, the committees under the aegis of G-10 Central Bank Governors have operated via international cooperation based firmly on home country (state) control, rather than through entrusting it to some international institution. Members of the various committees which meet at BIS negotiate positions among themselves, each reflecting more their national interests; each has also consulted with private sector actors, especially financial institutions, in his/her own country.[2] The aim is to reach a negotiated agreement acceptable to all G-10 countries, and to the public and private sector actors involved. These agreements are often ratified by ministers and central bank governors of the G-10 countries and, if required, are approved by G-10 legislatures.

Most of the agreements reached have also been accepted and implemented by developing countries. The acceptance by non-G-10 countries, of standards agreed by G-10 countries, has been encouraged by the fact that non-G-10 countries see them as broadly desirable. This is not only due to efforts made by various Basle Committees to disseminate their agreements, but also because private rating agencies consider meeting Basle capital adequacy standards as an important element in rating financial institutions. IMF, the World Bank and the regional development banks have also played a big role – especially through their surveillance and through conditions attached to their loans – in the spreading of the standards adopted by the Basle Committees. Indeed, it was stressed in several of the meetings held at BIS that there was a fairly sharp and important distinction, broadly seen as desirable, whereby institutions like BIS and the Committees linked to it formulated standards and norms for financial sectors and institutions such as IMF and the World Bank, which help to disseminate them and to survey their implementation in developing countries. As described below, the process of formulation of standards and norms is mainly done by G-10 representatives, though with the increasing participation – and especially consultation – of some developing countries.

The fact that basically the G-10 committees formulate standards and developing countries "accept" them assumes, possibly sometimes incorrectly, that the same standards are equally applicable to different categories of countries. Furthermore, the fact that developing countries are only partly represented in the deliberations on determining these standards could reduce their legitimacy for developing countries.

It needs to be stressed that even though the process has been functional in achieving very important international agreements, it has not really been successful in preventing crises, even when the risk that provoked or contributed to a crisis had already been identified before the crisis. Thus, the BCBS was only set up in the wake of the failure of the Bankhaus Herstatt in 1974, even though it had been recognized for some time that banks with large operations posed special problems. Concrete work on forging international capital adequacy standards was encouraged by the Mexican debt crisis of 1982. The G-10 Committee on Payment and Settlement Systems (CPSS) was set up in 1990 following various periods of financial distress with international repercussions, as well as a better understanding of the nature of risks in payments and settlements, particularly after a large increase in financial transactions occurred in the 1980s. On some occasions, the process has moved forward very slowly. Herstatt risk was identified (and named) in 1974, yet the first initiatives were promulgated by the CPSS only at the end of March 1996, that is 22 years later. Fortunately, Herstatt risk did not cause any major international problem during that period, arguably mainly due to luck. Thus, to a certain extent, the CPSS does provide an example of central bank preventative actions being implemented before a crisis happens.

More generally, the agreements which have been reached have probably contributed to prevent crises that would otherwise have happened or moderated ones that have occurred. Furthermore, it should be stressed that the tasks of regulators are made particularly difficult owing to two types of problems. First, information asymmetries normally identified for market actors also operate, to a certain extent, for regulators. When a new instrument or sector is developed, it is difficult also for regulators to determine precisely the nature and seriousness of the risks involved, although previous experience, as well as theory, can help sketch the broad contours of the risks involved. Secondly, when new financial markets or instruments are being developed, there is a sense of excitement in the markets, which is encouraged both by the novelty and the large profits that are normally made. A wave of "market knows best" sentiments is frequently transmitted to governments and regulators. Once an important failure, or crisis, has occurred, both information on the precise risks involved and awareness of the dangers increase substantially; as a result, regulatory action is usually taken.

It also seems interesting to mention that although the process broadly operates via consensus agreements among the G-10 countries, its more powerful members have, at various times, forced the process in rather unconventional ways. In the mid-1980s, progress in harmonizing approaches for capital adequacy standards were seen as "too slow" by United States authorities. The United States and the United Kingdom, representing the two largest financial centres by far, struck a bilateral deal, based on the British approach to risk-weighted capital standards. This sharply increased the intensity and speed of negotiations in the BCBS and contributed to the Capital Adequacy Agreements (Helleiner, 1994; Kapstein, 1994; White, 1996).

One important future challenge for the Basle process is the need to include participants from developing countries in the Committees on a more systematic and formal basis. Increased participation in the meetings should be achieved in a way that does not detract from the efficiency involved in making decisions through the Basle Committees. It has, for example, been argued that one of the reasons why the Committees are more efficient in reaching agreements than the worldwide organization of securities' regulators (IOSCO) is because the former have a far smaller membership, which has shared values and conceptual frameworks, and allows it to operate in a "club-like" atmosphere. However, these problems should not be over-stated, as mechanisms (such as a rotating membership) can be found to make consistent a far broader representation in the Basle process (to include different categories of developing countries, including poorer and smaller countries), with continued efficiency in decision-making.

It is also extremely important that not only offshore centres be increasingly incorporated into the Basle process, but also that mechanisms be found so that such offshore centres do not continue to make desirable changes in regulation difficult or impossible. Indeed, in recent discussions on the possible need to regulate institutional investors – such as mutual funds or hedge funds – it has been argued (even by those who see it as desirable to diminish the risks of currency crises) that any such regulations would be avoided by a flight to offshore centres. Therefore, a crucial element for improving global regulation is to explore ways – at least for those aspects, though also ideally for taxation purposes – for offshore centres to come onshore. It is very encouraging that one of the three Working Groups of the Financial Stability Forum is devoted to offshore centres. It is to be hoped that it will address not only its main brief, which is the important issue of whether offshore centres undermine global stability, but also the issue of whether offshore centres make desirable regulation less feasible.

III. How do BIS and the Basle Committees promote financial stability?

A.　*Financial regulation and the Financial Stability Forum*

Action to encourage financial stability can be broadly classified as directed either to prevention of crises and/or to crisis management and resolution. Clearly, crisis prevention is better, cheaper and more effective for sustaining growth than crisis management or resolution. However, good crisis management is also important if crises do occur. BIS and the Basle Committees have focused particularly strongly on activities relating to financial crisis prevention, especially on measures that strengthen the financial sector both within countries and internationally. BIS and the Committees are clearly the main focus of international coordination of financial-sector regulation. This is particularly true for banking systems, but is also true in relation to coordination with in-

surance regulators.[3] Links are also growing with IOSCO, particularly in the context of the Joint Forum (see below).[4] Consequently, BIS appears to be the obvious starting point for any future global financial regulation, such as an international supervisory surveillance secretariat – first proposed by the Canadian Government in April 1998 – built on in the Standing Committee for Global Financial Regulation proposed by Clare Short and Gordon Brown to the October 1998 Development Committee, or indeed for a super-regulator, that at a later stage would attempt to fully integrate global regulation between the different financial sectors and internationally.

In October 1998, the G-7 finance ministers and central bank governors approved this idea in principle and asked Hans Tietmeyer, then president of the Bundesbank, to develop the United Kingdom's proposal and more generally to consider cooperation and coordination between the various international regulatory and supervisory bodies, and to make recommendations for any new arrangements. Tietmeyer's report, released in February 1999, outlined areas where improvements to current arrangements were necessary, but stated that "sweeping institutional changes are not needed to realise these improvements" (Tietmeyer, 1999). It was proposed that a Financial Stability Forum, which would meet regularly to discuss issues affecting the global financial system and to identify actions needed to enhance stability, be convened. The Forum was formally endorsed by G-7 finance ministers and central bank governors at their February meeting in Bonn (see appendix 2), and met already for the first time in the spring of 1999.

The Tietmeyer report had outlined three main areas in which current arrangements should be improved: (i) identification of vulnerabilities in national and international financial systems and sources of systemic risk, as well as effective policies to mitigate them; (ii) development and implementation of comprehensive international rules and standards of best practice; and (iii) ensuring consistency of international rules and arrangements across all types of financial institutions.

Each G-7 country will have three representatives on the Forum, from the Finance Ministry, Central Bank and Supervisory Authority. The G-7 stated that while the Forum will initially be limited to G-7 countries, it is envisaged that other national authorities, including from emerging-market countries, will join the process at some stage. IMF and the World Bank will have two representatives each, as will the BCBS, IOSCO and the International Association of Insurance Supervisors (IAIS). BIS, OECD and the two BIS Committees will all have one representative on the Forum.

The Forum will initially meet twice a year, beginning in the spring of 1999. One of the key aims of the Forum will be to better coordinate the responsibilities of the main national and international authorities and supervisory bodies, and to pool the information held by these various bodies, in order to improve the functioning of markets and reduce systemic risk. Subsequent to its meeting in April, the Financial Stability Forum has defined three ad hoc working groups to tackle recommendations on three key subjects defined:

(i) To recommend actions to reduce the destabilizing potential of institutions employing a high degree of leverage (HLIs) in the financial markets of developed and developing economies;

(ii) To evaluate measures in borrower and creditor countries that could reduce the volatility of capital flows and the risks to financial systems of excessive short-term external indebtedness;

(iii) To evaluate the impact on global financial stability of the uses made by market participants of financial offshore centres, and the progress made by such centres in enforcing international prudential standards and in complying with cross-border information exchange agreements. As regards offshore centres, an assessment will be made of the additional efforts required to avoid underregulation or inappropriate disclosure in offshore centres contributing to global financial instability.

The working groups comprise officials from developed and developing market economies, international financial institutions and supervisory groupings, and will draw on work completed or under way in various public and private-sector forums. Senior officials from developing countries have been included where their expertise is seen as particularly relevant. For example, the group that will study measures to study volatility of capital flows includes senior representatives from Chile and Malaysia, two countries that have implemented measures to curb inflows and outflows (Malaysia for both, and Chile for inflows).

The setting up of the Financial Stability Forum is a very valuable first step towards improving the coordination and cooperation of the various bodies which work towards improving the way markets work in order to improve global stability. The question lies, however, in whether the Forum, as it has been proposed, will be representative and strong enough to address all these complex issues.

First, the omission of any developing country authorities in the initial years of the Forum itself appears to be an important error. It has been increasingly accepted that developing countries are important actors in the increasingly globalized financial system, and that currency crises in these countries pose systemic threats to the international financial system. Representation of developing countries on the Forum would be desirable both for legitimacy reasons and because it would provide the body with a wider range of expertise and perspectives.

Ways could easily be found to include developing countries in the Forum without making it too large. If three developing country representatives were included, the membership of the Forum would rise by less than 10 per cent. Developing country representatives from countries with large levels of private capital inflows or with major financial centres could, for example, be chosen on a regional basis, i.e. one representative each from Asia, Latin America and Africa. This would also ensure that the interests of poorer countries are represented. The representatives could be appointed for a fairly short period (e.g. two years) and then rotated. This type of representation by developing countries has been working rather well in other contexts, for example on the boards of the Bretton Woods institutions.

Second, doubts have been voiced over the institutional strength of the new Forum. With a very small secretariat in Basle (currently it has only three staff members), meeting only twice yearly, and no power of enforcement, will the Forum have sufficient institutional muscle to deal with the tasks that have been identified? Can its response be speedy and agile enough to a rapidly changing international private system? The setting up of the Forum represents a significant enhancement of the system of global regulation by agreement and peer pressure that has been shown to work reasonably well in the context of the BIS Committees, as discussed above. However, in the medium term, in a world of open financial markets, an international body whose Board meets regularly and has the power to make and enforce policy may well be needed. This would point towards a body more akin to some kind of World Financial Authority, which would be endowed with executive powers along the lines of a WTO for finance.

BIS already plays an important role in crisis management and resolution, especially as relates to crises affecting developing countries. The lead role here is played by IMF, which not only puts together the main financial package, but also imposes conditionality on developing countries in crises. However, even if secondary, the role which BIS plays in contributing to the financial packages has been growing for at least three reasons. Firstly, given the size of the financial packages required, particularly in the context of capital-account-led balance-of-payments crises, the contributions that BIS can assemble – drawing mainly on credits from the G-10 Central Banks – have the advantage of additionality and flexibility. The flexibility relates to the fact that the scale of the contributions is not linked to formal limits, such as the size of IMF quotas, but depends solely on the scale of the problem and the political willingness to lend. Secondly, the loans coordinated by BIS are not explicitly linked to additional conditionality for developing countries, although their disbursement may be linked to meeting IMF conditionality. Loans without policy conditionality are particularly appropriate for providing finance to developing countries with capital-account-led crises not caused by their own policy mistakes but by external factors, such as contagion and imperfections in international capital markets. Thirdly, the most recent loan coordinated by BIS – that for Brazil (see below) – was not a bridge loan as all other BIS loans to developing countries have been, but a proper credit facility granted for one year. This is an interesting innovation, as was the fact that the BIS loan was part of what could be called a preventive financing package rather than one of full crisis management.

B.   The role of BIS in crisis prevention

A central element in crisis prevention, both in developing countries and internationally, is strengthening financial systems. As White (1996, 1998) has suggested, the international financial system can be seen to be based on three pillars: financial institutions, financial markets, and payment and settlement systems. In this context, measures to prevent crises can be classified in a three dimensional matrix. The columns comprise the different categories of financial institutions, including banks, investment dealers, insurance companies, hedge funds and others. The rows are the markets for the individual operations, a growing proportion of which are tradeable. Behind this façade is a third dimension comprising the supporting infrastructure (or "plumbing" as it is known

in the jargon) for the international financial system, including the payment system, as well as the clearing, netting and settlement systems. The infrastructure is one of the most rapidly changing dimensions in the international financial system, as new systems emerge (e.g. in trading in derivatives) and others are greatly modified. Disturbances at the level of financial institutions, markets or infrastructure cannot only interact very negatively with each other (e.g. sharp changes in the prices of financial assets determined in financial markets can contribute to undermine the solvency of financial institutions, as occurred in East Asia); disturbances in some or all of these dimensions can also have very large and disruptive implications for key macroeconomic variables, such as interest rates and exchange rates.

A number of international agreements have been reached over the years to strengthen the three dimensions of the matrix, financial institutions, financial markets, and financial infrastructure. A very central part – but not all – of the work has been carried out by three BIS Committees; indeed, there exists a BIS Committee dealing with each of these individual pillars. Thus, the Basle Committee on Banking Institutions deals with one of the key sectors of financial institutions (banks), though not with other institutions, where coordination of the regulation is either carried out by other regulators (e.g. securities and insurance) or there are regulatory gaps (e.g. hedge funds). The former Euro-Currency Standing Committee deals with financial market developments thought likely to have systemic implications, as well as collecting crucial data on market developments. Finally, the Committee on Payments and Settlements Systems deals with international agreements on the crucial issue of strengthening the financial infrastructure.

1.   The Basle Committee on Banking Supervision

The BCBS, which is the best known of the Committees which have their secretariat at BIS, was established by the central bank governors of the G-10 countries in 1975. Since its creation, the BCBS has been working to improve banking supervision at the international level. Its work covers three areas. Firstly, it provides a forum for discussion on supervisory issues; secondly, it coordinates the supervision of international banking groups and their cross-border activities; thirdly, it aims to improve financial stability by improving standards of supervision. The Committee is made up of senior representatives of bank supervisory authorities and central banks from

12 countries: the G-10 plus Switzerland and Luxembourg.

While the work of the BCBS was originally centred on supervisory issues arising in the context of the G-10 countries, the rapid pace of globalization and the resulting need for international cooperation to involve a wider group of countries have been reflected in the recent efforts of the Committee to extend its reach. In the last few years, the BCBS has been expanding its links with non-member countries in order to strengthen prudential supervisory standards in all the major markets (for details, see below). For developing countries pursuing financial integration in the global economy, a sound banking system with an adequate regulatory and supervisory framework is one of the main prerequisites (World Bank, 1997). The BCBS has made a contribution to promote financial stability, through the definition of sound supervisory practices. It is also increasingly active in helping their implementation in non-member countries (see below). Owing in particular to the complexities of properly implementing banking supervision in developing countries, further efforts in this direction seem desirable and urgent.

(a) The Basle Concordat (1975) to the Supervision of Cross-border Banking (1996)

The early concerns of the BCBS focused on ensuring that all internationally active banks were adequately supervised on a consolidated basis. In 1975, the Committee issued the Basle Concordat which established the principle that no foreign banking establishment should escape supervision, and that the home supervisor is responsible for the global operations of banks headquartered in their territory and should supervise them on a consolidated basis. The Concordat has been revised a number of times since then, but the basic principles have remained the same.

In 1992, the Committee produced its report *Minimum Standards for the Supervision of International Banking Groups and their Cross-border Establishments*, in which basic standards were set out to ensure that home supervisors operate effectively and that they have adequate access to information about the cross-border activities of banks. If these standards are not met, host countries can refuse to grant a banking licence or home supervisors can close down a bank. However, continued concern over the adequacy of information available to supervisors prompted the preparation of a further

report by a joint working group of the BCBS and the Offshore Group of Banking Supervisors. This report, *The Supervision of Cross-border Banking*, presents 29 recommendations designed to strengthen the effectiveness of supervision by home and host-country authorities of banks which operate beyond their national borders.

(b) The Capital Adequacy Agreements

In 1987, the BCBS published proposed guidelines for the measurement and assessment of the capital adequacy of banks operating internationally. In 1988, the guidelines were approved by bank supervisors from the G-10 countries, plus Luxembourg and Switzerland. Under the agreement, known as the *Basle Capital Accord*, these countries' bank supervisors were obliged to impose by the end of 1992 a minimum risk-adjusted capital asset ratio of 8 per cent on all banks operating under their jurisdiction.

The agreement was intended to establish common regulatory conditions among the banks of participating countries in order to prevent unfair competition arising due to lighter regulatory conditions in some countries, and also to raise the levels of bank capital in the G-10 countries. Despite some drawbacks, which we shall examine below, the Capital Accord succeeded in establishing standards by which all banks can be compared, and resulted in a strengthening of bank capital among the G-10 countries. The widespread compliance with the Basle Capital Accord among the G-10 countries may be attributed to a combination of pressure from domestic supervisors, acting under international peer pressure, and market discipline (White, 1996). For reasons discussed above, the capital adequacy guidelines have been voluntarily accepted by an increasing number of countries, including many of the developing economies.

Originally, the Capital Accord centred on credit risk in the calculation of capital adequacy. During the 1990s, the BCBS has been working on refining the capital adequacy standards to take account of market risk, particularly that arising from the huge increase in bank trading in futures and options. A major revision was introduced in 1995 when the Committee issued a set of recommendations extending capital requirements to market risk, in which the Committee accepted the use of internal risk management systems (subject to certain restrictions) of financial institutions to determine their exposure to market risk. This was seen by some observers as an important step towards regulators working more closely with the market. There are, however, several concerns about this new approach, including worries that the internal analysis of risk for capital adequacy purposes may result in lower requirements than would a standard approach (Griffith-Jones, 1998a). Supervisors will need to bear this concern in mind when looking at the capital requirements of financial institutions.

While the Capital Accord has been an extremely useful tool for the universal comparison of financial institutions, it has been shown to have certain shortcomings, and further work on revising capital adequacy requirements will be necessary. One example, which became evident in the analysis of the recent international financial crisis, is that the current categories for risk weighting bank assets introduce a bias in favour of short-term lending. The risk weight currently recommended by BIS for claims on non-OECD institutions with a residual maturity of up to one year is 20 per cent, whereas claims over one year have a recommended risk weight of 100 per cent. This makes short-term lending to non-OECD countries more profitable than long-term lending for international banks, and this may have contributed to the heavy build-up of short-term debt in some East Asian countries immediately prior to the recent crisis. It may therefore be desirable to diminish the regulatory incentive towards short-term lending, for example by narrowing the difference between capital adequacy requirements for long- and short-term credits (Griffith-Jones, 1998b). A further distinction in the capital adequacy rules which may require revision is that between OECD and non-OECD countries, as has repeatedly been pointed out in G-24 communiqués. It may be more appropriate to base this distinction on the quality of banking supervision. In June 1999, the BCBS published a consultative paper outlining in the Capital Accord the planned shape of a broader reform of capital adequacy ratios. These proposals are still at an early stage of development, and have now been submitted for consultation.

As regards the acceptance of the capital adequacy guidelines by developing countries, problems have arisen due to the failure to adjust bank capital adequately for non-performing loans. This is because emerging market countries often have poorly developed accounting standards and insufficient information on the quality of bank assets (Fitzgerald, 1998). This problem was also highlighted by the recent crisis in East Asia, when apparently well capitalized banks were revealed as insolvent, as the crisis unfolded (BIS, 1998). This raises the broader issue that capital adequacy and provisioning requirements should possibly have either an explicit or an implicit countercyclical element whereby standards are tightened during periods of "booms" and surges of capital, and somewhat loosened during periods of "busts" and capital out flows (see Griffith-Jones et al., 1999). Such regulatory practice could help moderate excessive swings in bank lending, which currently exaggerate both overheating of the economy and recessions. Current practice – where regulation is introduced more rigorously during a crises – has the opposite and often undesirable procyclical effect.[5] The fact that developing countries seem to be more prone to crises – and that these often lead to numerous company bankruptcies – raises the issue of whether capital adequacy standards in those countries should be higher (as is the case for example in Argentina). The costs and benefits of such higher capital adequacy standards for developing countries need to be carefully evaluated, and it seems far more desirable that this be done by developing countries themselves, and not the imposition of general standards. However, analysis of international experiences in this area by the BCBS or BIS could be very valuable.

The Capital Adequacy Agreements will also face new challenges in the future, such as those presented by bank lending to hedge funds or for derivative operations, which may require further changes to regulation. Moreover, in the context of developing countries, it is important to bear in mind that standards set among G-10 nations, such as the capital adequacy standards, represent minimum requirements and that in the case of some developing countries it may be prudent to set higher capital/asset ratios.

(c)   The Core Principles

In April 1997, the BCBS released a set of *Core Principles for Effective Banking Supervision* backed by a three-volume Compendium of guidance documents. These guidelines, which were mainly based on the work and decisions of the Committee over the previous two decades, cover all aspects of banking and are intended to be applied to all banks. The 25 Core Principles, which are designed to serve as a basic reference for national agencies worldwide to use in the supervision of all banking organizations within their jurisdictions, cover seven broad topics: (i) the preconditions for effective banking supervision; (ii) licensing and structure; (iii) prudential regulations and requirements; (iv) methods of ongoing banking supervision; (v) information requirements; (vi) formal powers of supervisors; and (vii) cross-border banking (BIS,1997).

In developing the principles, the Committee worked closely with the supervisory authorities in fifteen emerging-market countries. The document was prepared by representatives of the BCBS and from Chile, the Czech Republic, Hong Kong (China), Mexico and the Russian Federation. Nine other economies were also closely associated with the work: Argentina, Brazil, Hungary, India, Indonesia, Republic of Korea, Malaysia, Poland and Singapore. This was a major step for the Committee towards increasing the participation of emerging-market countries in their discussions and decision-making processes.

The Asian crisis revealed distinct weaknesses in the supervisory structures in many emerging-market countries and highlighted the relevance of the Core Principles. The BCBS believes that achieving consistency with the Core Principles in all countries will be an important step towards improving financial stability. However, while the Principles represent a set of extremely useful minimum standards with which all countries can strive to comply, it is important not to see them as a panacea to financial instability. Additionally, implementing the Core Principles in all countries is likely to be a lengthy and complex process, complicated by issues such as varying accounting standards in different countries.

Thus, the main challenge for BIS, and other institutions such as IMF, is to ensure that the Core Principles are implemented globally. BIS began by asking supervisors around the world to endorse the Core Principles. To provide a forum for the discussion of problems associated with implementation, the BCBS has created a Liaison Group and a wider Consultation Group of G-10 and non-G-10 countries. In 1998, the Liaison Group conducted a survey on implementation designed to identify the steps that supervisory authorities are taking to implement the Core Principles, the problems they face, and the assistance which they may require (BIS, 1998). It would be very important and urgent for BIS to expand its activities in this field, so as to assist developing countries – including the poorer and smaller ones – with technical assistance in matters such as implementing the Core Principles for Banking. The BIS Financial Stability Institute described below would provide a natural basis for this, but complementary action – focused more on in-country training –

appears to be required. Given BIS's expertise and role in setting standards, it seems very well qualified to play a complementary role in that beginning to be developed by IMF and the World Bank.

(d) The "Joint Forum" and the involvement of non-member countries

In order to address new challenges presented by the breakdown of barriers between different sectors of the financial world and the growth of financial conglomerates, the BCBS has been strengthening its links with international supervisors working in other financial sectors. In early 1996, the Joint Forum on Financial Conglomerates was established, bringing together representatives from the BCBS, IOSCO and IAIS. Thirteen developed countries are represented in the Joint Forum: Australia, Belgium, Canada, France, Germany, Italy, Japan, Netherlands, Spain, Sweden, Switzerland, the United Kingdom and the United States.

The Joint Forum has reviewed the means to facilitate information sharing between supervisors, both within their own sectors and in different sectors, and ways to enhance supervisory coordination. The Joint Forum is also working on issues concerning intra-group transactions and exposures within financial conglomerates. In February 1998, the Joint Forum issued a package of consultative papers addressing several different aspects relating to the supervision of financial conglomerates. Despite these efforts to enhance supervisory coordination, progress in establishing a consolidated supervisory framework has been slow.

The BCBS has also been broadening its work in respect of expanding its links with non-member countries. As discussed above, the Core Principles were drawn up with the active participation of official representatives from emerging markets. This marked an important step in encouraging the formal involvement of non-member countries in the deliberations of the Committee. Other recent efforts to expand the work of the Basle Committee to non-member countries include: the dissemination throughout the world of policy papers on a wide range of supervisory matters; the creation of a network of supervisory authorities who meet at an international conference every two years; the creation of regional supervisory committees to enhance supervisory cooperation at the local level; and the provision of some supervisory training both in Basle and regionally.

2.   The Committee on the Global Financial System

The Committee on the Global Financial System (CGFS – until recently the Euro-Currency Standing Committee – ECSC) works on another of the three pillars of financial systems, that of financial markets. The Committee monitors developments in international financial markets and discusses issues which affect their functioning and stability. The tasks it performed have been recently redefined to fall into three categories (for details, see appendix 3): systematic short-term monitoring of global financial system conditions so as to identify potential sources of stress; in-depth longer-term analysis of the functioning of financial markets; and articulation of policy recommendations aimed at improving market functioning and promoting stability.

Originally, the ECSC was established to examine the expansion of bank lending, and was concerned with issues arising from the debt crisis during the 1980s. More recently, the Committee has been concerned with issues such as the growth of credit derivatives markets and capital flows to developing countries, as well as broader issues such as the implications for the banking industry of changes resulting from technological progress, increasing globalization and product innovation.

BIS compiles, analyses and publishes a wide range of statistical data on developments in international banking and financial markets under a mandate from the ECSC. The *BIS Consolidated International Banking Statistics* (formerly *The Maturity, Sectoral and Nationality Distribution of International Bank Lending*), which is a key source of information on creditor exposures and countries' external debt, is an important example. Under a mandate from the Committee, BIS collects and publishes these statistics from national (creditor) sources, so that risks arising from this area of market activity can be monitored.

The banking statistics produced by BIS can be used to draw attention to strains in international markets, as was the case in the period immediately preceding the recent troubles in East Asia. In the *1997 BIS Annual Report*, the financial fragility in some Asian countries – particularly Indonesia, Malaysia, the Philippines and Thailand – had been highlighted (see pp. 107–114). The report drew attention to the heavy exposure of some of the region's banks to short-term foreign currency financing, problems encountered by countries with recently liberalised financial sectors, and other issues, such as directed lending, which were later to feature in many analyses of the financial crisis in East Asia.

Unfortunately, although BIS was able to use its data to compile an extremely accurate picture of the weaknesses building up in some Asian economies, the low-key expression of their concerns, presumably designed not to be alarmist, caused the warnings to go unheeded. Partly in response to the Asian crisis, the Committee has to agree upon a number of proposals for improving the *BIS International Banking Statistics* in terms of coverage, quality and timeliness. It was decided that lags in the reporting of data to BIS and in the release of data to the public are to be reduced, reporting will now be on a quarterly best-efforts basis, there will be a move to report exposures on an "ultimate risk" basis, and efforts to add new reporting countries will be intensified (BIS, 1998, p. 174). While these improvements will be very valuable, there is also a case for an analysis based on this data to be made more widely available and for concerns to be more strongly voiced.

BIS is now also maintaining an extensive data base on international securities markets and has also expanded its coverage of derivatives markets. The growth of financial innovations, such as over-the-counter derivatives, while designed to facilitate the transfer of market risk and therefore enhance financial stability, have also made financial markets more complex and opaque. This has created difficulties in monitoring patterns of activity in these markets and the distribution of risks in the global financial system for regulators, central banks, market participants and other authorities. BIS studies have suggested that improved information on the size and structure of derivatives markets is needed to enhance their transparency and facilitate a more comprehensive monitoring for systemic risk.

In response to this situation, the CGFS has also drawn up a framework for the regular collection of statistics on over-the-counter derivatives markets on the basis of reporting by leading market participants. These statistics will be compiled by national central banks and published by BIS on a semi-annual basis. In addition, BIS also publishes the results of the triennial survey conducted by central banks (*Central Bank Survey of Foreign Exchange and Derivatives Market Activity*). These efforts to improve transparency, particularly in relation to derivatives, are widely welcomed. However, this sector is constantly evolving and there is a concern that regulatory reporting will never be able to keep pace with this complex and dynamic market. Difficulties are made greater by the fact that there are already many gaps in reporting derivatives; it would seem appropriate for major central banks and BIS to attempt to improve registration of derivatives by making it obligatory.

This Committee also works on longer-term analyses of structural developments which impact on financial stability. In 1997, the reports from two working groups, set up the previous year, were presented to the Committee. The first examined the implications for systemic risk of recent structural changes in financial markets, such as the emergence of non-bank financial institutions as providers of services traditionally carried out by banks. The second working group examined changes in portfolio management practices with the aim of developing a better understanding of cross-border capital flows.

3. The Committee on Payment and Settlement Systems

The CPSS works to identify, define and promote ways to reduce risks and improve the efficiency of national and cross-border payment and settlement systems, including those for securities and foreign exchange market transactions.

With the increase in the volume of financial transactions in recent years, the exposure of firms to possible non-payment by a counterparty has risen significantly, and the Committee has made many proposals on how payment and settlement systems could be strengthened. Much of the Committee's work focuses on interbank fund transfer systems, as banks continue to be at the centre of the international financial system. In 1997, the CPSS produced a *Report on Real-Time Gross Settlement Systems*. This report provides an overview of real-time settlement systems, which are now in place in most G-10 and some other countries, as well as looking at the risks associated with such systems.

In recent years, the CPSS has also extended its work to cover settlement systems for securities and foreign exchange, and clearing arrangements for exchange-traded derivatives. To further this work, the Committee has extended its cooperation with other international regulatory authorities, such as a recent joint initiative with IOSCO, which established a disclosure framework for securities and settlement systems. In 1996, the CPSS reached an agreement on exposure to settlement risk in foreign exchange markets (or Herstatt risk). In its report, the Committee established that such settlement exposures are much larger than had been estimated and also indicated ways in which market participants could reduce risks.

In order to further their work in these areas, the CPSS has also been fostering closer links with non-G-10 Central Banks, particularly those of developing economies. This has taken the form of meetings between the Committee and non-G-10 Central Banks, and payment systems seminars and workshops that have been organized in conjunction with BIS for various regional central bank groups. In developing the Core Principles for Payment and Settlements Systems, the Committee involved the central banks of a number of emerging market economies: Brazil, Hong Kong (China), Hungary, Malaysia, Mexico, Russian Federation, Saudi Arabia, Singapore and South Africa, as well as West African countries. It is important to note that countries which are at different stages of financial development have different concerns and priorities: whereas some emerging market countries are primarily concerned with establishing efficient and quick basic payment and settlement systems, such as cheque clearing, the G-10 countries are more concerned about reducing risk in payment and settlement systems. Therefore, some division of labour may be justified in the operation of this Committee.

4. The Financial Stability Institute

In response to the need to strengthen financial systems worldwide, BIS and the BCBS have recently established the Financial Stability Institute. This Institute will focus on promoting better and more independent supervision of banking, capital markets and insurance services; it will also promote the implementation of the Core Principles for Banking Supervision. It will achieve these objectives mainly through workshops, seminars and other activities that will disseminate best supervisory practice. The Institute will try to facilitate interaction between the private sector, central banks and supervisory authorities, and is hoping to establish close links with organizations such as IMF and the World Bank. It will also develop links with the Toronto International Leadership Centre for Financial Sector Supervision (the Toronto Centre), sponsored by the World Bank and the Government of Canada, which helps bank supervisors from emerging market countries to share experiences with other bank supervisors and facilitates the exchange of information.

As the blurring of the barriers between the different areas of the financial sector increases, the need for a coordinated approach to financial sector supervision becomes more pressing. It is planned that in the future the Financial Stability Institute will broaden its coverage to include other areas of the financial sector, looking at issues such as the implementation of Core Principles currently being developed for the securities and insurance sectors.

C.   The role of BIS in crisis management

Financial crises are unpredictable, and often unfold extremely quickly. It is therefore essential that good lines of communication be established and maintained between the major actors in a crisis (the central bank, the treasury, supervisory bodies of different countries) in order that each is well informed and decisions can be reached quickly. Indeed, as White (1998) points out, BIS's most important contribution to crisis management is ensuring that policy makers know each other well and have open lines of communication.

The international community, in particular the G-10 Central Banks, have also provided bridge loans through BIS to countries experiencing financial difficulties which are waiting for funds from the World Bank or other international financial institutions. Bridge loans can provide necessary liquidity and can also signal international support for policy changes undertaken by an economy which has run into financial difficulties.

In 1995, in response to the Mexican peso crisis, BIS coordinated two international financial support programmes for Mexico and Argentina. As part of the international support programme for Mexico put together in early 1995, BIS arranged a short-term credit facility of up to $10 billion in favour of the Central Bank of Mexico. This facility, which was backed by a group of participating central banks, was available from March to September 1995, but was never activated. In the same year, BIS granted a bridging loan of up to $1 billion to the Central Bank of Argentina. This facility was made available in six separate tranches, from April to September 1995, to pre-finance loans from the World Bank and the Inter-American Development Bank.

BIS has also played a role in the international response to the financial crisis which unfolded across the globe in late 1997 and throughout 1998. Firstly, BIS participated in a multilateral initiative of the G-10 and other Asian and European countries to provide

liquidity to the Bank of Thailand in the form of short-term bridging finance. However, this facility was not activated.

In addition to providing bridge loans, BIS has recently coordinated a credit facility of up to $13.28 billion in favour of the Central Bank of Brazil. This loan is part of the $41.5 billion international financial support programme put together by IMF in November 1998 to try to save Latin America's largest economy from financial collapse. The BIS credit facility had the backing of 19 central banks from the G-10 and certain other European countries. This facility, which has a draw down period of one year, is linked to disbursements under a Supplemental Reserve Facility provided to Brazil by IMF.

The role of BIS in crisis management may change in the near future. Firstly, the introduction of IMF's Emergency Financing Facility and especially the new Contingency Credit Line may mean that there will be less call for BIS bridge loans in the future. Secondly, the huge amounts now involved in cross-border private financial flows may well imply that IMF will not always have adequate resources to restore market confidence in troubled economies, as we saw recently in East Asia. This may mean that BIS will be called upon to provide some of the loans which make up an international rescue package.

IV. Membership and management; participation of developing countries

Before 1996, BIS membership was constituted by the G-10 and Switzerland, as well as other developed countries, the main East European countries and only two developing countries, South Africa and Turkey (see table 1). In 1996, several large developing countries were invited to join BIS: they were Brazil, China, Hong Kong (China), India, Mexico, Republic of Korea, Saudi Arabia and Singapore. The Russian Federation also joined that year. The developing countries invited to join were clearly the largest ones – both in GDP and population – as well as those which are very large financial centres and/or have very high incomes. Two issues may be raised in this context. Could and should this membership be broadened further? With what criteria? Should all categories of developing countries be represented (as, for example, the G-24), or should more key developing countries be included? Should at some point in the long term BIS aim at having, like IMF, universal

Table 1

MEMBERSHIP OF BIS, MARCH 1998

G-10 Members

Belgium	Canada	France
Germany	Italy	Japan
Netherlands	Sweden	Switzerland
United Kingdom	United States	

Other Pre-1996 Members

Australia	Austria	Bulgaria
Czech Republic	Denmark	Estonia
Finland	Greece	Hungary
Iceland	Ireland	Latvia
Lithuania	Norway	Poland
Portugal	Romania	Slovakia
South Africa	Spain	Turkey
Yugoslavia		

Joined in 1996

Brazil	China	Hong Kong (China)
India	Republic of Korea	Mexico
Russian Federation	Saudi Arabia	Singapore

Joined in 1997

Bosnia and Herzegovina	Croatia	The Former Yugoslav Republic of Macedonia
Slovenia		

membership, but with weighted and rotating representation on the Board? This seems particularly valuable, with the BIS having a very important role in the Financial Stability Forum, as it would facilitate its having a truly global perspective . Some of the changes suggested may require modifications of the BIS Statutes, particularly of its Article 8(3).

BIS has three administrative bodies: the General Meeting, the Board of Directors and the Management. At present, the Bank's Board of Directors is drawn exclusively from the G-10 countries. The Board of Directors comprises the Governors of the Central Banks of Belgium, France, Germany, Italy and the United Kingdom, and the Chairman of the Board of Governors of the Federal Reserve System, as ex-officio members, each of whom appoints another member of the same nationality. The Statutes of BIS also provide for the election to the Board of not more than nine governors of other member central banks (BIS, 1998). The elected members of the Board are currently all from developed countries. Presumably there are no restrictions in the BIS Statutes for having one or more representatives from developing countries on the Board of Directors, and this clearly seems a desirable step.

Recently BIS has taken a step to enhance its developing country work by opening a representative office for Asia and the Pacific in Hong Kong

(China), and reportedly BIS is also evaluating the possibility of establishing a branch in Latin America.

The staff of BIS (including temporary staff) is fairly small (around 500 people), but of an extremely high professional standard, as reflected in the very high quality of BIS's publications, and in particular of the BIS *Annual Report* (which has, for example, drawn attention systematically to risks in the international financial system, especially those relating to developing countries, often before other international institutions have done so). Though the staff is very international (drawn from 29 countries), developing countries are poorly represented. Indeed, senior BIS staff has expressed a positive interest in attracting more staff from developing countries. This seems highly appropriate, and special actions may need to be taken for this purpose. At a later stage, it seems important that some management positions too be allocated to colleagues from developing countries. There may also be a case to broaden the staff, from other perspectives (to include academics, private sector practitioners, etc.). Again new mechanisms, such as secondments or visiting staff, may be useful; this could build on the BIS Visiting Fellowship scheme for short-term seconders from emerging market central banks.

In section III, we have described the incorporation of developing countries in some of the work of the Basle Committees. The monthly meetings of governors discussed above are two-day events; most of the key sessions seem to be exclusive to G-10 central bank governors. Here, greater developing country participation seems desirable; however, there are a number of other international meetings at BIS in which developing countries are better represented. There is also a growing range of specific activities for developing countries, organized by BIS, such as the two regional conferences (one for Asia and one for Latin America). However, it seems even more essential to integrate developing countries more fully into the mainstream work of BIS and the Committees. An important question is whether developing countries wish to organize – probably best on a regional basis – BIS-like arrangements/meetings, beyond what already exists. Such arrangements/sets of meetings among regional regulators could be strongly linked to – but be broadly autonomous from – BIS and the Committees. The advantage of such complementary arrangements would be that they could draw more and better on common regional issues and features of financial systems within regions.

V.   The future: broadening BIS as a basis for enhancing its role in the new financial architecture

A.   *Increased role in global regulation*

BIS and the Basle Committees are the main focus of international coordination of regulation in banking. As the secretariat of the IAIS is now based at BIS, there are very close links with the international regulation of insurance. There are also growing links between BIS and the Committees with the securities' regulator, IOSCO, for example via the Joint Forum, on regulating the increasingly important financial conglomerates.

As a result, BIS together with the Committees and its links with other regulatory bodies would seem to make the Bank a natural base for the construction of a future body of global regulation. A very important intermediate step for the creation of such a body was the above-mentioned proposal made by the United Kingdom for a new and permanent Standing Committee for Global Financial Regulation, that would be charged with developing and implementing a mechanism to ensure that the necessary international standards for financial regulation and supervision are put in place and properly coordinated. The broader aim would be to deliver the global objective of a stable financial system. Indeed, the proposal suggested that this Standing Committee bring together not just the Basle Committees and other regulatory groupings but also the World Bank and IMF on a regular, perhaps monthly, basis. The President of the Bundesbank, Hans Tietmeyer, was in charge of preparing detailed recommendations on the operation of this institution. This report led to the creation of the Financial Stability Forum discussed above.

In the medium-term future, such a Standing Committee could evolve into a far more ambitious institution, a global super-regulator, along the lines suggested by Kaufmann (1992) and Eatwell and Taylor (1998). Such a body would have the authority and expertise to generate a level regulatory playing field between countries and sectors, as well as to fill the many existing regulatory gaps both within specific financial sectors (e.g. mutual funds, hedge funds) and within certain jurisdictions, such as for instance off-shore centres. More broadly, such a body would set mutually acceptable minimum risk-weighted capital or reserve requirements for different financial sectors, establish uniform trading, reporting and disclosure standards, and monitor the performance of markets and financial institutions. Such a global super-regulator would thus integrate and make compatible regulation between different financial sectors (to take account of growing de facto integration between markets of banking, securities and insurance) and deepen global regulation (to take account of the global nature of these markets). Though very desirable as it would correspond to the new needs of the global economy, such an institution might be complex to establish, and very difficult to agree internationally, especially if it would require an international treaty to be approved by national parliaments.

Therefore, it seems better to focus in the short term on the recently created Financial Stability Forum. As Brown (1998, p. 5) has pointed out, this will "not be an additional institution but a process of monitoring development in global finance, ensuring that necessary worldwide standards are put in place, and providing timely surveillance of financial conditions and international capital flows".

It seems appropriate that a leading role for the Forum rests on BIS and the Basle Committees, on the IAIS and on IOSCO, given the great accumulated technical expertise in each of their fields of regulation. As the ultimate aim is the pursuit of global financial stability, the perspective of BIS (drawing on its central bank constituents) examining financial markets from the angle of avoiding possible systemic risk seems particularly appropriate for this task. It would be complementary with a perspective focusing more on country (especially macroeconomic) problems, as possible causes of crises, which is the perspective that IMF adopts in its work. Thus, a fairly clear division of labour seems to emerge whereby BIS – jointly with IOSCO and IAIS in coordination with IMF and the World Bank – takes the lead on global financial regulation, with IMF and the World Bank playing a primary role mainly in helping dissemination and surveillance of the standards and norms formulated by the forum of global regulators. The central role of IMF will, however, continue to focus on monitoring of macroeconomic policies.

B. New possible roles in crisis management

BIS has also played a role of provision of official liquidity to developing countries either as part of a mechanism for crisis prevention, as recently in the case of Brazil, or more frequently, as part of a crisis management package. The financing provided by BIS is only in a small proportion based on its own resources, but is mainly based on pooling of financing from G-10 Central Banks. Until recently, financial facilities organized by BIS for developing countries had always been bridge loans (to IMF loans), whereas in the case of Brazil BIS organized a self-standing loan, although reportedly this was exceptional. Clearly, the lead role in providing official financing to countries in crises has up to now been taken by IMF.

The future of BIS in crisis management needs to be based on a diagnosis of the nature of developing countries' capital-account-led currency crises of today, which are different from the mainly current-account-led crises of the past. The recent ones have been partly caused by mistakes or problems in the countries themselves; however, a very significant cause of these crises – particularly in situations of contagion – is the imperfections in international capital markets, which can lead to rapid and large withdrawals of capital, even from countries whose underlying fundamentals are basically sound.

As markets can be not only very imperfect but also move very fast, it is essential that mechanisms for emergency official financing operate very speedily when a crisis erupts, to prevent its deepening and spreading to other countries.

A solution that may be appropriate therefore is to stress preventive programmes. One desirable strategy could be for the Fund, during Article IV consultations, to declare a given country to have good policies and not to be crisis-prone. Should, however, such a country nevertheless be hit by a crisis – owing, for example, to contagion – it would be appropriate for the country to receive emergency official financing quickly, but not appropriate for it to have additional policy conditionality imposed on it. One mechanism recently made available for this purpose is the IMF Contingency Credit Line (CCL). However, the CCL is not automatically disbursed, even if the crisis is caused by contagion, as it requires fresh approval by the IMF Board. An alternative or complementary mechanism could be for BIS to play a key coordinating role for rapidly assembling financial packages with resources mainly provided by G-10 Central Banks, combined where feasible with private credit lines; to a small extent, BIS could also draw on its own resources. Though BIS would take the lead in arranging the initial financing, IMF would have taken the lead in previously defining that the country's policies did not make it crisis-prone.

Such distinctions would provide strong incentives for countries to have good policies; this should make crises less likely. If, nevertheless, crises did occur, large lending without conditionality by G-10 Central Banks and commercial banks could possibly be quickly coordinated by BIS for countries deemed by IMF to have good policies; for countries having an IMF CCL, a crisis would also be followed by a speedily disbursed IMF loan, although that would still need to be ratified by the IMF Board (under the current terms of the CCL), which could imply some crucial delay.

The role of IMF conditionality would be far greater in crisis prevention, but smaller in crisis management, which would make it more effective and less controversial. Financing could be arranged speedily, which would also be extremely positive. A third advantage would be that policy conditionality would not be applied during crises situations if not caused by bad policies.

C. Widening the presence of developing countries in BIS

While an enhanced role of BIS and the Committees in global prudential regulation follows from its obvious leading expertise in this area, an enhanced role for this institution in crisis management may be desirable for the developing countries for two reasons: first, it may provide genuinely unconditional and rapid financing to countries following good policies, but suffering from crises caused by contagion or other external factors; and, second, unconditional lending by BIS may be particularly appropriate, because BIS is perhaps more technical and less "political" than IMF, because it has a greater tradition of sensitivity to, and analysis of, imperfections in international financial markets, and has not focused on imposing conditionality on developing countries. As a consequence, the above suggested division of labour may play to the strengths of both IMF and BIS, and would therefore be more beneficial for developing countries.

To provide an even more solid base for BIS to play these bigger roles in a future financial architecture, it seems very important to increase representation by developing countries in the Bank and the Committees. This would not only be appropriate for reasons of representation and legitimacy, but also because it would provide essential expertise and perspectives, given the increasing global integration of financial markets and the growing financial importance of developing countries; in particular, it would provide BIS with useful insights in those areas of the world where its work is likely to significantly expand.

Two caveats seem important in relation to intensifying the role of developing countries in BIS. Firstly, this needs to be done in ways that do not undermine the effectiveness and intimacy of the "Basle style", that reportedly much facilitates agreement and decision-making on the basis of consensus, though maybe the importance of small size for efficiency is overplayed. Instead of thinking of expanding too much – or expanding at all – membership of BIS's Board or the Committees, one might envisage developing country participation on a rotating basis. This should be more acceptable to the large G-10 countries, whose representation would not be affected, but might be less acceptable to some of the smaller G-10 countries, as they might have to yield some representation. However, this process could be somewhat facilitated by the creation of the European Central Bank, (which in some BIS fora could represent 11 countries). Secondly, there may be some aspects or issues such as regulating very sophisticated instruments used mainly in developed economies, or issues such as reducing risks in settlements systems – where developed countries do have greater concerns and/or expertise. In these, relatively rare, cases, it may continue to be appropriate for G-10 countries to play the dominant or even an exclusive role, though it always seems valuable for developing countries to participate, as this gives access to information on future trends and issues.

It seems important and urgent to: (i) ensure the participation of developing countries in the Board of BIS; (ii) ensure greater – and more formalized – participation of developing countries in crucial meetings, for example in monthly meetings of central bank governors; (iii) increase their participation in the three key Basle Committees, on a formal and not just on an ad hoc basis; (iv) increase developing country staff in BIS; and (v) expand the number and types of developing countries included in BIS and the Committees, thus including representation from low-income small countries.

D. Providing additional information on markets to developing countries

One of the valuable functions that BIS carries out is the provision of very useful and high quality information on trends in financial and banking markets. However, particularly during the Asian crisis, policy makers of emerging-market countries have found important limitations in the essential information available on the functioning of international capital and banking markets. The type of information required is both on more long-term structural changes in these markets – particularly on day-to-day changes in the functioning of markets – and their key actors, globally and regionally.

Just as IMF has led the way in improving information, and its dissemination, on emerging-market economies – particularly useful to markets – a parallel symmetric effort needs to be done to gather and provide timely information on market evolution to emerging-market policy makers. This task should obviously devolve on BIS, though inputs from other institutions, such as IMF, and from the private sector would be very valuable. Though possibly not giving it sufficient emphasis, suggestions in the October 1998 G-22 Report of the Working Group on Transparency and Accountability provide important elements for this task. These suggestions relate to the improvement of statistics and the compilation of data on the exposure not only of international banks but also of investment banks, hedge funds and other institutional investors; the latter would presumably include pension funds and mutual funds. It seems essential that developing countries should participate in the working group recommended by the G-22 and in other similar relevant groups.

Given the speed with which markets move, it seems particularly important that the frequency with which relevant data is produced be very high (and possibly higher in times of market turbulence, when it becomes particularly crucial), and that dissemination to all countries' central banks be instant. Indeed, a special additional service could be provided by BIS, in which it would play the role of a clearing house for information. For this purpose, it could draw not just on information gathered directly from markets, but could collect and centralize the information on their markets of individual central banks, and where the aggregate picture is not easily available to any individual central bank. This could include both quantitative and qualitative information. BIS might standardize information requirements, collect the information, aggregate it and disseminate it rapidly to all central banks, as well as to other relevant institutions. Such a service would be of the greatest usefulness to developing country policy makers, especially immediately before and during crises; naturally, it would also be very valuable to devel-

oped country policy makers and international institutions in handling crisis prevention and management.

VI. Conclusions and policy recommendations

This study has identified four key areas where the role of BIS should be modified and strengthened:

(i) BIS and the Committees are a natural base for the construction of a future body of global prudential regulation to promote financial stability globally and in individual countries, especially in developing economies. A crucial step in this direction is the creation of the Financial Stability Forum, in which BIS and the Committees work jointly with other key regulatory groupings, such as IOSCO and the IAIS, as well as with IMF and the World Bank. It seems appropriate for the small secretariat of this new Forum to be based at BIS, given the accumulated expertise there and that many central bankers and regulators already meet in this context.

This Financial Stability Forum should not only pool information, but also develop authority for the coordination of consistent prudential regulatory norms and for filling regulatory gaps, within both specific financial sectors and certain jurisdictions (see Eatwell and Taylor, 1998, and Kaufmann, 1992 for proposals on global regulation).

The Financial Stability Forum could reduce the likelihood of currency crises that are particularly damaging to developing countries. However, it is very important that developing countries' concerns and interests be appropriately and directly represented in the Forum. It also seems important that developing countries adopt a position on issues that should be excluded from such a Forum, such as capital account liberalization (see Griffith-Jones et al., 1999, for a discussion of these issues).

For the development of the Financial Stability Forum it may be valuable to draw on the recent British experience in establishing the Financial Services Authority, which coordinates and – as far as possible – integrates regulation across financial sectors in the United Kingdom.

(ii) Particularly for those developing countries with good policies (and approved by IMF as such during Article IV consultations), BIS could play an important role in assembling official financing if they were still hit by a capital-account-led crisis, and purely by external factors. This facility would be alternative to the recently created IMF CCL, which, although designed for countries with crises caused not by bad policies but by contagion, is still not fully automatic. A BIS-arranged facility could be fully automatic and would not have limits of scale other than those designed for each case by the lending central banks.

(iii) Greater participation of developing countries in BIS is important not only to strengthen further the legitimacy of BIS for its key tasks, but also to allow developing countries to access to discussions and expertise on issues that are becoming increasingly important for them, without burdening them with additional political demands. The participation of developing countries should be ensured on the Board of BIS, in other crucial BIS meetings and in the recently created Financial Stability Forum, and growing participation in the Committees should be formalized.

(iv) BIS seems ideally placed to build on the useful information it already provides, and on its network of links with central banks and markets by expanding it in two directions: (a) broadening coverage, for example to include more information on institutional investors and in rapidly growing instruments, such as derivatives; and (b) increasing significantly the frequency of information to provide timely inputs to policy makers on rapid changes in financial market trends.

This exercise would in some ways be symmetrical to the efforts being made by IMF to improve the availability of information on developing countries, essentially of use to markets; the proposed activity would improve information mainly for the use of policy makers, especially in areas of particular interest to developing countries.

Appendix 1

International Association of Insurance Supervisors

In 1994 insurance supervisors from around the world established their own association, the IAIS. Its membership now constitutes insurance supervisors from over 80 countries, who resolved:

* to cooperate together to ensure improved supervision of the insurance industry on the domestic as well as on an international level in order to maintain efficient, fair, sage and stable insurance markets for the benefit and protection of policyholders;

* to unite their efforts to develop practical standards for supervision of insurance that members may choose to apply;

* to liaise or cooperate with other relevant international entities;

* to provide mutual assistance to safeguard the integrity of markets; and

* to exchange information on their respective experiences in order to promote the development of domestic insurance markets.

The IAIS issues global insurance principles, standards and guidance, provides training and support on issues related to insurance supervision, and organizes meetings and seminars for insurance supervisors. Annually, it holds a conference where insurance supervisors, insurance industry representatives and other insurance professionals discuss topical issues affecting insurance regulation. The 1997 conference was held in Sydney, Australia; the next conference will take place in September 1998 in Cancun, Mexico.

The IAIS is headed by an Executive Committee whose members represent different geographical regions. It is supported by three main committees, the Technical Committee, the Emerging Markets Issues Committee and the Budget Committee. Eleven subcommittees and working groups – Accounting, Education, Electronic Commerce/Internet, Exchange of Information, Financial Conglomerates, Insurance Fraud, Insurance Laws Regulations Practices and Standards, Investment, Reinsurance, Solvency and Year 2000 Issue – report to the main Committees.

The IAIS is supported by a secretariat based at the BIS in Basle, Switzerland.

Appendix 2

Excerpt from the Communiqué of G-7 Finance Ministers and Central Bank Governors

20 February 1999, Petersberg, Bonn

Financial Stability Forum

15. We are grateful to Hans Tietmeyer for his report on international cooperation and coordination in the area of financial market supervision and surveillance. We welcome his proposal that the G-7 should take the initiative in convening a Financial Stability Forum to ensure that national and international authorities and relevant international supervisory bodies and expert groupings can more effectively foster and coordinate their respective responsibilities to promote international financial stability, improve the functioning of the markets and reduce systemic risk.

While the Forum will initially be the initiative of the G-7 countries, we envisage that over time additional national authorities would be included in the process. The issues to be addressed affect all countries, including both industrial and emerging market economies, and the G-7 regards this initiative as a step toward broader participation.

- We agreed that the Forum will meet regularly to assess issues and vulnerabilities affecting the global financial system and identify and oversee the actions needed to address them, including encouraging, where necessary, the development or strengthening of international best practices and standards and defining priorities for addressing and implementing them.

- We agreed that the Forum will be comprised of representatives of national authorities responsible for financial stability, the relevant international financial institutions and organizations as well as the relevant international supervisory bodies and expert groupings. The Forum will be supported by a small secretariat located in Basle. Its first Chairman will be Mr. Andrew Crockett, General Manager of the BIS, for a term of three years. We ask our Deputies to make the necessary preparations so that the first meeting of the Forum could be held in Spring 1999.

Appendix 3

Committee on the Global Financial System

On 8 February 1999, the Governors of the Central Banks of the Group of Ten countries decided to clarify the mandate of the Euro-Currency Standing Committee (ECSC) in order to strengthen the effectiveness of the overall Basle-based process in promoting monetary and financial stability. Concomitantly, the Committee was renamed Committee on the Global Financial System.

* * *

After having acted in the 1960s as an informal forum for the regular exchange of views on international monetary and financial issues among senior central bank officials, the ECSC first received a formal mandate from the governors in 1971. This mandate was stated publicly in 1980, when the governors announced their intention to monitor international banking markets more closely. The initial focus of the Committee was on the monetary policy implications of the rapid growth of the Euromarkets. In the late 1970s, attention shifted to concerns relating to financial stability. After the international debt crisis had subsided, the Committee's work was principally devoted to an examination of financial innovation and of the longer-term changes in the structure of the financial system, with particular reference to their potential impact on systemic risk. Over the years, the Committee has published a number of reports on issues addressed within its remit. In addition, it has been responsible for developing and overseeing the implementation of the various sets of BIS statistics on international banking, derivatives and foreign exchange market activity.

Besides its regular monitoring tasks, the Committee is currently working on a number of initiatives. Following the recommendation of a template for the disclosure of foreign currency reserves and potential drains on them endorsed by the governors in late 1998, the Committee is now investigating ways of enhancing the transparency of the financial activities of market participants more generally. Two working groups, including representatives of emerging market countries, are addressing this issue. One group is concerned with disclosure practices by individual financial institutions. Building on a previous report issued by the ECSC in 1994, it is focusing on the disclosure of information that would allow users to form a meaningful view of the institutions' risk profile. The second group is examining what kind of aggregated information would help improve the functioning of markets. These efforts are a natural complement to initiatives undertaken by the Basle Committee on Banking Supervision in related areas, including its recent report on banks' interactions with highly leveraged institutions. In addition, a third working group is exploring the possibility of aggregating information drawn from risk management models of individual firms in order to facilitate the assessment of market vulnerabilities. These efforts run parallel to other initiatives aimed at studying the preconditions for well-functioning and liquid markets and which could serve as a basis for future policy recommendations in this area.

* * * *

The Committee on the Global Financial System is a central bank forum for the monitoring and examination of broad issues relating to financial markets and systems with a view to elaborating appropriate policy recommendations to support the central banks in the fulfilment of their responsibilities for monetary and financial stability. In carrying out this task, the Committee will place particular emphasis on assisting the governors in recognizing, analysing and responding to threats to the stability of financial markets and the global financial system. More specifically, the Committee's primary objectives will be the following:

- To seek to identify and assess potential sources of stress in the global financial environment through a regular and systematic monitoring of developments in financial markets and systems, including through an evaluation of macroeconomic developments;

- To further the understanding of the functioning and underpinnings of financial markets and systems through a close monitoring of their evolution and in-depth analyses, with particular reference to the implications for central bank operations and broader responsibilities for monetary and financial stability;

- To promote the development of well-functioning and stable financial markets and systems through an examination of alternative policy responses and the elaboration of corresponding policy recommendations.

In its analysis, the Committee should pay particular attention to the nexus between monetary and financial stability, to the linkages between institutions, infrastructures and markets, to the actual and potential changes in financial intermediation and to the incentive structures built into markets and systems. The Committee should seek to increase the transparency of financial markets and systems by promoting the design, production and publication of statistics and other information by central banks – including through the BIS – and by recommending the adoption of appropriate disclosure standards by both the official and private sectors. Where relevant, the Committee should also contribute to the development of an international consensus on sound principles and norms.

The Committee is encouraged to cooperate with other national, supranational and international institutions with responsibilities for pursuing related objectives. In particular, it shall coordinate its activities with other Basle-based committees, such as the Basle Committee on Banking Supervision and the CPSS, in order to strengthen the overall effectiveness of the process.

Notes

1   Referred to as "the [BIS] [Basle] Committees".
2   As matters are – and above all are perceived to be – broadly "technical", there tends to be little consultation at a more general level in national contexts. The question needs to be asked whether, in the interests of greater democracy and accountability, consultations should be broader at the national level to include, for example, discussions in parliament.
3   The secretariat of the International Association of Insurance Supervisors (IAIS) is now based in Basle, in the BIS building (for summary of IAIS activities, see appendix 1).
4   Several senior BIS officials even expressed the hope that the IOSCO secretariat could move to – or at least be permanently represented in – Basle, so that the regulators of the three main official sectors would be fully represented there.
5   Remarks by Joseph Stiglitz at the UNCTAD G-24 Meeting on the Future of the International Monetary and Financial System, Geneva, January 1999.

References

BIS (1997), *67th Annual Report* (Basle: Bank for International Settlements).

BIS (1998), *68th Annual Report* (Basle: Bank for International Settlements).

BROWN, G. (1998), *Rediscovering Public Purpose in the Global Economy*, Chancellor of the Exchequer's Lecture at the Kennedy School, Harvard University, 15 December.

EATWELL, J., and L. TAYLOR (1998), "International Capital Markets and the Future of Economic Policy: A proposal for the creation of a World Financial Authority", mimeo.

FITZGERALD, V. (1998), "Global Capital Market Volatility and the Developing Countries: Lessons from the East Asian crisis", paper prepared for the East Asian Crisis Conference at the IDS and reproduced in the *IDS Bulletin*, January 1999.

GIOVANOLI, M. (1989), "The Role of the Bank for International Settlements in International Monetary Cooperation", *The International Lawyer*, Vol. 23, No. 4.

GRIFFITH-JONES, S. (1998a), Global Capital Flows: Should they be regulated? (London: Macmillan and St. Martin's Press).

GRIFFITH-JONES, S. (1998b), "Stabilising Capital Flows to Developing Countries", paper prepared for the East Asian Crisis Conference at IDS and reproduced in the *IDS Bulletin*, January 1999.

GRIFFITH-JONES, S., and J.A. OCAMPO, with J. CAILLOUX, (1999), "Proposals for a New International Financial Architecture, with Special Emphasis on Needs of Poorer Countries", http://www.ids.ac.uk/ids/global/finance/intfin.html.

GROUP OF TEN (1997), *Financial Stability in Emerging Market Economies: a strategy for the formulation, adoption and implementation of sound principles and practices to strengthen financial systems* (Basle: BIS), April.

HELLEINER, E. (1994), *States and the Re-emergence of Global Finance, from Bretton Woods to the 1990s* (Ithaca, NY: Cornell University Press).

KAPSTEIN, E.B. (1994), *Governing the Global Economy* (Cambridge, MA, and London: Harvard University Press).

KAUFMANN, H. (1992), "Challenges for global regulation", mimeo, paper presented to 1992 IOSCO Conference, Montreal.

TIETMEYER, H. (1999), "Evolving Cooperation and Coordination in Financial Market Surveillance", *Finance and Development*, September.

WHITE, W. (1996), "International Agreements in the Area of Banking and Finance: Accomplishments and outstanding issues", BIS Working Paper, No. 38, October.

WHITE, W. (1998), "Promoting International Financial Stability: The Role of the BIS", in Jan Joost Teunissen (ed.), *Regulatory and Supervisory Challenges in a New Era of Global Finance* (The Hague: FONDAD).

WORLD BANK (1997), *Private Capital Flows to Developing Countries: The Road to Financial Integration* (New York: Oxford University Press).

ADEQUACY OF INTERNATIONAL LIQUIDITY IN THE CURRENT FINANCIAL ENVIRONMENT

Aziz Ali Mohammed

Abstract

This paper reviews current arrangements for the supply of liquidity through the IMF and explores the possibilities for improvements in the management of an international financial system that would contribute to greater efficiency and equity in the reserve-creation process.

Since the last SDR allocation in January 1981, major shareholders of the Fund have argued that international capital markets generated sufficient liquidity to permit growth of world trade and finance. The lack of access of a large number of developing countries to such liquidity has been attributed to insufficient creditworthiness, rather than being regarded as evidence of "global need" which would justify new SDR allocations under the current Articles of the IMF. This argument has been contested on the ground that reserves borrowed through capital markets are costly to hold and that they are not a reliable and stable source of liquidity in the face of sudden and unpredictable changes in market sentiment.

While the IMF's ability to provide conditional liquidity has been constrained by the insistence of major shareholders that the Fund remain a catalyst rather than becoming the predominant source of funding for countries encountering balance-of-payments difficulties, the Fund has moved over the years from being a crisis manager to becoming a crisis lender. Whether it can move beyond its present role to becoming a genuine lender of last resort depends on whether and how it can mobilize resources to deal with the problems of all its members. This paper argues that, in a world where private markets can mobilize enormous sums in very short order, the IMF can successfully face down market speculators only if it has the power to freely create international reserves itself. It is recognized that any type of pre-qualification credit facility in the Fund immediately raises issues of moral hazard. The case for an international-reserve-creating mechanism to provide unconditional liquidity is buttressed by both efficiency and equity considerations. The efficiency argument is based on the superiority of "owned" reserves over "borrowed" reserves and the fact that "owned" reserves under current arrangements can only be accumulated by adjusting current account positions, which is typically achieved through compressing imports.

It is also argued that it might not be premature to review the possibility of moving away from the multiple currency reserve system towards one based on an international reserve asset, by conversion of excess reserve-currency balances through a substitution account.

I. Introduction

The adequacy of international liquidity has been discussed in recent years largely in the context of the resources of the International Monetary Fund (IMF) for the provision of *conditional* liquidity and of the merits of an SDR allocation to supply *unconditional* liquidity. This paper reviews current arrangements for the supply of both types of liquidity[1] with a view to exploring the possibilities for improvement in the current arrangements that could help to better manage an international financial system that has come to be dominated by massive flows of capital through highly integrated private capital markets.

II. The IMF as provider of unconditional liquidity

Despite the original Keynesian concept that the Fund was meant to provide unconditional liquidity, it was not until 1969 that the Articles explicitly recognized that role through the First Amendment by launching the SDR system to "meet the long-term global need, as and when it arises, to supplement existing reserve assets" (Article XVIII of the IMF Article of Agreement). Allocations were made in two "basic periods", the second and last being made in January 1981; cumulative allocations totalling SDR 21.4 billion have been made to that date. Since then, the Managing Director of the IMF has been unable to report a consensus requiring 85 per cent of voting power to make additional allocations on the basis of "global need". Major Fund shareholders have argued that the development of international capital markets has enabled sufficient liquidity to be generated to permit the growth of world trade and finance unimpeded by constraints of a monetary reserve character. The lack of access to the international capital markets experienced by a large number of developing and transition countries has been attributed to their lack of creditworthiness rather than being regarded as evidence of "global need". This claim has been supported by the increasing access – until quite recently – to private capital markets obtained on highly competitive terms by a selection of countries in the developing world, designated as "emerging markets" that have been perceived by private capital market participants to have sound "fundamentals" and to operate liberal capital account policies.

The IMF has tried to keep the issue of an SDR allocation alive over the years through Management Statements from time to time and through seminars, the last one having been held in March 1996 (IMF, 1996). Developing countries have consistently supported general allocations in their policy pronouncements (Group of 24, 1998) and, alone among the major shareholders of the Fund, Japan has proposed consideration of the merits of an SDR allocation on several occasions, the last in December 1998. The sole outcome of these efforts to date was the adoption in April 1997 of a proposal to amend the Fund's Articles to provide for an "equity allocation", primarily to help more than 40 members that never received an SDR allocation because they joined the Fund after the last allocation had been made in January 1981. The proposed amendment (the fourth) had not been ratified by the required large majority at the time of writing.[2]

The argument that the growth of private capital markets has obviated the case for a general SDR allocation has been contested on the ground that "borrowed" reserves – as opposed to "owned" reserves – are subject to an "intertemporal budget constraint that requires that they be paid for sometime, provided they are costly to hold – which they are" (Fischer, 1999). The argument has intensified in the face of the massive reversals in private capital flows in recent years that have underlined the "fair weather" quality of a system based on "borrowed" reserves and the need for "owned" reserves to provide an element of stability in the face of sudden and unpredictable changes in market sentiment affecting "emerging market" countries. A succession of financial crises have been triggered by large-scale capital outflows, starting with the Mexican crisis at the end of 1994,[3] which produced contagion (the "tequila effect") in the form of a cumulative process of capital flight from Latin America. The onset of the East Asian crisis in mid-1997, with the forced depreciation of the Thai baht and the spread of its impact to Malaysia, Indonesia, the Philippines and the Republic of Korea, strengthened the perception of unreliability of private markets for the supply of reserves. These misgivings were intensified by the almost global impact of the Russian Federation's debt default in August 1998, the concerted attack on the Hong Kong dollar a month later and the extraordinary intervention undertaken by the United States Federal Reserve authorities in October 1998 to prevent a seizing up of global capital markets as a consequence of the difficulties of a private hedge-fund (i.e. Long-Term Capital Management Inc.). The saga of widespread turbulence has continued apace in the massive capital flight out of Brazil, with the potential for contagion spreading to other Latin

American countries. While in each country case the contagion could be attributed to domestic weaknesses, the fact that the impact was so widespread and so disproportionate in the economic dislocations it produced has suggested that a more "systemic" set of factors might be at work. Among the factors underlying these events is the role played by current arrangements for the supply of reserves, including the role of the IMF as a provider of liquidity in conditions of financial crises.

III. The IMF as provider of conditional liquidity

As noted earlier, a regular focus of international discussion in the course of the quinquennial review of Fund quotas has been the size of the Fund as a measure of its ability to provide conditional liquidity to members to deal with their balance-of-payments problems. These problems were long regarded as originating primarily in current account imbalances, and the criteria for evaluating the adequacy of Fund quotas were therefore framed in relation to trade variables, including the adequacy of a country's foreign exchange reserves measured in terms of the number of months of imports that could be covered by such reserves. The shrinking capacity of the Fund to meet its responsibilities in a growing world economy was clear enough on the basis of the traditional criteria, but as pointed out by Stanley Fischer, the IMF's First Deputy Managing Director, "since the Fund was set up at a time when private capital flows were very small, it is safe to conclude that its scale relative to private capital flows has declined even more than its size relative to trade flows".[4]

These propositions about the Fund's shrinking resource base relative to the potential demand for its resources have been repeatedly advanced by developing countries on the occasion of the periodic quota reviews but have not found favour with some of the Fund's major shareholders,[5] which have insisted that the Fund remain a catalyst rather than being the predominant source of funding for countries encountering balance-of-payments difficulties. The major shareholders have sought to ameliorate the resultant strains on the Fund's ordinary resources through various arrangements under which the Fund could borrow from its members, the first of these arrangements having been set up as long ago as 1962 under the name of General Arrangements to Borrow (GAB). Under the latter, 11 industrial countries or their central banks agreed to lend up to specified amounts of their respective currencies in special circumstances at market-related rates of interest. The GAB has been renewed for successive five-year periods (the last time in December 1998) and the potential amount of credit available to the IMF currently totals SDR 17 billion, with an additional SDR 1.5 billion available under an associated arrangement with Saudi Arabia. Activation in support of GAB participants is conditioned by a need "to forestall or cope with an impairment of the international monetary system". Stricter criteria apply for GAB support to the Fund in connection with arrangements with non-participants: not only must drawings be in connection with an upper credit tranche purchase but also the IMF must be deemed to face an inadequacy of resources to meet actual and expected requests for financing that reflect "an exceptional situation associated with balance of payments problems of members of a character or aggregate size that could threaten the stability of the international monetary system".[6] Developing countries have not regarded the GAB as a general addition to Fund resources, given the highly restrictive criteria for access, and because the decision to activate lies not with the IMF but with the GAB participants.

A second round of borrowing was inaugurated in the wake of the "oil crisis" of the 1970s through the establishment of the First and Second Oil Facilities, which borrowed from the oil-exporting countries and re-lent the same amount to the major oil-importing countries on close to commercial terms, including to two major industrial countries, the United Kingdom and Italy. However, the Fund's role turned out to be marginal, with much the larger share of recycling the oil surpluses being intermediated by international banks operating in the Euromarkets and with most of the medium-income developing countries finding it "easier and more attractive to borrow from banks than from international institutions" (James, 1996). In 1979, the IMF was permitted to conclude a series of borrowing agreements with a group of 14 industrial and oil-exporting countries to finance the Supplementary Financing Facility for an amount of SDR 7.8 billion. The full commitment of these lines of credit in an environment of serious payments imbalances – and this even before the onset of the Latin American debt crisis in 1982 – led to the creation in 1981 of another borrowing arrangement to finance higher access than could be sustained from quota resources. Under this arrangement to finance the Enlarged Access policy, the Fund raised SDR 15.3 billion in the period 1981–1984 from the Saudi Arabian Monetary Agency, the Bank for International Settlements (BIS) and some central banks;

this line of credit was subsequently increased to SDR 18.3 billion following an additional SDR 3 billion borrowed from the Government of Japan in 1986. The Enlarged Access policy was terminated in 1992 following the completion of the Ninth Quota Increase exercise.

The 1990s have seen the Fund moving decisively beyond reliance on its own resources, whether derived from quota subscriptions or by borrowing. And this movement has occurred despite the completion of the Eleventh Quota Increase exercise (which raised Fund quotas to approximately the equivalent of $300 billion) and notwithstanding the approval of the New Arrangements to Borrow (NAB). Under the NAB, 25 participating countries and institutions declared their willingness to lend to the IMF up to SDR 34 billion (about $45 billion) to cope with an impairment of the international monetary system or to deal with an exceptional situation that threatens the stability of the system, i.e. under circumstances closely parallelled by those envisaged under the GAB. The NAB became effective just in time to be used in connection with the drawings for Brazil in November 1998. However, in all the more recent cases of dealing with countries in financial crises, the Fund has had to rely on other multilateral institutions (the World Bank Group and the regional development banks) as well as on bilateral official sources, disbursing in tandem directly, or indirectly through the BIS. In addition, the Fund has used its good offices to help debtor countries obtain rollovers of short-term inter-bank lines of credit (as in the Republic of Korea) and negotiate for debt relief from various bank and non-bank creditors (as in Indonesia). Table 1 provides estimates on the additional resources mobilized by the Fund in connection with its recent crisis-related transactions.

IV. The Fund as crisis lender

The Fund has functioned as a crisis manager ever since the Latin American debt crises of the 1980s. It has moved into the role of crisis lender within the constraints of its Articles through a gradual evolution in three aspects of its operations: (i) the level of access to its resources; (ii) the speed with which it responds to a member facing a financial crisis; and (iii) its ability to mobilize resources additional to its own. As regards (i), the issue has been framed in terms of access beyond accepted quota limits, i.e. annual limit of 100 per cent of a member's quota and a cumulative limit of 300 per cent. This limita-

tion was set as long ago as 1977, when the Fund included a provision in one of its facilities that credits larger than the specified limits could be granted in "special circumstances" by drawing on resources borrowed by the Fund; subsequent Board decisions have rephrased the clause to refer to "exceptional circumstances" and without restricting it to Fund borrowing. While the clause was invoked from time to time to accommodate moderate deviations from the traditional limits, its first significant application came in connection with the approval for the financing package for Mexico when the Fund initially agreed to lend approximately $7.8 billion, or approximately four and a half times the country's quota. However, when Congressional difficulties arose in respect of United States loan guarantees requested by the United States Administration, the Fund increased its commitment almost overnight by $10 billion "in an impressive display of the Fund's ability to escape from its customary constraints when it judges the case to be compelling enough" (Williamson, 1996). Since the outbreak of the Asian crisis, such multiple-of-quota commitments have become more frequent, the standby arrangement for the Republic of Korea in December 1997 amounting to nearly 20 times the country's (admittedly low) quota. The Supplemental Reserve Facility (SRF) adopted in December 1997 places no quantitative limits on access but enunciates certain qualitative criteria, namely that access will be determined "taking into account the financing needs of the member, its capacity to repay, including in particular the strength of its programme, its outstanding use of Fund credit, and its record in using Fund resources in the past and in cooperating with the Fund in surveillance, as well as the Fund's liquidity". The SRF applies higher rates of charge and shorter repayment periods than apply to drawings under its normal facilities[7] and it expects members to "maintain participation of other creditors, both official and private, until the pressure on the balance of payments ceases".

As regards the speed with which the IMF responds to a member facing a financial crisis, the recognition that dealing with financial crises required not only a larger but a more rapid commitment of Fund resources has led to several initiatives. The first was a Management proposal in September 1994 to establish a short-term financing facility within the Fund that would be fast-disbursing and that would help to counter capital outflows judged to be speculative and destabilizing (IMF, 1998a). While that initiative proved premature, it did result in the adoption in September 1995 of a set of procedures, designated as the Emergency Financing Mechanism

Table 1

COMPOSITION OF RECENT IMF RESCUE PACKAGES[a]

($ billion)

	IMF	*World Bank*	*Regional dev. banks*	*Bilateral*	*Total*
Mexico, 1995	17.7	-	-	31.1[b]	48.8
Thailand, 1997	4.0	1.5	1.2	10.5	17.2
Indonesia, 1997	11.2	5.5	4.5	21.1	42.3
Republic of Korea, 1998	21.1	10.0	4.2	23.1	58.4
Russian Federation, 1998[c]	15.1	6.0	-	1.5	22.6
Brazil, 1998	18.1	4.5	4.5	14.5[d]	41.6

Source: M.S. Ahluwalia, "The IMF and the World Bank: Are overlapping roles a problem?" in this volume.

   a The rescue packages for each country represent resources available over differing periods for each case.

   b Comprises $20 billion from the United States, $1.1 billion from Canada and $10 billion credit line from the BIS.

   c Conditional commitments through end 1999. Of these, $1.5 billion (shown under "Bilateral") constitute Japanese support in co-financing the World Bank.

   d From industrial countries, including direct assistance from Japan, and from others through the BIS.

to facilitate rapid Executive Board approval of financial support while ensuring the conditionality necessary to warrant such support (IMF, 1998c). Following the onset of the Asian crises, the Fund moved, as noted above, to establish the SRF at the end of 1997 to be activated "in cases where the magnitude of outflows may create a risk of contagion that could pose a potential threat to the international monetary system". The SRF has been used three times to date – for the Republic of Korea, the Russian Federation and Brazil – and while the first case represented a partial switching from regular Fund facilities and the second case, an augmentation of an existing extended arrangement, the point of interest is that in all cases the SRF arrangements were negotiated rapidly and approved by the Executive Board within weeks of the initial request from the member in crisis.

V. Can the IMF evolve into an international lender of last resort?

The discussion has moved further in recent months to the possibility of developing contingency lines of credit as a precautionary instrument to stem the threat of possible crisis, i.e. without waiting for the onset of an actual crisis, as required in the case of the SRF. In considering the practicality of such arrangements, and in particular the ability of the IMF to graduate into a genuine lender of last resort (LLR) at the international level, a proposition recently advanced by Stanley Fischer, we turn to the institution's ability to mobilize adequate resources to help its members deal with system-threatening crises, especially those deriving from the spread of contagion. It has been noted already that the Fund's quotas have not kept pace with the growth of the world economy. Its major shareholders have not agreed to a general SDR allocation under the current Articles after 1981 and have tended to hold the growth of its quota resources on a tight leash, relying on borrowing arrangements to bridge the periodic insufficiency of the Fund's ordinary resources. Although the Fund has the power under the Articles to borrow in capital markets, its borrowing operations to date have been confined within the circle of official institutions.

Whether the Fund can play the role of a genuine LLR depends crucially on whether it can mobilize resources to deal with the problems of all those members that do not have access, or have lost access, to private capital markets, and whether it can do so by itself, and not only with the help of resources additional to its own. A number of poor countries have been hit just as hard by problems of contagion and there is a real question whether the Fund would be prepared to make the effort – or would succeed even if it were prepared to make it – on behalf of its smaller members that it has expended on behalf of the "systemically significant" ones. The second qualification for an LLR goes to the heart of the issue: can the Fund create international reserves in much the same way as central banks are able to do in order to deal with liquidity crises within their own domestic markets through their power to expand both sides of their balance sheets? It has been argued that institutions have served as LLR in the past without having that power. However, it is pertinent to ask whether, in a world where private markets can mobilize enormous sums in very short order to attack any country's currency, the Fund can successfully face down market speculators without having the power to create international reserves freely and without having to spend time on mobilizing other sources of funding. Can IMF judgements in support of a crisis-affected country be sustained if the market knows, or can guess, what the limits of Fund support are likely to be? A predictable limit tends to act as a challenge, in much the same way as a pegged exchange rate becomes a target for speculators.

Any type of unspecified credit commitment from the Fund immediately raises issues of moral hazard on the borrower's side, and hence a *sine qua non* for eligibility for such a facility must be a solid track record of the borrowing country as pursuing, and as firmly committed to pursue, prudent and consistent financial policies, so that a judgement can be rendered in advance of a crisis that the country is eligible for Fund support. There is also a question of moral hazard on the investor's side that might result from any pre-qualification facility, and to minimize such a hazard there is a need for preventive arrangements for adequate private sector involvement in forestalling crises. These arrangements involve a number of measures, e.g. effective insolvency and debtor-creditor regimes,[8] an efficient legal infrastructure, particularly for implementing bankruptcy legislation at the national level, and mechanisms for orderly debt workouts, including the activation of temporary debt standstills and collective action provisions in international bond agreements, these being just some of the measures featured in the current discussion on the reform of the international financial architecture (see the paper by Radelet in this volume). Such measures and many others will require prolonged negotiations with a vast array of private interests and it may be years before they are implemented, if they can be implemented at all. In the meantime, to deny the option of developing an international LLR for fear of moral hazard leaves the

international financial system open to the risk, if not the certainty, of recurring financial crises.[9]

VI. The case for an international reserve asset to provide unconditional liquidity

There are both efficiency and equity arguments favouring the deployment of an international reserve asset to provide unconditional liquidity which need to be brought into the debate, even if they might appear too impractical for implementation at this stage. In the remaining part of this paper these aspects are discussed without regard to the constraints on the IMF as it is currently constituted, with the SDR being treated simply as a prototype of an international reserve asset that could be developed further in order to better serve the international community as it evolves beyond the current multi-currency reserve system. It is important to emphasize that some of the applications envisaged would involve the automatic cancellation of SDRs when the need for their creation has passed and would thus not carry the inflationary risks that have contributed to the past reluctance of industrial country policy makers to agree to SDR allocations that remain outstanding as part of international reserves once they have been created. We take up first the efficiency argument for reserve creation in relation to the choice of exchange regimes and the deflationary bias of the global economy.

The choice of exchange regime has a bearing on the question of international liquidity at two levels: at the individual developing or transition country level and at the global regime level. With regard to the former aspect, the adoption of a freely floating currency should absolve the need, in theory, to hold reserves. In practice, the move to greater flexibility in exchange regimes has gone hand in hand with the continued holding of large reserves of foreign currencies; indeed, a decision to accept greater flexibility, as in the Brazilian case, has been motivated in part by the desire to protect reserves. It has also been noted that in recent crises "countries with large reserves have done better in dealing with crisis than those with small reserves" (Fischer, 1999) and this has resulted in a determination "to set their reserves on the basis of capital, as well as current account variables".[10]

The need for reserves becomes greater when countries choose to move to the other extreme of fixing their exchange rate to another currency under a currency board arrangement. On the assumption that the demand for reserves is apt to increase in the next few years – independent of whether countries opt for one or the other extreme – there arises the question of how this demand should be met. Reserves can be built up under the current system either by "earning" them through running current account surpluses or by "borrowing" them on international capital markets. It can be argued that if countries accumulate reserves efficiently, the costs of acquiring reserves through different channels would be equated at the margin. However, many countries are not able to optimize at the margin because they face credit rationing in international capital markets (Mohammed et al., 1996) and find no representative interest rate for the cost of external borrowing. Even countries with previous access to portfolio capital, especially sovereign bond finance, might find themselves cut off by a sudden shift in investor sentiment, as experienced by many developing and transition countries in the past couple of years. Once that happens, their reserve supplementation requirements can be met only by adjusting current account positions to the lower level of capital inflows through either increasing current account surpluses or reducing deficits. Such adjustments require the reduction of domestic absorption in order to expand net exports, typically achieved through compressing imports. The costs of forgone absorption in order to generate any required current-account change are apt to be high relative to the costs that countries with access to capital markets would pay for their borrowed reserves, but these differential costs, as noted in the last paragraph of section II, are not trivial and become much higher for countries lacking access altogether or losing access during a crisis. These costs would be saved if reserve supplementation could be achieved through a mechanism creating international reserves such as the SDR, and these savings would not come at the expense of other participants in the system (see also Fischer, 1999, pp. 208–209).

The implications for aggregate demand of reserve creation depend on whether recipients choose to spend, rather than on average to hold, such reserves. The aggregate demand effects are also different, depending on the prevailing and prospective global economic environment. In past years, much industrial country resistance to SDR allocations was based on the argument that they would contribute to global inflationary pressures. In the current phase of little or no inflationary pressure in the world economy, there can be little apprehension on this score. Indeed, meeting the increasing demand

for reserves through generating current account surpluses "in the next few years will impart a deflationary impact to the world economy",[11] providing a significant efficiency argument in favour of an internationally created reserve asset.

It was noted above that the implications for international liquidity of the choice of exchange regimes could be explored at two levels. We turn next to liquidity aspects of the global regime that is emerging with the advent of the euro and with renewed Japanese official efforts to internationalize the use of the yen, and to the impact these developments might have on the dominant role of the United States dollar in world reserves. The facts about the current pattern of official reserve holdings are well known: the United States dollar accounts for around 65 per cent of total non-gold reserves, the deutsche mark and the French franc together for another 16 per cent, and the Japanese yen for about 9 per cent. The distribution of private sector holdings is not precisely known, but the fact that something like 80 per cent of offshore bank loans and over 40 per cent of external bond issues are denominated in dollars (Polak, 1998, table 1) would suggest that the share of the dollar in total holdings should be higher than in official holdings. The introduction of the euro will inevitably cause changes in reserve-holding behaviour on the part of both official and private agents, with the likely outcome of making the euro a major international currency. A principal component of these changes will be a redirection of demand for international reserves from dollars to euros. To start with, national central banks in the euro area will no longer need to hold international reserves to back their intra-European trade, resulting in an "overhang" of anywhere between $50 billion and $230 billion in their reserves, which are largely held in United States dollars.[12] Central banks outside the euro area are also likely to reduce their dollar positions (which amount to approximately $775 billion), particularly if the risk-return characteristics of euro-denominated assets become more competitive with the dollar as euro-area financial markets deepen. The speed of the shift will be reinforced by bandwagon effects if the euro exchange rate vis-à-vis the dollar is expected to appreciate over time and depending on the degree to which investors perceive the euro to be a stable source of value.

At the same time, a greater volatility is apt to develop in the movements of the exchange rates of the three major currencies. As pointed out by the IMF staff, "the weight placed by the European Central Bank on the euro's external value in formulating its monetary policy may be less than the weight placed by its predecessor central banks possibly resulting in greater variability of the exchange rate".[13] The recent experience of volatility in the dollar-yen rate, which was such an important contributory factor in the East Asian crises, is illustrative of the potential for growing instability in a regime characterized by the possibility of large-scale portfolio shifts among the three reserve currencies.

While proposals for coordinating mechanisms designed to reduce such volatility are under consideration,[14] it might not be premature to revive the possibility of modifying the multiple currency reserve system by reviving the possibility of establishing a "Substitution Account" that would absorb an excess supply of currency reserves by replacing them with an international reserve asset, such as the SDR. Proposals for the conversion of currency reserves through a Substitution Account failed in the late 1970s for many reasons, of which one was the fact that the United States was the issuer of the main reserve currency and was unprepared to accept an obligation to maintain the financial integrity of the account. With three currencies now operating as reserves, and with the United States dollar's share in the SDR basket rising to 40 per cent or beyond, a Substitution Account's claims on the United States, if denominated in SDR, would impose a guarantee burden closer to only one-half of the total value of the corpus in the account. A Substitution Account would serve as a means of preventing, or at least dampening, the excessive variability of exchange rates associated with portfolio shifts among reserve holders.

VII. Equity aspects of current international liquidity arrangements

Issues of "fairness" have been a feature of debate on international liquidity. In the earlier stages, reference was made to the "advantage" presumably enjoyed by the United States because of its reserve currency status that enabled it to finance its balance-of-payments deficits by issuing foreign liabilities denominated in its own currency, thereby avoiding the necessity to balance its external accounts through "asset settlement". This "advantage", as noted in the preceding section, has gradually been extended to a few other currencies, including the newly introduced euro. The distinction of being a reserve currency has

been further eroded by the growth of international capital markets which have enabled more countries to borrow against their own IOUs. The floating of major currencies and the removal of distortions in domestic credit markets has allowed reserve currency countries to argue that all those that hold their currencies do so voluntarily at market-determined exchange and interest rates.

However, two elements of "unfairness" have persisted in that several countries with access to capital markets can still not denominate their IOU external obligations in their own currency, but have to denominate them in a reserve currency. The consequences of this deficiency have proved very costly when sudden shifts in investor sentiment have blocked access to private capital markets and forced massive depreciations of exchange rates, which have driven governments as well as business firms into virtual bankruptcy when they failed to properly hedge their borrowings in foreign currencies. Moreover, poor countries without access to private markets have been required to build up their reserve holdings through running current account surpluses, which entailed import compression in most cases, and were costly in terms of consumption or investment forgone.

A second element of inequity has resulted from the growing "dollarization" of many developing and transition economies, a result of the liberalization of capital accounts which has enabled financial institutions to offer deposits not only in their own domestic currency but also in other key currencies. There has also been a redirection of seigniorage in the increasing use of the dollar or the deutsche mark in hand-to-hand transactions, which will inevitably extend to euro currency issues as well. This redirection will be even greater if countries adopt the Panama model (as Argentina is reportedly considering quite seriously) of abandoning their own national currency in favour of the dollar. It is not obvious what can be done to minimize the equity implications of these trends, except perhaps to suggest that an internationally created reserve asset that could be held privately as well as in official-to-official transactions might begin to redistribute some of the benefits obtained by the issuers of the dominant currencies. However, bringing such equity issues into the debate calls for an exercise of international solidarity that may be difficult to visualize in an environment dominated by private financial interests determined to push market solutions even when the problems that have to be dealt with are the outcome of market failure – as they surely are in the international financial sphere.

Notes

1   The distinction made in this paper between conditional and unconditional liquidity is without prejudice to the position espoused by many students of the subject, namely that only if it is unconditional can it be liquidity, and that "conditional liquidity" is an oxymoron.

2   If and when the amendment is ratified, it would provide for a one-time allocation of SDR 21.4 billion and would raise all participants' ratios of cumulative SDR allocations to their quotas (under the Ninth General Review of Quotas) to a common benchmark ratio of 29.3 per cent. Developing countries were strongly opposed to the proposal when it was initially tabled as a United Kingdom-United States initiative, for fear that it would rule out the possibility of general SDR allocations based on a finding of a long-term global need to supplement reserves. Their acceptance in 1997 of the proposal for an "equity allocation" followed a period of intense acrimony, culminating in a joint refusal by the developing country members of the Interim Committee at the Madrid meeting in September 1994 to agree to the United Kingdom-United States proposal. The G-24 communiqué of September 1997 maintains their position that "this one-time measure does not diminish or preclude the need for a general allocation". For a discussion of the Madrid meeting controversy, see Buira and Marino (1996).

3   Presciently characterized by the IMF's Managing Director, Michel Camdessus, as the "first crisis of the 21st century".

4   Fischer points out that "If the Fund were today the same size relative to the output of its member states as it was in 1945, it would be more than three times larger than it will be when the present quota increase is completed; if the quota formula applied in 1945 were used to calculate actual quotas today, the Fund would be five times its size; and if the size of the Fund had been maintained relative to the volume of world trade, it would be more than nine times larger, i.e. over 2.5 trillion dollars" (Fischer, 1999).

5   This has been the traditional position of the United States, which has a veto, since any quota-increase decision requires a qualified majority of 85 per cent of total voting power, while the United States share in total votes is currently 17.78 per cent.

6   Given these strict criteria, it is not surprising that the first activation of the GAB in support of a non-participant occurred in July 1998 to support the Russian Federation with a credit line of SDR 6.3 billion.

7   The rate of charge on SRF resources during the first year is 300 basis points above the basic rate of charge, and the surcharge increases by 50 basis points at the end of that period and every six months thereafter, up to a maximum of 500 basis points. As to repayment periods, repurchase expectations arise in two equal semi-annual installments one to one and a half years from the date of purchase, but the Fund may extend each repurchase expectation by up to one year. Repurchase obligations arise in two equal semi-annual installments between two and two and a half years after the purchase. For additional detail, see IMF (1998a).

8   See Annexes A and B to the G-22 Working Group Report on International Financial Crises.

9   Relying on market solutions presupposes a whole series of other preconditions that market supporters take for granted as being already in place, when they surely are not in the international sphere. To take one example quoted by Boughton, market solutions require bankruptcy procedures to avoid prisoners' dilemmas and credit races for the exit. An international lender of last resort provides a viable alternative to potentially much more costly international bankruptcy procedures. See Boughton (forthcoming).

10 Fischer adds that "it is very likely that countries seeking to draw the lesson of the present crisis will decide they should hold larger reserves than before. This is already happening in the case of Korea – and it will not be the only country to move in that direction" (Fischer, 1999).

11 Fischer has argued that "It is possible – indeed, it was very much possible a few months ago – to envisage circumstances under which a general increase in reserves would be useful, for instance, at a time of a seizing up of flows of credit in the world economy" (Fischer, 1999).

12 See IMF (1998b). The rest of this paragraph draws heavily on that material.

13 *Ibid*. At the same time, however, the IMF staff notes that "in the near term at least, the euro's exchange rate may take on added importance as an indicator of monetary policy decisions owing to the potential instability in money demand and in the relationships between money growth and future inflation".

14 Notably proposals reportedly advanced by Prime Minister Obuchi of Japan during recent visits to Europe for new international arrangements to stabilize exchange rates among the key international currencies. His ideas have received support from President Chirac of France.

References

BOUGHTON, J.M. (forthcoming), "From Suez to Tequila: The IMF as crisis manager", *Economic Journal*.

BUIRA, A., and R. MARINO (19969), "Allocation of special drawing rights: The current debate", *International Monetary and Financial Issues for the 1990s*, Vol. VII, United Nations publication, sales no. E.96.II.D.2 (New York and Geneva).

FISCHER, S. (1999), "On the need for an international lender of last resort", mimeo, paper presented at a joint session of the American Economic Association and the American Finance Association, New York, 3 January 1999.

G-24 (Intergovernmental Group on International Monetary Affairs) (1998), *Communiqués of the Group of 24* (Caracas: Banco Central de Venezuela).

IMF (1996), *The Future of the SDR* (Washington, DC: IMF).

IMF (1998a), *Annual Report* (Washington, DC: IMF), pp. 143–144.

IMF (1998b), *World Economic Outlook* (Washington, DC: IMF), October, pp. 141–155.

IMF (1998c), *IMF Survey Supplement*, September.

JAMES, H. (1996), "International monetary cooperation since Bretton Woods" (Washington, DC: IMF and Oxford University Press), pp. 317–319.0

MOHAMMED, A.A., M. JACUB, and I. ZAIDI (1996), "A focused SDR allocation", in IMF, *The Future of the SDR* (Washington DC: IMF), pp. 202–220.

POLAK, J.J. (1998), "The significance of the euro for developing countries", *International Monetary and Financial Issues for the 1990s*, Vol. IX, United Nations publication, sales no. E.98.II.D.3 (New York and Geneva).

WILLIAMSON, J. (1996), "A new facility for the IMF?", *International Monetary and Financial Issues for the 1990s*, Vol. VII, United Nations publication, sales no. E.96.II.D.2 (New York and Geneva).

ORDERLY WORKOUTS FOR CROSS-BORDER PRIVATE DEBT

Steven Radelet*

Abstract

This paper explores proposals for improved procedures and institutions to facilitate orderly workouts of international private sector debt. It focuses on systematic episodes of cross-border bankruptcies (rather than cases of individual firms) in which firms and banks are abruptly threatened with illiquidity and possible insolvency because of a sudden event that may be largely out of their control (such as a massive and sudden exchange-rate depreciation). The paper addresses the question as to how standstills and workout arrangements can be designed that would help stop a panic and an overshooting of capital withdrawals from emerging markets, and subsequently provide a framework to close insolvent firms and reorganize more viable enterprises. The paper first explores the dynamics of a financial panic, and then examines the basic logic behind domestic bankruptcy regimes and international sovereign debt workout procedures (such as the Paris Club and the London Club). It examines a variety of proposals for international versions of the three basic components of a debt workout: a debt payments standstill, provisions for new finance, and the framework for restructuring.

In the absence of a true international lender of last resort, the key to stopping an international financial panic is a temporary standstill on international debt payments, much like the payments standstill that features prominently in most domestic bankruptcy proceedings. An important step would be to encourage the use of collective action clauses in international bond contracts, which would help to coordinate creditor action on standstills and debt rollovers. However, while voluntary standstills and rollovers should be strongly encouraged, they should be backed by a credible mechanism to invoke a mandatory standstill when necessary. In certain extreme cases the IMF should be prepared to support a country's temporary imposition of broader capital controls and exchange restrictions that would temporarily suspend foreign currency debt service payments owed by banks and private corporations. The more credible the threat to use such mandatory controls, the easier it should be to reach a voluntary agreement with creditors on a payments standstill.

With respect to new financing, the IMF should explore new facilities through which certain countries can prequalify for fast-disbursing, low conditionality loans. The private sector should play a much larger role in providing fresh funds to countries in distress. Somewhat paradoxically, a key ingredient to establishing the stable environment needed to encourage new private sector financing is an effective payments standstill mechanism. New private financing to countries in distress should be voluntary, not mandatory. Government guarantees should not be provided on new financing provided by private sector creditors to private sector debtors.

*   The author is grateful to Matthew Cuchra for excellent research assistance, to Jeff Sachs for helpful discussions, and to Yilmaz Akyüz for comments on an earlier draft.

I. Introduction

For at least a century, it has been widely recognized that completely open and unregulated financial markets are prone to panic. Wide-open financial markets have been accompanied by panics and manias since the introduction of banking systems several centuries ago (Kindleberger, 1996). The United States, of course, faced a long string of major domestic bank panics in the late nineteenth and early twentieth centuries, and essentially all industrialized countries have faced similar crises at one time or another.

In the past several years, the emerging markets have taken their turn. In the 1990s, a number of emerging markets were hit by financial crises, including Argentina and Mexico in 1995; Indonesia, the Republic of Korea, Malaysia, the Philippines and Thailand in 1997; and the Russian Federation and Brazil in 1998. In each case, very large capital inflows suddenly stopped, and creditors (both foreign and domestic) rushed for the exits. The reversals were partly due to weaknesses in these economies that led to a change in perceptions about their creditworthiness. In each case, however, it is clear that markets overreacted both in their exuberance with the initial inflows (which often came in with little analysis or risk management) and in their haste with the subsequent outflows. The resulting economic contractions in these countries were much deeper than was either inevitable or necessary.

Early in the twentieth century, industrialized countries began to respond to repeated financial sector crises by carefully and prudently regulating financial markets and by developing public sector institutions to help prevent major crises. Today's industrial country financial markets are far from being completely free and open, with several key institutions helping to prevent or mitigate market failures. One critical institution is the lender of last resort (usually the central bank), which provides liquidity to financial institutions hit by sudden withdrawals, and which assures depositors (or creditors) that they need not rush for the exits. Closely related are supervisory and regulatory institutions (usually also housed in the central bank), which ensure that financial entities meet certain minimum operating conditions and that they are not involved in excessively risky activities. Deposit insurance systems give further comfort to depositors that might think of running. Finally, the industrialized countries developed well-defined and relatively transparent systems for managing bankruptcies, liquidations and other forms of debt workouts. These bankruptcy systems help to prevent risky borrowing (by providing a credible threat to firms that they might be liquidated if they are poorly managed), stop panics from getting out of control (through debt standstills) and provide a framework for ultimate restructuring when necessary. Also, they try to ensure some equity in the sharing of the burden of bankruptcy between creditors and borrowers, recognizing that in most cases both sides bear some of the blame when loans go bad.

Of course, these institutions and procedures are far from perfect, and do not always ensure smooth operation of financial systems, as the United States found out with the crisis of the savings and loan associations in the 1980s. Generally, however, they have succeeded in preventing extreme panics and crises in industrialized country domestic financial markets, and have helped these markets to operate more smoothly and efficiently. It is worth noting, for example, that the last major bank panic in the United States was in 1933, just before the creation of the Federal Deposit Insurance Corporation.

To a very large extent, parallel institutional arrangements do not exist in international financial markets, and so these markets remain relatively prone to panic. Without a true international lender of last resort, international banking standards, international bankruptcy laws and deposit insurance, international financial markets are as volatile as were financial markets in the industrial countries before these institutions were put in place. In the aftermath of the Asian financial crisis, the debate on redesigning the international financial architecture has touched on several of these institutional issues. This paper explores one segment of this debate: the possibility of developing improved procedures or institutions to facilitate orderly workouts of international private sector debt.

Our focus is not on individual cases of cross-border bankruptcies, which are best handled by developing stronger insolvency codes and more effective courts in emerging markets. Rather, we focus on systemic episodes where firms and banks across an economy are abruptly threatened with illiquidity and possible insolvency because of a sudden event that may be largely beyond their control. The relevant case, of course, is a massive exchange rate depreciation resulting from a sudden shift in capital flows that undermines both well run and poorly run firms alike, weakens banks and interrupts the payments system, and threatens to plunge a country into deep recession. How can standstills and workout arrangements be designed that would help stop a panic and an overshooting of capital withdrawals from emerging markets, and subsequently provide a framework to close insolvent firms and reorganize more viable enterprises?

The next section of the paper briefly explores the dynamics of a financial panic. Section III examines the basic logic behind domestic bankruptcy regimes and international sovereign debt workout procedures (mainly the Paris Club and the London Club), and reviews the few recent cases of workouts of private sector cross-border debt. Section IV is the heart of the paper, examining a variety of proposals for international versions of the three basic components of a workout procedure: a debt payments standstill, provisions for new finance and the framework for restructuring. The final section offers some recommendations and conclusions.

II. Financial crises in emerging markets

The hallmark of international financial crises is a sudden and rapid reversal of large-scale capital flows. An economy that had been the recipient of large inflows is suddenly faced with the cessation of these inflows, and demand for immediate repayment of outstanding loans. Firms and banks are pushed near to or into default, a situation that is typically exacerbated by the large exchange rate depreciations that ultimately accompany such large swings of foreign capital.[1]

The Asian crisis economies were true to form. According to estimates by the Institute of International Finance, capital flows to the five most severely affected Asian countries (Indonesia, the Republic of Korea, Malaysia, the Philippines and Thailand) shifted from an *inflow* of $103 billion in 1996 to an *outflow* of $1 billion in 1997 (Institute of International Finance, 1999a). This shift of $104 billion is the equivalent of about 9 per cent of the pre-crisis gross domestic product (GDP) of these economies. The Russian Federation and Brazil faced similar reversals of investor sentiment.

The effects of such economy-wide reversals in capital flows and large exchange rate movements can be devastating. Large numbers of firms suddenly become illiquid and face the prospect of shutting down. Commercial bank capital can be quickly wiped out, threatening the operation of the payments system. Poorly run firms and banks tend to be the most vulnerable, and many deserve to be merged or shut down. It is important to recognize, however, that even well-run firms and banks are threatened, not through any fault of their own, but because of large and unanticipated exchange rate movements and their collateral effects.

Creditor panic

It is worth briefly exploring the circumstances under which such large reversals of capital flows can occur. The withdrawals can be sparked by rapid changes in international market conditions, such as the large swings in commodity prices and the sharp increases in dollar interest rates that brought about the 1980s debt crisis. Domestic economic mismanagement, or an abrupt change in economic policy or political leadership, can likewise cause credit withdrawals, as with Mexico in 1994. In addition, and most importantly for this discussion, recent financial crises point to intrinsic instability in international financial markets as a key part of the problem.

The basic idea is that under certain conditions, international financial markets can become prone to self-fulfilling crises.[2] Individual creditors acting rationally in their own self-interest can together generate sharp and fundamentally unnecessary panicked reversals of capital flows. Both creditors and borrowers find themselves collectively worse off as a result, even though each was acting rationally on an individual basis. Consider, for example, a solvent but illiquid borrower. Normally, because the borrower is solvent, it should be able to borrow fresh funds from the capital markets to relieve the liquidity problem. Since the firm is solvent, the creditors could reasonably expect that both the old and the new loans would be fully serviced. However, it is possible that creditors will be unwilling to provide fresh funds, not because of concerns over the fundamental strength of the borrower, but because they fear that *other* creditors may not provide sufficient new funds to the firm to ease the liquidity problem. Suppose that the borrower requires credits so large that no single lender can provide all of the necessary funds. Each creditor recognizes that if the other creditors do not make new loans, the firm will not be able to meet its debt service obligations. Thus, any creditor that lends new funds on its own risks losses on both its old and new loans. Therefore, each creditor will be unwilling to make a new loan if it believes that other creditors will not lend as well, and in fact will begin to demand repayment of existing loans. A creditor "grab race" ensues in which each creditor tries to be the first in line to be repaid or to seize assets. The borrower, even though it was solvent, will ultimately default on its loans and face possible bankruptcy proceedings.

In international capital markets, entire economies can become susceptible to a similar kind of "grab race" (Radelet and Sachs, 1998a; Chang and Velasco, 1998). Economies are especially vulnerable when borrowers (be they firms, banks or the government) build up aggregate short-term foreign exchange liabilities in excess of available liquid foreign exchange assets. In this case, international lenders know that there is not enough foreign exchange available to repay everyone, but they are willing to continue lending as long as they believe that other creditors will do the same. However, if something happens to make them believe that other creditors will withdraw their credits, they will rush to be the first to demand repayment, since they do not want to be the last in line to be repaid.

In each of the recent severe crises in emerging markets – Mexico (1994), Argentina (1995), Thailand (1997), Indonesia (1997), the Republic of Korea (1997), the Russian Federation (1998) and Brazil (1998) – aggregate short-term foreign exchange obligations exceeded liquid foreign exchange assets, setting the stage for panicked withdrawals by foreign creditors. Although information on total foreign exchange liabilities and assets is not available, in each of the crisis economies short-term debts owed to foreign commercial banks far exceeded the foreign exchange reserves of the central bank (Radelet and Sachs, 1998a). This situation posed no problems as long as confidence in Asia remained high and the banks believed that everyone else would continue lending. However, once confidence shifted following the float of the Thai baht in July 1997, the rush for the exits was on. The more the exchange rates depreciated, the more the creditors demanded to be repaid, which itself put additional pressure on the Asian currencies and accelerated the process of withdrawals. Creditors knew that there was not enough foreign exchange to pay everyone, and no one wanted to be last in line. Sure enough, those who got out of Asia early were more or less paid in full, while those who waited suffered large losses. The result was widespread liquidity problems among Asian banks and firms, which undermined the capital base of the banks and pushed many firms to the edge of bankruptcy. With no mechanisms in place to deal with these problems, the panicked withdrawals could not

be effectively stopped. The workouts that followed were disorderly and far from optimal, at great and unnecessary cost to the creditors, the debtors and the Asian economies.

III. Current debt restructuring procedures

In considering the design of workout procedures for cross-border private debt, there are two main parallels from which to draw: domestic bankruptcy procedures dealing with individual private firms, and workout mechanisms for cross-border sovereign debt (mainly the Paris Club and the London Club).

A. *Bankruptcy proceedings*

We begin with the basic procedures used in the case of a firm facing financial distress.[3] Bankruptcy procedures, at their core, establish a collective forum both to sort out the rights of creditors and debtors and to address the "collective action" problem of individual creditors acting rationally to the detriment of creditors (and the debtor) as a group. They temporarily hold the assets of the firm in a common pool. A primary objective is the maintenance of the value of the firm's assets (which is ultimately in the interest of the creditors as a group), rather than addressing concerns about individual creditor rights (Jackson, 1986). At the same time, bankruptcy procedures should not be so lenient that debtors can easily walk away from their obligations. Thus, ideally, the goal of maximizing the value of the firm assets should be balanced against the objective of encouraging adherence to the *ex-ante* terms of the debt contract as much as possible (Eichengreen and Portes, 1995). Although bankruptcy proceedings differ in important ways across countries, most have four key elements in common:

(i) an arbitrator or administrator, usually a court or tribunal;

(ii) provisions for a standstill on payments to prevent a creditor "grab race";

(iii) provisions for the possibility of the firm borrowing new money to continue operations during the standstill; and

(iv) a workout arrangement (following a period of time for information gathering and negotiation) consisting of some combination of a rollover/ extension of existing loans, a reorganization of the firm and/or the debt contracts, or a closure of the firm.

The arbitrator/administrator acts as umpire, supervisor and facilitator during the restructuring process, and when necessary imposes a binding settlement on the competing claims of the creditor and debtor. Essentially, the arbitrator supervises a legal framework in which a settlement between the debtor and creditor can be negotiated. In most cases, a bankruptcy court or a judicial tribunal plays this role. A key point is that in domestic bankruptcy proceedings, the debtor and the lenders all fall under a single judicial authority, giving the court the legal power to impose a settlement on all parties involved. The arbitrator must be neutral, able to balance the competing claims of both sides, and free from political or other influence that could give an unfair advantage to one of the competing parties. The arbitrator specifically, and bankruptcy law more generally, would not be necessary in a world of perfect information where all parties could forecast all future contingencies (Cornelli and Felli, 1995). The market failure of lack of complete information is what leads to imperfectly specified contracts and the inability of the two sides to negotiate an agreeable solution outside the courts. The arbitrator helps induce the two parties to share relevant information and reach a final settlement.

One of the critical powers of the arbitrator is the authority to impose a standstill (called the "automatic stay" in section 362 of the United States bankruptcy code) on debt service payments for a specified period of time. The core role of this provision is to stop actions by individual (or groups of) creditors acting in their individual self-interest that could lead to a creditor grab race and undermine the common good of all the parties involved (Jackson, 1986; UNCTAD, 1998). The standstill provides the time necessary for a more rational workout process. *Note that the standstill is mandatory, imposed by the court, and is not left as a voluntary choice of the creditors* (since the market, left to its own, could devolve into a grab race). Note further that during the standstill, no distinction is made between "good" firms and "bad" firms – both good and bad firms receive the initial protection, except in a few extreme cases in which the judge refuses to grant temporary protection. The standstill provides the time necessary to distinguish between viable and unviable firms, and to choose the appropriate course of action. However, standstills should not be so long as to allow unviable firms to avoid liquidation. The length of the standstill period varies widely across countries. Bankruptcy codes in the United Kingdom and Germany provide for a three-month moratorium, whereas in the United States the court has wide discretion regarding the length of the stay, which can extend for several years (Franks, 1995).

The principle of maintaining the value of the firm suggests that in some cases it may be in the collective interest of the creditors to allow the firm to continue operations during the standstill period, provided that it can generate a positive cash flow. Thus, bankruptcy codes generally contain an arrangement that allows firms to tap private capital markets for interim financing (in the United States Bankruptcy code, this is the so-called debtor in possession financing provision, found in section 364). The general idea is to enable the debtor to tap the private capital markets by granting *priority* to the new loans in the repayment queue. Creditors may be willing to grant new loans, to the extent that they believe the firm is solvent, as long as the new claims are senior to most existing claims. This provision helps the firm avoid a premature cessation of operations, thus helping to preserve its value as a going concern. *Unlike the standstill, the provision of new financing is voluntary*: creditors can choose whether or not to provide funds, with presumably the better firms receiving funds, but not the weaker firms.

The ultimate workout arrangement can vary widely. There are at least three broad cases. First, a firm that is solvent but illiquid should be able to ultimately resume full debt service payments without a writedown or reorganization. The primary need for such firms is temporary protection and access to new financing to alleviate the liquidity crunch. Second, insolvent firms may be able to return to solvency after financial and/or managerial reorganization. Management is often replaced, and the ownership structure of the firm may change, sometimes during the standstill period. In this case, a return to solvency typically requires debt relief, certainly in the form of rollovers during the standstill, and probably debt reduction and/or debt-to-equity conversions. A key problem is to get the creditors to agree to the form of the restructuring. Bankruptcy proceedings make provisions to guard against the possibility of a minority group of creditors holding up the agreement, usually by allowing for the approval of the reorganization with a majority, rather than unanimous, approval of the creditors. In the United States code, approval is required by a simple majority of creditors by number, and by two-thirds by value in all classes of creditors

(Franks, 1995). The court has the authority to "cram down" the provisions of the agreement to dissenting creditors. The third case is that of an insolvent firm that has no hope of returning to a positive cash flow. In this case, the firm should be shut down, with remaining assets distributed to the creditors in priority order.

B.   Sovereign debt restructuring arrangements

Restructuring procedures for sovereign foreign debt are not as formalized as those for domestic bankruptcy. Nevertheless, operating procedures are in place for sovereign debt owed to other governments (through the Paris Club) and to commercial banks (through the London Club). The Paris Club and the London Club coordinate their actions with each other and with the IMF. Together, their operations can be thought of as a rough equivalent of domestic bankruptcy proceedings, with the presence of an arbitrator, a standstill period, provisions for new finance, and workout arrangements.

The Paris Club is a forum for creditor governments to restructure the debts owed to them by debtor governments. The specific creditor governments vary by case, but are all members of the Organization for Economic Co-operation and Development (OECD). The Paris Club maintains a permanent secretariat in Paris, and operates with a set of standard conventions and policies (Vitale, 1995; Sevigny, 1990). The IMF plays something akin to the role of the arbitrator in Paris Club negotiations, although there are important differences. Countries do not approach the Paris Club for rescheduling without the support of the IMF. Indeed, the Paris Club requires that debtor countries conclude an agreement with the IMF before a formal restructuring can proceed. The IMF acts in some sense as a referee, and plays the important role of supplying each side with the relevant information needed to restructure the debt. The IMF programme in a debtor country can be thought of as an approved "reorganization plan", since it details the policy and institutional changes that are seen as necessary in order to return the debtor to a sound economic footing (Eichengreen and Portes, 1995). Of course, the IMF does not play the exact same role as a bankruptcy court. It is clearly not as neutral as a court, since the creditor countries have much larger voting power than do the debtor countries within the IMF (UNCTAD, 1998). Moreover, the IMF does not have the legal authority to impose a binding agreement on either the creditors or the debtors.

As in the case of bankruptcy procedures, the Paris Club has provisions for a standstill on at least some debt service payments during a specified time period (called the consolidation period). Only payments falling due during this period (rather than the entire stock of debt) are eligible for rescheduling. Payments on short-term debt (with maturities of less than one year) and previously rescheduled debt are generally not eligible. Similar to the way in which a bankruptcy standstill helps stop a panic and preserve the value of a firm, the Paris Club standstill supports the economic prospects of a debtor country by taking immediate pressure off the exchange rate (or, in a fixed exchange rate system, it takes the pressure off foreign exchange reserves) and mitigates the extent to which the debtor country must make dramatic adjustments to reduce absorption.

The Paris Club itself does not generally provide new senior financing during the consolidation period. However, the IMF, unlike a bankruptcy court, provides immediate financing to the debtor, almost always supplemented by additional funds from the World Bank, one of the regional development banks and some of the same governments that are members of the Paris Club. These new funds provide the debtor government and the economy as a whole with a certain amount of liquidity to purchase imports and meet other foreign currency obligations.

The precise terms of the Paris Club restructuring differ depending on the economic situation and bargaining power of the debtor. Historically, most cases involved a rollover of debt rather than any writedown. Since 1988, however, debts have been written down, sometimes substantially, for eligible low-income debtor countries. Although the Paris Club itself does not include all of a country's creditors, the terms of the agreement specify that the debtor is expected to seek similar treatment from all its creditors, including commercial banks and other private creditors (but not multilateral agencies). Unlike in the case of bankruptcy proceedings, the Paris Club requires the unanimous consent of all the creditors, and therefore does not make provisions for a "cramdown" on dissident creditors.

The London Club provides a mechanism for sovereign debtors to restructure their debts owed to commercial banks. Since there are many more creditor commercial banks than there are creditor governments, the London Club typically consists of a larger and more variable group of creditors than does the Paris Club. The London Club usually specifies a creditor committee of about 15 banks to negotiate with the debtor (Eichengreen and Portes, 1995). As with the Paris Club, an IMF agreement is a prerequisite for negotiation. The IMF facilitates flows of information between the debtor and the creditors and provides the foundation for determining how much and when a country might be expected to pay.

Members of the London Club can play a role in providing fresh financing for debtor countries undergoing an adjustment programme. For example, foreign commercial banks provided financing (sometimes following heavy arm-twisting from industrial country governments) to distressed Latin American governments during the early stages of the 1980s crisis and later during the Baker Plan. Occasionally, members of the London Club might provide new financing ("bridge" financing) while a country is negotiating with the IMF in order to allow the country to discharge overdue debt payments to the IMF and/or the World Bank.

The London Club differs from the Paris Club in that the ultimate agreement needs the approval of banks holding 90–95 per cent of total exposure, rather than the unanimous agreement required in the Paris Club. Unlike in a typical bankruptcy procedure, there is no legal authority that can "cram down" the agreement on dissident creditors or arbitrate a deadlocked negotiation. Since there are so many creditor banks to deal with (each with its own group of lawyers) and since a small minority can hold out and delay the process, London Club reschedulings can drag out over a period of years (Eichengreen and Portes, 1995). Terms of the ultimate agreement can vary widely from a rollover to a significant writedown, as was the case with some of the Brady Plan restructuring in the aftermath of the Latin American debt crisis.

Note that sovereign debt owed to the IMF and the World Bank is not rescheduled. Thus, not all creditors are subject to a standstill. Moreover, unlike in the case of domestic bankruptcy procedures where fresh financing is not used for debt service (since all creditors are subject to the standstill), in sovereign cases some new financing is used to repay the most senior creditors.

C. *Private debt workouts*

Currently, there are no institutions to deal with private sector cross-border workouts that parallel those for domestic bankruptcy or sovereign debts.

Cross-border insolvencies differ from domestic cases in at least two important ways. First, there is no clear legal jurisdiction that has ultimate authority over creditors and debtors. Moreover, in many emerging markets legal institutions and bankruptcy laws are very weak and ineffective. Second, cross-border cases are vulnerable to particular kinds of systemic shocks (like large exchange rate depreciations) that have less effect in a purely domestic context. With the Paris Club and the London Club, there is some experience in cross-border cases, but private cross-border cases differ from sovereign cases in at least two important ways. First, in systemic private cases there are many debtors and many creditors, whereas in sovereign cases there is one debtor and generally far fewer creditors. Thus, organizing debt workouts is more complicated in the private case. Second, in the sovereign case there is little concern about the government getting involved in the workout, since the government is the debtor. Private cases raise the issue of the proper role of the government in imposing solutions, guaranteeing new debt contracts or otherwise effectively nationalizing private sector liabilities. The case for public sector involvement is stronger when the debtors are banks, since the payments system may be threatened; it is weakest for purely private sector non-financial debtors.

There are some recent examples of workouts of private sector cross-border debt, although they tend to be ad hoc rather than orderly workouts. Perhaps the most relevant example is the rollover of the commercial bank of the Republic of Korea debt in early 1998. After the Republic of Korea's first programme with the IMF (signed on 3 December 1997) failed to stem the flight from the won and to calm markets, the country found itself on the brink of default in mid-December. The United States Government, rather than continuing to hope that market confidence would return through a traditional IMF programme, dramatically changed tack and decided to press the foreign commercial banks to roll over their short-term credits to Republic of Korea banks. On 24 December, a new IMF programme for the Republic of Korea was announced, together with the rollover initiative and new immediate financing. The first step was an immediate standstill on debt servicing, pending a formal agreement. Within just a matter of weeks, an agreement was reached between the commercial bank debtors of the Republic of Korea, the government, and the foreign bank creditors on a complete rollover of $22 billion in debts falling due in the first quarter of 1998, converting these short-term debts into claims with maturities of between one and three years.

Although the rollover was not mandatory in the legal sense, the Treasury of the United States used its authority to pressure the creditors into what the creditors called a "quasi-voluntary" rollover (Institute of International Finance, 1999b). In a sharp departure from traditional bankruptcy proceedings, the debts effectively became nationalized via a guarantee by the Government of the Republic of Korea, even though the debts involved private sector debtor banks. Notably, on the strength of the rollover, the government was able to quickly return to the international financial markets, floating a strongly oversubscribed bond issue for $4 billion in early April 1998.[4] There is little question that the rollover was critical to the Republic of Korea's relatively rapid turnaround. The foreign creditors actually came out better *after* the rollover than before: there was no writedown, the new loans carried higher interest rates than the original loans, and they carried a guarantee by the Government of the Republic of Korea. The Republic of Korea had certain advantages favouring a rollover that other debtors may not have: its political importance brought strong pressure from the United States to get a deal done, and there were a relatively small number of creditor banks. The country's rollover was not a true orderly workout, since it was done through informal and uncertain mechanisms that were not in place during the most intense phase of the panic in December 1997. Nevertheless, the experience shows that workouts, while perhaps not perfect in all the details, can be successful.

In June 1998, Indonesian commercial banks restructured $9 billion in short-term debts into new loans with maturities of between one and four years, all guaranteed by the Indonesian Central Bank. The restructuring, while generally seen as successful as far as it went, came much too late (eight months after the first IMF programme) to help stave off the Indonesian panic. In Thailand, the first 16 financial institutions suspended in mid-1997 defaulted on $2 billion in loans, and an additional $2 billion owed by 40 other financial institutions was exchanged for five-year notes (at 5 per cent interest) guaranteed by the government. These amounts were also too small to stop the panic in Thailand.

Examples of successful corporate debt workouts are harder to find. Mexico (1983), the Philippines (1983) and Indonesia (1998) established frameworks for corporate debt/restructuring. The mechanisms focused on the final restructuring phase; they did not include provisions for a standstill or fresh financing. In each case, firms were eligible to participate only *after* they had reached a restructuring agreement with their creditors. Essentially, the plans established a mechanism which locked in the exchange rate (in either nominal or real terms) so that the government took on the risk of subsequent further exchange rate depreciations. Mexico's FICORCA[5] system also gave the Mexican firms some front-end cash flow relief for their peso payments. While FICORCA is generally seen as at least partially successful, Indonesia's system has had no participants (by early 1999), partly because it offered firms no real cash flow relief, and partly because the rupiah had already depreciated so much by the time the system was established that firms simply could not make their payments.

IV. Proposals for orderly workouts

Several recent analyses of various aspects of the architecture of international financial markets at least touch on proposals for workouts for private sector cross–border claims. These proposals have been put forward by academics (e.g. Eichengreen, 1999; Radelet and Sachs, 1998a, b; Litan et al., 1998; Buiter and Silbert, 1998; Calomiris, 1998; Sachs, 1995), private organizations (e.g. Institute of International Finance, 1999b, which represents commercial banks) and intergovernmental groups (e.g. Group of 22, 1998a-c; UNCTAD, 1998; Group of Ten, 1996). (The reports of the Working Groups of the Group of 22 [G-22] are especially notable since they include substantial input from representatives of emerging market countries.)

A. Crisis prevention

Clearly, the most attractive way to deal with financial crises and panics is to take strong steps to prevent them. A thorough analysis of crisis prevention, however, would take us away from the focus of this paper. Instead, we shall briefly note two of the most important steps towards prevention.

First, emerging markets with underdeveloped domestic financial systems should strongly consider taking steps to limit inflows of short-term capital. The best way to avoid panicked withdrawals of short-term lines of credit is to avoid building up these kinds of liabilities in the first place. The basic rationale for controls on short-term debt is as follows. Most emerging market countries will require many years to develop the regulatory, supervisory and private sector institutions to make financial markets function relatively smoothly. Partly as a result of this, these countries are vulnerable to large inflows of short-term, volatile capital. Therefore, during the interim period when financial institutions are being developed, these countries should take step to mitigate the risks from large short-term exposure. Modest controls on inflows can be introduced during periods of large capital inflows, and eased either when inflows subside (as happened recently in Chile) or as financial systems develop more fully. Chile's experience with modest controls in the early 1990s showed promising results; Malaysia's more limited experiment in 1994 and 1995 is another relevant example (Eichengreen, 1999; Group of 22, 1998a; Eichengreen and Mussa, 1998; Helleiner, 1998; McKinnon and Pill, 1996).

Second, pegged exchange rates, especially if not fully backed by foreign exchange reserves, invite trouble. Some advocates of fixed exchange rates have pointed out that when the Asian crisis countries suddenly adopted flexible rates in mid-1997, the bottom dropped out of their currency markets. But that misses the crucial point. Had the Asian countries adopted more flexible exchange rate systems in the early 1990s, before the period of large capital inflows, they would have built up far less short-term debt. Volatile exchange rates tend to deter short-run capital flows, but have much less impact on longer- term capital. In a world of highly mobile capital, apparently the best options for emerging markets are either flexible exchange rates (suitable for most countries) or very rigid systems such as currency boards (in a few cases, such as those of small, open, resource-poor economies, or for limited periods following a hyperinflation) (Eichengreen, 1999; Sachs, 1998).

Beyond prevention and turning to workouts, there are three general issues for consideration: temporary payments standstills, mechanisms for new finance, and restructuring.

B.   *Temporary payments standstill*

The key to stopping a full-fledged creditor panic is the temporary payments standstill (UNCTAD, 1998). As in domestic insolvency cases, the standstill is designed to halt creditors from racing to strip a firm of its assets for the benefit of a few creditors, but to the detriment of creditors as a group, the debtor and the economy as a whole. In the international context, the standstill plays a larger role. *A standstill helps relieve the intense pressure on the exchange rate from a systemic creditor panic, thus mitigating the possibility of a substantial overshooting of the exchange rate and minimizing the corresponding damage to bank capital and corporate balance sheets.* With a successful standstill and less exchange rate overshooting, the subsequent dimensions of the workout process (providing new finance and ultimate restructuring where necessary) become much easier. In addition, an effective standstill mechanism is likely to contribute to crisis prevention, since the threat to use it will probably dampen short-term capital inflows in the first place (UNCTAD, 1998).

There is widespread agreement on the general notion of the desirability of some kind of a standstill mechanism that can be employed during the extreme circumstances of an international financial panic. As with domestic bankruptcy, a standstill is generally warranted even when the debtor bears some (or even a large portion) of the blame for the loans going bad. The standstill period is not the time to discriminate between "good" and "bad" firms, but rather it is designed to provide the time necessary so that those kinds of judgements can be made more accurately. There are, however, wide differences of opinion about the appropriate design of the standstill mechanism, the circumstances under which it should be employed, and who would have the authority to trigger it.

1.   *Voluntary standstills*

The G-22 Working Group emphasizes its view that in most cases traditional IMF programmes and the accompanying financial support will normally be sufficient to avert a payments crisis (Group of 22, 1998a). In slightly more difficult cases, it advocates making available extraordinary IMF financing through drawings from the IMF's Supplemental Reserve Facility. Creditor banks agree with this view, arguing that policy adjustment programmes together with extensive official financial support are much more appropriate than standstills and reschedulings (Institute of International Finance, 1999b).

However, the G-22 Working Group recognizes that in certain extreme cases an interruption of normal debt servicing by either the government or the private sector, accompanied by an orderly, cooperative restructuring, may be the best course of action in the context of a payments crisis. It concludes that:

> A government should consider initiating a temporary suspension of debt payments only when it is clear that, even with appropriately

strong policy adjustments, the country will experience a severe fiscal, financial or balance of payments crisis and the government *or a substantial portion of the private sector* will be unable to meet its contractual obligations in full and on time. In such circumstances, the initiation of an orderly, cooperative, and comprehensive workout, while inherently costly, could best serve the collective interest of the debtor, its creditors, and the international community [emphasis added]. (p. 28)

The Group of 22 recommends that governments avoid unilateral actions, and instead favours voluntary cooperation whenever possible. It argues that unilateral actions run the risk of damaging a country's reputation in financial markets, adversely affecting a country's market access or generating litigation against the debtors. Moreover, if one emerging market suspends debt service payments, there is a risk that creditors would react by quickly withdrawing their credits from *other* similar markets, thus spreading the crisis. The Group of 22 suggests that creditors are most likely to agree voluntarily to a standstill (or rollover) when the scope of the liabilities included is relatively narrow, the time frame is relatively short and when the IMF and key creditor governments signal their support, either verbally or through new lending. The Group argues that although the scope of the suspensions should be as narrow as possible, "no category of debt should be granted an automatic exemption from the suspension if it is contributing substantially to the payments crisis" (p. 31).

The Working Group of the Institute of International Finance (IIF), representing commercial banks, strongly argues that any private sector participation must be voluntary, and rejects any kind of mandatory participation (IIF, 1999b). Curiously, however, in the same report, the Group praises the Republic of Korea's rollover as having been a "relatively good one" (p. 65), even as it refers to the arrangement as "quasi-voluntary". It does not specifically endorse or reject standstills per se, arguing instead that crises should be dealt with on a case-by-case basis, and recognizing that voluntary rollovers may be appropriate in some circumstances. The Group argues that whatever form the voluntary private sector participation takes, it should involve higher spreads and (probably) public guarantees on the relevant debt instruments (p. 8). It concludes that mandatory standstills would be counterproductive because they would delay a country's restoration of market access.

Of course, if voluntary approaches actually worked well in practice, there would be no need for

standard bankruptcy proceedings and imposed standstill arrangements. The damage from a creditor panic occurs precisely because of problems in coordinating the creditors. Individual creditors generally – or at least in most circumstances – will not voluntarily roll over their credits if left on their own.

In the absence of an international court with the power to impose a standstill (a proposal discussed later), analysts have looked for mechanisms that could automatically trigger a standstill. The most common suggestion is the introduction of clauses into bond contracts aimed at achieving better coordination amongst creditors (Eichengreen, 1999; Group of 22, 1998a; Group of Ten, 1996; Eichengreen and Portes, 1995). The G-22 Working Group recommends the inclusion of three such clauses in *sovereign* debt contracts, and suggests consideration of (while avoiding explicitly recommending) including such clauses in *private* debt contracts. The three key collective action clauses are: (i) collective representation clauses, aimed at coordinating the actions of creditors and facilitating communication among them as well as between creditors and debtors; (ii) majority action clauses, allowing a majority of creditors to change the payment terms of a debt contract, without the unanimous consent of all creditors; and (iii) sharing clauses specifying that creditors will divide proportionally with all other creditors any and all payments received from the debtor. The 1996 report of the Group of Ten added non-acceleration clauses to the list, which would preclude creditors from voting to accelerate repayment of outstanding debt, an action that effectively turns long-term debts into short-term obligations. Eichengreen (1999) suggests a fifth clause: a minimum voting threshold for creditors to bring lawsuits, requiring at least 10 per cent of creditors to agree to take action against the debtor. This would avoid the possibility of a lone creditor taking legal action against the debtor, which could threaten a rollover or rescheduling agreed to by everyone else.

The IIF agrees that it may be useful to include clauses in bonds that allow for qualified majority rescheduling (IIF, 1999b, p. 77). It argues, however, that any sort of officially mandated inclusion of these clauses would be counterproductive "in the view of most market participants".

An important consideration is how such clauses would affect the cost of borrowing. The IIF concludes that bond issuers would have to expect to pay more for the inclusion of such clauses. The Group of 22 argues that the price effects are ambiguous. Creditors might perceive the inclusion of such clauses as increasing the probability of default, leading to a higher price as the IIF suggests. However, these clauses also reduce the uncertainty about the debt workout process and partially protect against the large downside risk of a creditor being stuck at the end of the line in a panic and therefore receiving nothing. This latter assurance should help reduce the price.

Most likely, these clauses would increase the cost of borrowing. After all, such clauses are effectively a form of insurance for both creditors and debtors, and like most insurance will come at a small cost. And, as with all insurance, while this mechanism is in the collective interest of creditors and debtors, each individual creditor and debtor may resist paying for the insurance. However, as Fischer (1999) notes, a higher price on debt instruments with these clauses simply reflects a more appropriate pricing of risk. Moreover, raising the cost of borrowing may reduce the risk that countries "overborrow" in international capital markets in the way that most of the crisis countries did in the early 1990s.[6] *To the extent that the problem in the crisis countries has been too much foreign borrowing, measures that increase the cost of borrowing may be appropriate, even if they raise the cost of investment.* A slightly higher price would also favourably change the maturity mix of borrowing. The price penalty is likely to be highest on short-term debt, since potentially the entire amount would be subject to rollover, whereas only a portion of a longer-term maturity (the amounts falling due during the roll-over period) would be affected. Thus, such clauses may raise the price of short-term debt relative to long-term debt, increasing their attractiveness.

Eichengreen (1999) argues that these clauses are unlikely to be introduced voluntarily without specific legislation and regulation; otherwise, the first country to introduce them might be perceived as signalling its own lack of confidence in its capacity to fully service its debts. He suggests that the IMF urge all its member countries to make the inclusion of such clauses a requirement for issuing international bonds on the domestic market. He further proposes that the IMF could provide additional inducement by lending at more favourable rates to countries that require such provision in their own contracts and those of commercial banks and corporations in their country (Eichengreen, 1999, p. 113). To that might be added that the World Bank and the regional development banks could also be encouraged to lend to such countries at more favourable rates. Of course, these institutions lend in much larger amounts than the IMF, especially outside crisis situations.

These clauses, as suggested, leave it to the creditor to trigger the standstill by a majority vote. This still leaves the question of facilitating the necessary communication amongst the creditors, and between the debtor country and the creditors, to invoke the clauses. One way to do so would be to establish standing representative creditor committees (Eichengreen, 1999; Sachs and Radelet, 1998; Eichengreen and Portes, 1995). Standing creditor committees would facilitate communication between the debtors and creditors, make it easier to quickly begin negotiations with creditors early in the crisis, and ease the process of triggering the collective action clauses described above. Such committees are unlikely to appear on their own (otherwise they would already exist), and so suasion and pressure may be necessary from the IMF and creditor country governments to put them in place (Eichengreen, 1999).

2. *Mandatory standstills*

In the absence of collective action clauses, many analysts (but not all, with the major exception of the IIF) argue that a purely voluntary approach will not always work. In what is perhaps the most striking feature of the G-22 report, the Working Group holds out the possibility of (while staying clear of explicitly recommending) *a mandatory payments suspension in certain circumstances.* A voluntary approach will not work, it argues, if the government does not have sufficient bargaining power to obtain sustainable terms, if certain creditors refuse to participate (hoping to free-ride on the restructuring of others), or if the negotiations in a purely voluntary approach take too much time. It indicates that mandatory debt suspensions could come in several forms, such as (a) suspension of government debt service payments, (b) restrictions on outward payments by commercial banks or (c) with respect to private sector debt payments, the use of capital and exchange controls. It stresses that the latter should be undertaken only in very exceptional circumstances and only in conjunction with an IMF programme. The risks to a country in imposing temporary capital controls would be reduced if the move was supported by the international community, rather than made alone. Thus, when capital controls are seen as the least bad option facing a country, the Group of 22 suggests that the international community could provide credibility by signalling its support and by supplying limited and conditional financial assistance, even in the context of suspended debt payments (i.e. the IMF could "lend into arrears", discussed further in the next section).

One implication (not spelt out by the Group of 22) is that a government's announcement that it was suspending debt service payments would be interpreted as an exchange control as covered in the IMF's Articles of Agreement (Sachs, 1995; Eichengreen and Portes, 1995; UNCTAD, 1998). Article VIII (2)(b) states that "exchange contracts which involve the currency of any member and which are contrary to the exchange control regulations of that member maintained or imposed consistently with this Agreement shall be unenforceable in the territories of any member". The question is whether or not this clause (and specifically the term "exchange contract") can be interpreted broadly enough to include a suspension of debt service payments as a form of exchange controls (see UNCTAD, 1998, for a discussion). Eichengreen and Portes (1995) conclude that this was not the original intent of the clause or the interpretation of various courts, but they hold out the possibility that the IMF Executive Board could give the clause a new definitive interpretation that would include a standstill. Explicitly amending the Articles of Agreement would also be possible. In this spirit, the Canadian Government has suggested that IMF members agree to legislate an "Emergency Standstill Clause" that would apply to all cross-border financial transactions (Canada, Department of Finance, 1998). However, either amending the IMF Articles of Agreement or pushing for legislation that would have to be passed by most of its member governments is highly unlikely.

In both the voluntary and mandatory cases, the Group of 22 approach relies heavily on the IMF to play at least part of the role of the arbitrator/administrator in standard insolvency proceedings: that of the referee who can verify when a standstill is warranted. Of course, the IMF (and the broader international community it represents) does not have the ultimate legal authority of a bankruptcy court, but its judgement would be critical in providing support to a suspension of payments. There is no question that the backing of the IMF and the broader international community would be critical in easing concerns about the motives of the debtor country and in helping reach a standstill, as was so clearly the case in the Republic of Korea's rollover in early 1998. Nevertheless, the reliance on the IMF raises at least two issues. First, the IMF in its current form is not a truly neutral body in the sense of a bankruptcy court, since voting power in the Executive Board lies heavily with the creditor countries. Thus, politically favoured countries are likely to receive different treatment than countries that are perceived to be less strategically important. Second, at present the IMF's analytical

strengths and core objectives lie in traditional fiscal, monetary and exchange rate policies, not bank or corporate finance, and so it may not be in the best position to judge when a standstill is the best course of action. It is possible that at least the second of these weaknesses can be corrected. In the end, even with these drawbacks, the IMF is probably the best-positioned institution to take on this role.

Buiter and Sibert (1998) have proposed a different kind of clause to be included in debt contracts that would put much more power in the hands of the borrower. They propose that *all* foreign currency lending ("private or sovereign, long or short, marketable or non-marketable, including overdrafts and credit lines") be required to include what they call a *universal debt roll-over option with a penalty* (UDROP). The borrower would be able to exercise the option automatically, at its own discretion, to roll over the debt for a specified period (three to six months) at a penalty rate. The option could be exercised a second time at a higher penalty rate. Buiter and Sibert argue that this clause would have to be included in all debt contracts, and not just by request, otherwise a request for the option would signal that a borrower had inside information about its impaired ability to service the debt; they emphasize that the debtor be allowed to unilaterally trigger the clause at any time; they argue that debtors would only do so in extraordinary circumstances, because otherwise he would quickly lose all market access; they argue against waiting for the support of an IMF programme, which they believe takes too much time to put in place; they conclude that UDROP would increase the cost of borrowing by differing amounts, depending on the market perception of the risks of a particular country actually triggering the mechanism (for the safest countries there may be no increase at all).

The advantages of this mechanism are that it can be triggered quickly, and that it does not require negotiations with the IMF or other governments (although the support of the international community would clearly be helpful). It avoids the potential problems of other schemes that rely on the neutrality and judgement of the IMF. The biggest problem with the scheme is to work out a way to mandate that the relevant clause be included in all debt contracts. The authors propose doing so via an agreement amongst members of the Bank for International Settlements (BIS) that would make foreign currency debt contracts without the rollover option unenforceable in participating countries' courts. They do not assess the likelihood of whether BIS members would agree to this proposal. Realistically, it seems extremely unlikely that the countries of the creditor banks would agree to this kind of scheme.

The Shadow Financial Regulatory Committee (an informal private group made up mainly of academics that meets at the American Enterprise Institute) goes beyond a rollover in its proposal, advocating instead a mechanism that would allow for an automatic across-the-board debt *reduction* if a rollover cannot be achieved. It recommends that borrower countries enact legislation that would allow the country, when it is receiving IMF assistance, to elect to impose a minimum automatic reduction of the principal of all foreign currency loans extended to banks in their countries (Litan et al., 1998). These "haircuts" would be imposed on the creditors only if and when they either withdrew or failed to rollover their claims before the IMF loans were paid back. Creditors would not be allowed to charge penalty rates on extended loans. It is also proposed that the IMF make the enactment of such legislation one of the conditions for all countries receiving its assistance. Countries that did not enact such legislation would either be ineligible for IMF assistance or would be made to pay a substantially higher penalty rate for such assistance. This mechanism would increase the cost of credit for borrowing banks, which in turn would discourage them from taking on excessive risks. Litan and his co-authors also foresee that it would encourage governments to strengthen their banking systems and therefore lower the premium which foreign creditors would attach to such loans in their country.

The idea behind this proposal is that it would provide a stick that would make creditors more willing to negotiate a rollover so that they would not be faced with the possibility of actually triggering the writedown. In some sense it envisages an even stronger role for the IMF than does the G-22 proposal, since the IMF would require member countries to adopt the appropriate legislation for the scheme. However, given the voting power within the IMF, it is hard to believe that it would require countries to impose a scheme that mandated a haircut for creditors. Moreover, it is possible that a mandatory haircut could induce creditors to panic even *faster* than is the case now, since they would want to flee as soon as there was any sign that the debtor country was considering triggering the haircut. The authors of the proposal narrowly apply it to banks, apparently seeing debt owed by banks as the key to financial crises because of the inherent threat to the payments system. Bank debt is also much easier to deal with than

corporate debt, simply because there are fewer commercial banks than corporations. Beyond this, however, it is not clear why the mechanism should be applied to one class of creditors and not to others. Triggering this mechanism for debt owed by banks, for example, could set off a withdrawal of credits from other debtors in the country (e.g. corporations), which would simply displace the focus of the panic (while perhaps to some extent safeguarding the payments system). Moreover, since this would increase the cost of borrowing for banks, but not for corporations, more debt would be channelled through corporations.

Indonesia's recent experience in this regard is telling. In 1991, facing a growing current account deficit, Indonesia imposed quantitative limits on the amount of borrowing allowed by commercial banks. This worked in the narrow sense, in that the banks did not build up significant debt exposure, but one consequence was that domestic corporations borrowed directly overseas in larger amounts. This is a key reason why Indonesian corporations had much heavier foreign exposures than their counterparts in the Republic of Korea and Thailand (which borrowed through their local banks), while Indonesian banks were much less exposed. However, when the financial panic hit, it was much more difficult to deal with the diverse body of corporate borrowers in Indonesia than the narrower group of commercial bank borrowers in the other countries. This episode is indicative of the kind of unforeseen problems that can develop in schemes focused on just one type of creditor.

3. *An international debt restructuring agency*

Some have gone further in the mandatory approach, suggesting variations on establishing a quasi-legal international debt restructuring agency (Cohen, 1989; Raffer, 1990; Williamson, 1992; Greenwood and Mercer, 1995). Williamson (1992) recommends including clauses in future loan contracts specifying that this agency could revise the terms of the loan in the event of unforeseen contingencies. These clauses would presumably allow the agency to impose a simple rollover, or even a debt reduction. The agency could have a range of powers, perhaps including the authority to enact a standstill on creditors, to "cram down" on dissenting creditors revised terms agreed between the debtor and a majority of the creditors, or to award debt relief in arbitration even over the objections of a majority of creditors (Williamson, 1992).

Almost all commentators have concluded that establishing an international body with these legal powers is simply not realistic (Group of 22, 1998a; Eichengreen and Portes, 1995; Group of Ten, 1996). It is hard to believe that the governments of the creditor countries would be willing to cede any legal authority for debt contracts to an international tribunal. Even if they were willing to do so in principle, they would have great difficulty in agreeing on the specifics, since each of the major creditor countries has important differences in its own domestic insolvency laws.

Sachs (1995) advocates that the IMF take on some (but not all) of the roles of a bankruptcy court, rather than establishing a new bankruptcy agency. Writing explicitly about sovereign rather than private debt, he suggests that the IMF could have the authority to impose a temporary standstill on debt servicing, perhaps through Article VIII (2)(b), as discussed previously. Moreover, he suggests that the IMF may not need to lend new money at all, but instead could supervise the extension of new senior private sector loans and play the role of coordinator among the creditors.

An alternative proposal calls for debtor countries to be able to unilaterally impose a debt standstill via capital controls, and then submit the decision to an independent international panel that would determine whether the standstill is justified under Article VIII (2)(b) (UNCTAD, 1998). This proposal is designed to avoid the potential problem of relying on the judgement of the IMF Board, whose voting power lies heavily with the creditor countries. However, the panel's ruling would need to have legal force in international courts, leading to some of the same problems noted above. Also, the time lag needed between a country's decision and the ruling of the panel would be problematic. Moreover, it is not clear what the penalty for a country would be if it imposed the standstill and the panel later ruled that it was not justified.

C. Fresh financing

The second major component of any workout process is the ability of at least some debtors to obtain new finance in order to remain in operation and maintain the value of the firm, or in the case of a country, to avoid an unnecessary economic contraction. In domestic bankruptcy, debtors which gain the approval of the bankruptcy court can go to the markets and at least try to obtain new loans, which

become senior to the old loans. In international situations, most analysts see the IMF and the OECD governments continuing to be the main channel for new finance, augmented to varying degrees by private sector finance. The IMF also plays the role of "approving" a debtor to go to the markets for new finance, in the form of agreeing with the debtor country on an adjustment programme.[7]

1. IMF and other official finance

As stated earlier, the G-22 Working Group concluded that traditional IMF programmes and the attendant financing package will be sufficient to ward off a crisis, at least in most cases. However, a major problem with IMF financing is that it is provided in tranches over an extended period of time, and is highly conditional. As a result, IMF funds are generally inadequate to relieve an intense liquidity crisis, both because they are disbursed slowly and because there is always doubt that the next tranche will arrive.[8] There are at least three ways in which IMF funds could be made available more quickly to crisis countries. First, the borrowing country could draw on the Supplemental Reserve Facility, which was approved by the IMF Board in December 1997 at the outset of the Asian crises. Along the same basic lines, the United States proposed (in October 1998) the establishment of additional contingent financing facilities within the IMF that could be disbursed more quickly and with less conditionality than traditional IMF loans – in effect the same approach that was used to bail out Mexico in early 1995. Second, the IMF could "lend into arrears" (that is, disburse new funds to a debtor country that is in arrears to its private creditors) in a broader set of circumstances. In the early 1980s, the IMF had a strict policy of not lending into arrears, which ultimately limited its ability to provide new money. This put great pressure on the borrower to reach an accommodation with its creditors, otherwise it would not be able to receive new funds. The IMF began to allow for the possibility of lending into arrears on commercial bank debt in 1989 in the context of Brady Plan restructurings. In September 1998 the IMF Executive Board agreed that the IMF could consider lending in arrears in a broader set of circumstances than previously considered, including arrears on bonds and other non-bank credits. The Group of 22, the G-7 and others supported this step. Not surprisingly, commercial banks are opposed to this policy shift, seeing it as a form of mandatory "binding in" of the private sector, which they argue would be ultimately counterproductive in facilitating capital flows (IIF, 1999b).

Third, the IMF could disburse more of its pledged funds at the beginning of the programme, with fewer conditions attached, at least for certain countries. The basic idea is that certain countries that meet a variety of policy conditionalities in normal circumstances (e.g. on banking standards, fiscal policy and a range of other issues) would "pre-qualify" for rapid IMF disbursements in the event of a crisis (Fischer, 1999; Radelet and Sachs, 1999; Williamson, 1998). Just as commercial banks must first meet a variety of standards to operate, and thus be eligible for lender-of-last-resort financing from the central bank, the idea is that countries which are judged to have appropriate policies should be able to get low-condition financing more quickly. Calomiris (1998) goes much further, suggesting that countries must meet such conditions to be eligible for membership of the IMF. This latter version seems unrealistic, because it is hard to believe that so many countries would be excluded from IMF membership, and that the international community would stand by if an excluded country was experiencing a crisis with potential systemic implications. But the more limited proposal of allowing pre-qualified countries to receive funds more quickly has merit.

Relying heavily on the IMF for fresh financing raises several issues. First, the IMF alone cannot disburse enough funds quickly enough to forestall a full-blown crisis, even with these proposed changes. Everyone knows there are ultimate limits on how much the IMF, unlike a true lender of last resort, can feasibly lend, and these amounts increasingly seem small relative to private sector capital flows. Second, if the funds are provided in an attempt to support unsustainable or unwise policies (such as the defence of Brazil's overvalued currency, or the abrupt and clumsy closure of Indonesia's banks), they will not stop the creditor withdrawals.

A third problem is that official funding ultimately converts private sector debts into public sector debts, in effect nationalizing some of the debt (UNCTAD, 1998; Radelet and Sachs, 1998b). This issue was especially relevant for Asia, where most foreign debts were owed by the private sector (but less so in Brazil, where most debts were public sector debts). In a typical situation, the IMF lends funds to a country's central bank, which sells the foreign exchange in the market where it is used to retire private sector debts. Total foreign debt is not reduced but shifted from the private to the public sector. Effectively, IMF money is used to repay foreign creditors, bailing them out of the crisis. *The key to avoiding this problem is the payments standstill.* With a standstill in place, new financing (from either the IMF or other creditors) will not be used to repay foreign debts, and instead will be available for current account transactions or to replenish reserves, and is thus similar to debtor-in-possession financing in domestic bankruptcy proceedings.

On balance, these proposals regarding IMF disbursements all seem to be small steps in the right direction to make some funds available more quickly to crisis countries. Even together, however, they will not go far in generating substantial amounts of new finance or in solving the problem of stopping a creditor panic.

In short, it has become clear that with the substantial increase in private sector capital flows into emerging markets in the 1990s, the IMF and other official creditors simply do not have deep enough pockets, nor are they willing to lend freely enough, to ward off a creditor panic. IMF funds are likely to continue to play a central role but will be insufficient on their own. The IMF's Interim Committee acknowledged the need to "involve private creditors at an early stage, in order to achieve equitable burden sharing vis-à-vis the official sector and to limit moral hazard".[9] These issues have led to growing calls to "bail in" private sector creditors during a crisis.

2. Private finance

The earlier proposals on standstills and rollovers are one way of involving the private sector. There are fewer explicit proposals on how to encourage private creditors to actually provide new funding. New private financing could be provided to the government, or individual banks and firms, or to both. One possibility is for the central bank to arrange with private creditors for contingent financing facilities under which it would pay a commitment fee to a consortium of international banks for the right to draw predetermined amounts therefrom as needed. Argentina recently arranged such a facility with 13 commercial banks that provides $13 billion in standby credits, and Mexico has an arrangement with 31 commercial banks for $2.5 billion (Eichengreen, 1999). Indonesia's central bank has had facilities ranging from $500 million to $1.5 billion since the late 1980s, and it drew $1.5 billion in two tranches in early 1998. Commercial banks favour expanding these facilities, although they argue that after Mexico unexpectedly drew down its facility in late 1998, more aggressive pricing might be necessary (IIF,

1999b). Contingent facilities would make a certain amount of new financing available, and might also make the creditor banks more amenable to restructuring their other loans. These types of facilities can be helpful, but clearly on their own cannot be of the scale necessary for forestalling a panic. Moreover, the extent to which these facilities would provide true additional financing is not absolutely clear. Creditors that have committed themselves to providing these resources might be more likely to withdraw other lines of credit in order to limit their overall exposure to a country.

The Group of 22 calls for an enhanced private sector role through some combination of "providing new credits, extending the maturities or rolling over existing credits, otherwise restructuring payments, and perhaps even, in certain extreme cases, debt reduction" (Group of 22, 1998a, p. 27). Its report stays clear of specific recommendations on precisely defining this private sector role, instead suggesting that this should be worked out between the creditors and the debtor government. It does, however, suggest the possibility of creating a privately funded standing facility that would be available to provide credits in the event of a crisis or payments suspension. These new credits could be given some effective senior status in relation to existing credits (as an extra inducement to creditors) by an IMF decision that it would not lend to countries that fell into arrears on these loans.

The IIF concludes that private participation in either rollovers or providing new money may be feasible on a case-by-case basis. It concludes that a combination of risk mitigation (i.e. government or multilateral guarantees), "credible conditionality on policy reform, and spreads above pre-crisis levels would seem to offer the best chance for mobilizing private sector financing on a voluntary basis in the face of a crisis" (IIF, 1999b, p. 73).

Whereas the case for some kind of mandatory mechanism for a payments standstill is strong, the case for mandating the private sector to provide new financing is much weaker. Private creditors are not required to provide new money in traditional bankruptcy cases. They have the option to do so in cases where the borrower has been approved by the court and where the creditors believe the borrower is solvent. Creditors receive the extra incentive of supra-seniority (and usually higher interest rates) on the new loans. Fischer (1999) cautions that any requirement for mandatory private sector financing could be inadvertently destabilizing, since creditors

might rush for the door even more quickly at the mere hint of a crisis, and so they would not be around to be expected to contribute new financing. He suggests that private creditors be given some inducement to lend voluntarily, perhaps by the IMF agreeing not to "lend into arrears" on these new loans or by making these new loans exempt from future standstills.

The willingness of private creditors to voluntarily lend new money probably depends to some degree on the effectiveness of the initial standstill mechanism. Once the panic stops and some calm and predictability return to the market, private creditors may be willing to lend to both the government and individual debtors that are deemed to be creditworthy. As described earlier, the Government of the Republic of Korea was able to float a new bond issue within months of its commercial bank debt rollover and the corresponding end of the panic. Tellingly, the Republic of Korea's standstill and rollover enabled it to regain access to international capital markets much more quickly than any of the other crisis countries, which were subject to more prolonged panics.

Should the government provide guarantees on new loans to private sector debtors or, for that matter, on debts rolled over during the initial standstill? The argument in favour of guarantees is that they would encourage private creditors to extend more loans more quickly and at lower interest rates than without guarantees. This is undoubtedly true, as far as it goes. The Republic of Korea's initial rollover on debts owed by its commercial banks came with complete government guarantees, which helped facilitate a fast negotiation. The IIF concludes that public sector guarantees (either from the local government or through multilateral organizations) are probably necessary in order to secure private sector participation. The obvious problem with guarantees, however, is that they effectively turn private sector debt into public sector contingent liabilities, creating substantial distributional and moral hazard problems (UNCTAD, 1998; Group of 22, 1998a; Radelet and Sachs, 1998b). The Group of 22 is circumspect about government guarantees, leaving open the possibility of using them in some circumstances without specifically recommending their use. It highlights the dangers of guarantees, and suggests that they be used sparingly and be as limited in scope as possible. The Shadow Financial Regulatory Committee states that it is strongly against government guarantees on any portion of bank liabilities. It argues that if they are extended to foreign loans, they should be limited to the amount of principal minus the mandatory "haircut" that the group proposed, as discussed earlier (Litan et al., 1998).

For new financing provided to private firms, the case for guarantees is very weak. For new loans to banks, the case is a little stronger, since there is a public interest in ensuring that at least some banks remain operational. However, the costs of guarantees on bank liabilities can be huge, as the Republic of Korea, Thailand and Indonesia have found. Moreover, they can distort future lending decisions. In Asia, effectively all foreign lending to banks in the crisis countries will be fully repaid because of these guarantees, while many loans to private firms will be written down or written off. As a result, foreign creditors are in the future likely to be more than happy to lend heavily to banks in emerging markets, but less willing to lend to firms. All else being equal, then, it would be preferable to have the debtor banks pay a higher interest rate on new loans than to provide a government guarantee. *With an effective standstill mechanism in place, accompanied by new IMF and other official financing and appropriate policy changes, government guarantees on new private financing should not be necessary.*

D. Restructuring

The third major component of bankruptcy proceedings is corporate and financial restructuring. At the economy-wide level, restructuring generally takes place through the implementation of appropriate adjustment policies in cooperation with the IMF. Thus, the IMF plays at least four key roles in the workout process: signalling the appropriateness of a debt servicing standstill; providing some new financing; facilitating communication and negotiation between creditors and debtors; and structuring the policy reforms needed to put the economy back on track.

As with domestic bankruptcy, in a systemic crisis the combination of a standstill and fresh financing may be sufficient for some banks and corporations to continue operations without further restructuring. At the other extreme, the weakest banks and firms with no hope of regaining solvency should be closed. In the intermediate cases, more substantial corporate, managerial or financial restructuring may be needed in order to return firms to solvency. This may include more significant refinancing or rescheduling of loans, writing down loans or debt-equity swaps. The basic framework for corporate restructuring should be strong bankruptcy and other related laws

and court institutions in the debtor countries. For example, the Group of 22 strongly recommends that debtor countries establish the appropriate legal codes and supporting institutions for insolvency proceedings.

Domestic insolvency regimes are seen, in the first instance, as contributing to crisis *prevention* by providing a predictable legal framework that includes the credible threat to debtors of removal of management, reorganization and liquidation. These regimes therefore provide appropriate incentives for prudent corporate behaviour. They are also an important part of crisis *resolution,* since they establish a framework for eventual restructuring or liquidation, in line with the principles outlined earlier. Moreover, appropriate insolvency laws help facilitate out-of-court settlements. *However, in most emerging market countries, introducing the appropriate legislation and developing the strong supporting institutional base to make bankruptcy regimes operate effectively will take many years.*

The Group of 22 recognizes that even with good systems in place, in some cases systemic crises could overwhelm bankruptcy courts simply because of the speed with which they hit and the number of cases involved. In these circumstances, it recommends that governments facilitate the process of debtor-creditor negotiations and possible out-of-court settlements through the establishment of creditor committees, removing existing legal and regulatory obstacles to restructuring (e.g. tax penalties), and possibly establishing a mechanism for exchange rate insurance to protect against further extreme depreciations. The international community could play an indirect role in such a mechanism by facilitating contacts, channelling information and exerting some moral suasion on both sides of the negotiation. Such procedures were followed with some success with Mexico's FICORCA system in the early 1980s, as discussed earlier. They met with less success in Indonesia, partly because of the sheer volume of the claims involved, but primarily because the exchange rate had depreciated much further in Indonesia, making workouts much more difficult.

In some circumstances where the economy and the court system are overwhelmed by a systemic crisis, governments may have to explore somewhat more dramatic measures, such as across-the-board debt-equity swaps and other mechanisms to wipe out the debt overhang of otherwise profitable firms. One solution in the Asian context, especially where domestic banks have borrowed from abroad and then on-lent to corporations, would be to convert existing corporate debt into equity, so that the domestic bank creditors would become part owners of the firms (Radelet and Sachs, 1998b). The reduction of debt would ease the borrowing firms' cash flow burdens, enabling them to re-enter the loan markets for working capital and long-term loans. As part of the procedure the existing owners could receive an option to repurchase the shares from the banks at some premium over current market prices; this would maintain incentives to improve the performance of the firm. The banks would be required to sell off these shares in a limited period of time, perhaps two years.

Although this would provide some relief for corporations, it would add to the financial burdens of domestic banks, which would presumably already be under tremendous strain from the crisis. Some banks would have to be closed or merged, and other more promising banks would require a capital injection. In some cases (as in Asia), the private sector (either domestic or foreign) cannot be reasonably expected to inject sufficient capital quickly enough. This leaves the government the only realistic option of injecting new capital into the subset of promising banks. The new capital would presumably be in the form of bank equity, which would give the regulatory agencies special control over and supervision of the banks. The injection of new capital would allow the banks to begin lending again. Over time, the government would sell off its shares in the banks to foreign and domestic investors, including the current owners. The restructuring of the Republic of Korea's banks and corporations has been roughly consistent with these proposals, albeit on an ad hoc basis.

V. Conclusions and recommendations

The basic objective in designing mechanisms for orderly workouts of cross-border debt should be to limit the damage to bank capital, corporate balance sheets and economic activity from the massive credit withdrawals and overshooting of the exchange rate that accompany an international creditor panic. Workout options should not be made too attractive or too easy for borrowers to activate, since the original loan contracts should be honoured as much as possible. But when a country is threatened by systemic default, a well-designed workout mechanism can help limit the collective losses of the creditors and debtors and speed the stabilization process.

In the absence of a true lender of last resort, the key to stopping a panic is an effective standstill

mechanism. A well-designed standstill mechanism can help ease the intense pressure on the exchange rate, calm the markets, set the stage for obtaining fresh financing and help establish some of the stability for successful restructuring. Voluntary standstills and rollovers should be encouraged, but they should be supported by a credible mechanism to invoke a mandatory standstill when necessary, backed by the IMF. Fresh financing should be obtained from both official sources (IMF, World Bank and bilateral agencies) and private creditors. Fresh financing from the private sector should be provided on a voluntary basis. The ultimate restructuring of private firms and banks should take place as much as possible through well-designed bankruptcy regimes, supported by frameworks to facilitate reorganization where bankruptcy institutions remain weak or where they are overwhelmed by the sheer magnitude of the crisis. More specifically, the most promising avenues for strengthening the procedures for orderly workouts of private sector debt include the following:

Standstill arrangements

- The international community generally, and the IMF specifically, should encourage all member countries to enact legislation that requires that specific collective action clauses be included in all international bonds issued in the domestic market. The IMF should consider requiring its member countries to enact legislation mandating the inclusion of such clauses in bond contracts. The BIS could help to encourage the introduction of these clauses. The key clauses include provisions for collective action, majority action, payments sharing, non-acceleration and minimum thresholds for law suits. It should be recognized, however, that it will take many years for the use of these clauses to become widespread.

- The international community generally, and the IMF and the BIS specifically, should encourage member countries to establish standing creditor committees which include the major public sector and private sector creditors. These committees should help facilitate communication between the debtors and the creditors, and in the event of an imminent default they can accelerate the process of negotiating and implementing standstills and rollovers.

- Given the problems of international law, a true mandatory standstill mechanism is probably not feasible. Partial mandatory standstills can be implemented, with the support of the IMF, on debt service payments owed by governments and by commercial banks. However, in certain extreme cases, the IMF should be prepared to support a country's temporary imposition of broader capital controls and exchange restrictions that would temporarily suspend all foreign currency debt service payments. The more credible the threat to use such mandatory controls, the easier it should be to reach agreement with creditors on a voluntary payments standstill.

Fresh financing

- The IMF should establish a facility whereby countries can "pre-qualify" for fast-disbursing, low-conditionality disbursements. Eligibility should be based on the strength of a country's economic policies and institutions, not its strategic and political importance. Countries that do not pre-qualify would remain eligible for existing IMF facilities.

- The international community generally, and the IMF and the BIS specifically, should encourage emerging-market governments and private creditors to further develop contingent financing facilities. Although meant primarily for government borrowers, drawing on such facilities would help private debtors by easing overall liquidity constraints and taking some pressure off the exchange rate. Commercial banks, especially state-owned banks, and private corporations could also be encouraged to explore the use of these facilities.

- Government guarantees should not be provided on new financing by private sector creditors to private sector debtors.

Insolvency regimes

- The international community generally, and the IMF specifically, should encourage the development of effective bankruptcy laws and related creditor-debtor laws. The IMF should be encouraged to require the introduction of such legislation in member countries over an appropriate period of time. It should be recognized, however, that it will take many years to develop effective insolvency regimes in most emerging markets.

- The IMF should develop guidelines for effective mechanisms for systemic restructuring outside formal insolvency regimes which, amongst other things, provides for creditor-debtor communication, exchange rate insurance, and the possibility of across-the-board debt/equity swaps and public recapitalization of distressed but viable commercial banks.

Notes

1 Some countries, such as Brazil in 1998 and Thailand in 1996/97, can postpone depreciation for a period of time if they have sufficient foreign exchange reserves or receive new financing. If the capital outflows continue, however, reserves will eventually be exhausted, and depreciation is inevitable. Note that the primary force behind the crisis is the reversal of capital flows, *not* the depreciation of the exchange rate as is often supposed.

2 Diamond and Dybvig (1983) develop the basic theory behind this model in the context of explaining bank runs. They show how rational depositors can suddenly withdraw their deposits, not because they believe the bank is unsound but because they believe other depositors are withdrawing their funds and they fear there will not be enough to go around. In the end, most depositors cannot be fully repaid, and so everyone is made worse off. Chang and Velasco (1998) develop a similar model for emerging markets.

3 For other analyses that draw the parallel between domestic bankruptcy procedures and international debt workouts, see Eichengreen (1999), Radelet and Sachs (1998b), UNCTAD (1998), Sachs (1995), Eichengreen and Portes (1995), Williamson (1992), Raffer, (1990) and Cohen (1989).

4 The government issued $1 billion in five-year notes (priced at 345 basis points over comparable United States securities) and $3 billion in ten-year notes (with a spread of 355 basis points). It had originally planned to issue a total of $3 billion in bonds, but increased it to $4 billion as customer orders topped $12 billion.

5 Fideicomiso Para la Cobertura de Riesgo Cambiaros.

6 For an insightful analysis of the "overborrowing syndrome" in Asia written before the crises, see McKinnon and Pill (1996).

7 The IMF can thus "approve" a government to seek new funding, or in some sense an economy as a whole, but of course not individual private creditors.

8 For example, despite international pledges in 1997 of $17 billion, $40 billion and $57 billion respectively for Thailand, Indonesia and the Republic of Korea, that made impressive headlines, by the end of December 1997 Thailand had received just $7 billion, and by the end of March 1998 Indonesia and the Republic of Korea had received just $3 billion and $13 billion respectively (Radelet and Sachs, 1998a).

9 Communiqué of the IMF Interim Committee, 17 April 1998, section 3(e).

References

BUITER, W.H., and A.C. SIBERT (1998), "UDROP or you drop: A small contribution to the new international financial architectures", unpublished paper (November).

CALOMIRIS, C. (1998), "Blueprints for a new global financial architecture", unpublished paper (New York: Columbia University Business School), 23 September.

CANADA, DEPARTMENT OF FINANCE (1998), "Canada's six point plan to restore confidence and sustain growth", at http://www.fin.gc.ca/ncwsc98/data/98-094cl.html (30 September).

CHANG, R., and A. VELASCO (1998), "Financial crises in emerging markets: A Canonical model", NBER Working Paper No. 6606 (Cambridge, MA: National Bureau of Economic Research), June.

COHEN, B. (1989), "Developing country debt: A middle way", Princeton Essays in International Finance No. 173 (Princeton, NJ: Princeton University).

COOPER, R., and J. SACHS (1985), "Borrowing abroad: The debtor's perspective", in G. Smith and J. Cuddington (eds.), *International Debt and the Developing Countries* (Washington, DC: World Bank).

CORNELLI, F., and L. FELLI (1995), "The theory of bankruptcy and mechanism design", in Barry Eichengreen and Richard Portes, *Crisis? What Crisis? Orderly Workouts for Sovereign Debtors* (London: Center for Economic Policy Research).

DIAMOND, D., and P. DYBVIG (1983), "Bank runs, liquidity, and deposit insurance", *Journal of Political Economy*, Vol. 91, pp. 401-419.

EICHENGREEN, B. (1999), *Toward a New International Financial Architecture: A Practical Post-Asia Agenda* (Washington, DC: Institute for International Economics), February.

EICHENGREEN, B., and M. MUSSA (1998), "Capital account liberalization: Theoretical and practical aspects", Occasional Paper No. 172 (Washington, DC: IMF), October.

EICHENGREEN, B., and R. PORTES (1995), *Crisis? What Crisis? Orderly Workouts for Sovereign Debtors* (London: Centre for Economic Policy Research).

FISCHER, S. (1999), "On the need for an international lender of last resort", paper presented at the annual meetings of the American Economics Association, New York, 3 January 1999; available at the IMF website (http://www.imf.org/external/np/speeches/1999/010399.htm)

FRANKS, J. (1995), "Some issues in sovereign debt and distressed organizations", in Barry Eichengreen and Richard Portes, *Crisis? What Crisis? Orderly Workouts for Sovereign Debtors* (London: Centre for Economic Policy Research).

FURMAN, J., and J. STIGLITZ (forthcoming), "Economic crises: Evidence and insights from East Asia", Brookings Papers on Economic Activity, 2nd edition (1998) (Washington, DC: Brookings Institution).

GOLDSTEIN, M. (1997), "The case for an international banking standard" (Washington, DC: Institute for International Economics), April.

GREENWOOD, C., and H. MERCER (1995), "Considerations of international law", in Barry Eichengreen and Richard Portes, *Crisis? What Crisis? Orderly Workouts for Sovereign Debtors* (London: Centre for Economic Policy Research).

GROUP OF TEN (1996), "Resolving sovereign liquidity crises" (Washington, DC).

GROUP OF 22 (1998a), "Report of the Working Group on International Financial Crises" (Washington, DC: World Bank); available from the World Bank website (http://www.worldbank.org/html/extdr/ifa-reports/index.htm).

GROUP OF 22 (1998b), "Report of the Working Group on Transparency and Accountability" (Washington, DC:

World Bank); available from the World Bank website (http://www.worldbank.org/html/extdr/ifa-reports/index.htm).

GROUP OF 22 (1998c), "Report of the Working Group on Strengthening Financial Systems" (Washington, DC: World Bank); available from the World Bank website (http://www.worldbank.org/html/extdr/ifa-reports/index.htm).

HELLEINER, G. (ed.) (1998), *Capital account regimes and the developing countries* (New York: St. Martin's Press).

IIF (Institute of International Finance) (1999a), "Capital flows to emerging market economies" (Washington, DC), January.

IIF (Institute of International Finance) (1999b), "Report of the Working Group on Financial Crises in Emerging Markets" (Washington, DC), January.

JACKSON, T. (1986), *The Logic and Limits of Bankruptcy Law* (Cambridge, MA: Harvard University Press).

KINDLEBERGER, C.P. (1996), *Manias, Panics, and Crashes: A History of Financial Crises*, 3rd edition (New York: John Wiley and Sons).

LITAN, R., R. HERRING et al. (1998), "International Monetary Fund Assistance and International Crises", statement of the Shadow Financial Regulatory Committee of the American Enterprise Institute, Washington, DC, 4 May 1998; available at www.aei.org/shdw/shdw145.htm

McKINNON, R.I., and H. PILI (1996), "Credible liberalizations and international capital flows: The 'overborrowing syndrome'", in Takatoshi Ito and Anne O. Krueger (eds.), *Financial Deregulation and Integration in East Asia*, National Bureau of Economic Research East Asia Seminar on Economics, Vol. 5 (Chicago: University of Chicago Press).

RADELET, S., and J. SACHS (1998a), "The East Asian financial crisis: Diagnosis, remedies, prospects", Brookings Papers on Economic Activity, 1st edition (Washington, DC: Brookings Institution).

RADELET, S., and J. SACHS (1998b), "Towards a new strategy for Asian recovery", *Singapore Straits Times*, 24 July.

RADELET, S., and J. SACHS (1999), "What have we learned, so far, from the Asian financial crisis?", paper presented at the American Economics Association meetings, New York, January 1999.

RAFFER, K. (1990), "Applying Chapter 9 insolvency to international debt: An economic efficient solution with a human face", *World Development,* Vol. 18, No. 2.

SACHS, J. (1984), "Theoretical issues in international borrowing", Princeton Studies in International Finance No. 54 (Princeton, NJ: Princeton University Press).

SACHS, J. (1995), "Do we need an international lender of last resort?", Frank D. Graham Lecture, Princeton University, April.

SACHS, J. (1998), "Creditor panics: Causes and remedies", unpublished paper available at the Harvard Institute for International Development website (http://www.hiid.harvard.edu).

SACHS, J., and S. RADELET (1998), "Next stop: Brazil", *New York Times*; 14 October.

SEVIGNY, D. (1990), *The Paris Club: An Inside View* (Ottawa: North-South Institute).

UNCTAD (1998), *Trade and Development Report, 1998*, United Nations publication, sales no. E.98.II.D.6 (New York and Geneva).

VITALE, G. (1995), "Multilateral sovereign debt restructuring: The Paris Club and the London Club", in Barry Eichengreen and Richard Portes, *Crisis? What Crisis? Orderly Workouts for Sovereign Debtors* (London: Centre for Economic Policy Research).

WILLIAMSON, J. (1992), "International monetary reform and the prospects for economic development", in J.J. Teunissen (ed.), *Fragile Finance: Rethinking the International Monetary System* (The Hague: Forum on Debt and Development).

WILLIAMSON, J. (1998), "A new facility for the IMF?", in Gerald Helleiner (ed.), *Capital Account Regimes and the Developing Countries* (New York: St. Martin's Press).

STANDARDS FOR TRANSPARENCY AND BANKING REGULATION AND SUPERVISION: CONTRASTS AND POTENTIAL

Andrew Cornford*

Abstract

This paper is concerned with various issues involving the disclosure of financial information to both supervisors and market participants. The issue of the availability of financial information to supervisors has multiple connections to that of its public disclosure. The latter is intended to enable the exercise of market discipline by lenders and investors which can reinforce (or even, as some have argued, at least partly replace) banking supervision.

The strategy of the paper is to review briefly some of the (sometimes conflicting) ideas concerning the role of transparency, and then to survey the actual position in the recent past regarding the availability of financial information (principally concerning banks) to supervisors and to market participants in a number of countries, including those where financial transparency and the stringency of supervision have attained relatively high levels. For this purpose the paper contains a review of two surveys of various features of the regimes of financial reporting, regulation and supervision during 1992–1994. The countries covered by the surveys mostly have relatively advanced financial sectors. Amongst the issues covered by the surveys are various features of the regimes for financial reporting, auditing and its relation to bank supervision, disclosure beyond that required in annual accounts, and provisioning for bad loans.

Perhaps the most important point to emerge from the surveys is that while arrangements for the provision of financial information are clearly being strengthened in the countries covered, they frequently still fall well short of levels corresponding to what is now considered to be best practice. Moreover, unsurprisingly, where there are still disagreements as to best practice regarding bank regulation and supervision, these are often reflected in divergences of approach in different countries. Another point is that the quality of arrangements for financial reporting reflect not only the regulatory regime but also standards, especially those relating to accounting, and the norms of industry practice.

On the question of the extent to which disclosure to lenders and investors leads to levels of market discipline which can act as a useful complement to financial supervision or even as a partial substitute for it the discussion here points to likely limitations of disclosure's potential. This would appear to depend significantly on the extent to which a bank's balance sheet consists of marketable assets and liabilities. Regarding entities still heavily involved in traditional commercial banking long-standing limitations are still relevant to consideration of what disclosure can reasonably be expected to achieve, and this would appear to apply to the great majority of countries, even though securitization and other innovations are making significant inroads in traditional commercial banking in many of them. In the case of entities whose balance sheets consist to a much greater extent of marketable items the discipline that can be exercised by disclosure is likely to be more important (though this statement is subject to caveats).

* The author is grateful for the wide-ranging comments of Yilmaz Akyüz and for more general discussion with Raymond Glasgow. However, he is solely responsible for any remaining errors.

I. Introduction

Different dimensions of transparency have been the subject of much attention in the context of the international policy response to the Asian crisis. Initiatives as part of this response are now under way to improve the timeliness and quality of information concerning key macroeconomic variables, the reporting of financial and non-financial firms, and transparency regarding the views and operations of multilateral financial institutions.[1]

Few would attribute a major role in the outbreak of the Asian crisis to the absence of pertinent information on the balance of payments, external financial flows, trends in domestic bank lending, corporate governance, and external assets and liabilities (although there were gaps in what was publicly disclosed regarding the scale and certain other important features of the last of these matters).[2] And if the existence of such data failed to deter capital flows associated with the build-up of eventually unsustainable external financial positions in the case of certain Asian countries, the same applied *a fortiori* to the behaviour of international lenders and investors in Russia prior to the crisis of the summer of 1998. Such remarks are not in contradiction with the view that improvements in macroeconomic and financial information have the potential for contributing to action reducing the likelihood of financial crises and enabling better management of them when they occur. But this contribution should not be exaggerated.

The starting-point of the discussion here is the relation between information and financial regulation and supervision. But the issue of the availability of financial information to supervisors also has multiple connections with that of its public disclosure. The latter is intended, *inter alia*, to enable the exercise of market discipline by lenders and investors. Thus, while this paper does not provide an exhaustive treatment of the extent to which publicly disclosed information can reinforce (or even, as some would argue, at least partly replace) banking supervision, it takes up several matters involving both the advantages and the disadvantages of public disclosure of data concerning banks.

Good financial information is like oxygen for banking supervision, since without it effective supervision is impossible. However, even when supervision is based on the levels of disclosure to be found in countries with state-of-the-art regimes of financial regulation, there are still limits to what such

regulation be expected to achieve. These limits are partly due to the dependence of the quality of loans on business conditions in the economy as a whole or in particular regions. But they are also a reflection of inevitable imperfections in regulation and supervision themselves which even implementation of recent international recommendations on best practice cannot be expected to eliminate. Many of these imperfections are connected with shortcomings in the information available to supervisors, shortcomings which in many cases are due to recent financial innovation.

In consideration of determinants of the strength of financial systems much attention is paid to the discipline on financial firms which can be exerted by well-informed investors and lenders. Typically, investors and lenders dispose of information about such firms which is somewhat different from, and generally more restricted than, that available to regulators and supervisors. There have recently been proposals to move in the direction of more extensive disclosure. This would dovetail with, and in some cases perhaps overlap with, initiatives for improved transparency regarding macroeconomic variables. Improved information on these two fronts would make possible better management of credit risk but, as the reference to the Russian crisis above suggests, realization of its potential contribution is not assured. Moreover, even if all these initiatives come to fruition, important lacunae on the information front can be expected to remain and to continue to affect the quality of cross-border as well as domestic lending and investment. These lacunae refer not only to the information available from banks and other financial firms which are within the jurisdiction of existing regulatory systems but also to firms whose coverage by such systems is at most partial.

Initial global initiatives for strengthened financial regulation and supervision have their origin in greater awareness since the 1970s of the potential cross-border effects of insolvencies and other sources of financial instability in particular countries. Such perceptions have of course been heightened by the Asian crisis. The current emphasis on improvements in regulation and supervision, and on the levels of transparency required for this purpose, is an integral part of current plans for reform of international financial governance: access to borrowing from multilateral financial institutions and other external financial support, for example, is likely increasingly to be dependent on such improvements. Underlying this emphasis is the idea that with sufficiently good information for lenders, investors and supervisors, financial markets will allocate resources efficiently and will avoid boom-bust cycles. In this way, such information can be expected to reduce the need for (and thus the cost of) packages of international financial support such as those mobilized in recent financial crises. At the same time, according to this logic, improved transparency serves to strengthen the case for financial liberalization as well as arguments against intervention in financial markets in forms such as capital controls.

Faith in such efficacy of information reflects partly awareness of its importance for financial supervision. But it is also influenced by some variant of the hypothesis of efficient financial markets, a subject which has generated a large conceptual and empirical literature.[3] This paper, however, concentrates on the different issues of the quality of banking supervision likely to be associated with typical existing arrangements regarding the availability of financial information, and of certain aspects of the way in which these arrangements can be reasonably expected to generate disciplined behaviour in financial markets (and thus, *inter alia*, reduce financial instability). The strategy of the discussion is to review briefly some of the (sometimes conflicting) ideas concerning the role of transparency in this context, and then to survey the actual position in the recent past regarding the availability of financial information (principally concerning banks) to supervisors and to market participants in a number of countries, including those where financial transparency and the stringency of supervision have attained relatively high levels.

Several points emerge from this survey. Perhaps the most important is that while arrangements for the provision of financial information are clearly being strengthened in the countries covered, they frequently still fall well short of levels corresponding to what is now considered to be best practice (which itself is unlikely to provide anything approaching failsafe protection against financial instability and crises). Moreover, unsurprisingly, where there are still disagreements as to what is best practice regarding bank regulation and supervision,[4] these are often reflected in divergences of approach in different countries. Another point, pertinent to decisions about the pace of financial liberalization, is that the quality of arrangements for financial reporting reflects not only the regulatory regime but also standards, especially those relating to accounting, and the norms of industry practice. Such standards and norms are generally not quickly or easily acquired: they develop as a result of the efforts of both participants in financial markets and regulators and supervisors to solve the problems of management and control which are generated by the development of financial markets as this process unfolds. They tend to reflect the stage reached by this process and the length of time during which it has taken place (an important determinant of the opportunity to find successful solutions).

II. The utility and limits of transparency

At first sight, recommendations for greater transparency on the part of financial firms[5] have an almost self-evident quality, and the value of improvements in this area seems incontrovertible. Yet on closer scrutiny the issues become less simple. As mentioned above, the quality of information made available to financial supervisors has an important bearing on the effectiveness of their work, and it is often argued that improvements should be pushed to the point where additional benefits would be outweighed by the costs which such improvements would entail. There is less consensus on the benefits of disclosure to market participants. Whereas financial firms are usually subject to several of the same obligations with regard to reporting as non-financial firms, disclosure of information submitted to supervisors is typically subject to limits resulting from the argument that it could undermine the confidence in the financial system that regulation is intended to promote.[6] This argument would appear to be intended to apply not only to situations of crisis for individual banks (where it is susceptible to counter-arguments such as that put forward in the statements of the Basle Committee on Banking Supervision, discussed below, that greater disclosure would reduce the incidence of such crises) but also to other conditions in financial markets. Regarding the latter, scepticism about the benefits as opposed to the costs of something more closely approximating full disclosure than today's practices derives from such problems as that of defining the rules without which increased disclosure might be accompanied by increased difficulties of interpretation, and from the prospect of increased volatility in financial markets.[7]

Other questions are now often raised about just how great is the value of the information made available by financial firms not only for decisions by lenders and investors but even for supervisors. There is not, of course, any suggestion here that such information is of negligible value. However, financial liberalization and innovation have greatly increased the speed at which financial firms in many countries can now alter the assets and liabilities on their balance sheets as well as their scope for taking off-balance-sheet positions of an opaque nature (in both cases changing the risks they face in ways which can be difficult for outsiders to identify). For example, William McDonough, President of the Federal Reserve Bank of New York and current chairman of the Basle Committee on Banking Supervision, has made this point in surprisingly strong terms as follows: "formerly, you could look at the balance sheet of a financial institution and quickly get a sense of exposure and risks. Today balance-sheet information is clearly inadequate for this purpose ... the fast pace of activity in today's market renders financial statements stale almost before they can be prepared" (Leach et al., 1993, pp. 15–16). McDonough's statement refers to particular kinds of information – the data traditionally included in balance sheets – and in view of its importance for banking regulation, some of its implications are worth spelling out at greater length. Banks' assets and liabilities are unlikely ever to be stationary. Loans are repaid, and new ones are made. Similarly, the identities of banks' depositors and other creditors is subject to change, as are the scale and terms of their different liabilities. But supervisors and participants in financial markets could until recently generally anticipate a reasonably high degree of stability in the qualitative character of banks' balance sheets, a stability which facilitated evaluation of their condition. McDonough's statement indicates that such stability can no longer be counted on. This change by no means affects all banks and other financial firms equally. Considerable differences will be found both among different types of financial firm and among firms in different countries (in particular, countries at different levels of financial development). McDonough's statement is applicable primarily to banks with substantial trading operations,[8] a common but nevertheless far from universal feature of their activities but one that can be expected to be increasingly widely pertinent with the trend towards the marketability of different items on their balance sheets.

Unsurprisingly, the difficulties stemming from, as well as the benefits of, transparency are extensively discussed in the statements of those responsible for developing international standards for bank regulation and supervision. One place to begin a brief review of their discussion is Principle 21 of the *Core Principles for Effective Banking Supervision* of the Basle Committee on Banking Supervision: "Banking supervisors must be satisfied that each bank maintains adequate records drawn up in accordance with consistent accounting policies and practices that enable the supervisor to obtain a true and fair view of the financial condition of the bank and the profitability of its business, and that the bank publishes on a regular basis financial statements that fairly reflect its condition" (BCBS, 1997, pp. 35–37). Implications of this principle are fleshed out in greater detail in the Basle Committee's subsequent statement, *Enhancing Bank Transparency* (BCBS, 1998a, paras. 53–102). Here are elaborated the qualitative characteristics of information critically contributing to banks' transparency, namely comprehensiveness, relevance and timeliness, reliability, comparability, and materiality.[9] The statement also identifies six categories of information which need to be addressed clearly and in appropriate detail as part of achieving the same objective: financial performance; financial position (including capital, solvency and liquidity); risk management strategies and practices; risk exposures; accounting policies; and basic business, management and corporate-governance information.

In both cases the statement identifies both market participants and supervisors as users of the information to which the recommended standards are to apply. The role thus accorded to market participants is a natural extension of that described in an earlier discussion paper, entitled *Public Disclosure of Market and Credit Risks by Financial Intermediaries,* of another committee linked to the Bank for International Settlements (BIS), namely the Eurocurrency Standing Committee of the Central Banks of the Group of Ten Countries. The recommendations of this paper too are based on the assumption that "Financial markets function most efficiently when market participants have sufficient information about risks and returns to make informed investment and trading decisions ... [thus facilitating] the prompt and accurate pricing of assets" (BIS, 1994, paras. 1.2 and 2.1).

However, as might be expected, statements of the BIS-related bodies have also expressed awareness both of the limits of what improved transparency can be expected to achieve and of the argument that public disclosure of certain information about financial firms can be a source of instability. Thus, regarding the latter point, for example, the Basle Committee's statement entitled *Enhancing Bank Transparency* notes: "In promoting transparency, supervisors and other policy makers need to take into account the potential drawbacks that public disclosure can have in certain circumstances ... In particular, when the market becomes aware that a bank is in a weakened position it may react more harshly than is desirable from the point of view of the authorities who have responsibilities for depositors' protection and for managing systemic risk ... the bank may fail as a result of a liquidity crisis, even if it is solvent in terms of net assets. The market's lack of confidence in a bank may spread to other banks, leading to a systemic disturbance". However, the Basle Committee subscribes to the view that generally the benefits of greater disclosure to market participants are likely to outweigh their costs. As the Committee continues in the same statement, "However, in an environment of adequate ongoing disclosure, the likelihood of this kind of contagion is less likely. Moreover, in many countries banks are already required to disclose substantial information about their financial condition, performance, risk profile and risk management in their annual reports, and most stock exchange rules require listed banks to disclose market-sensitive information promptly" (BCBS, 1998a, para. 31). In this statement the emphasis is less on the dangers of disclosure than on its potential for causing banks to correct problems quickly. In an earlier paper (BIS, 1994), the BIS-related body had in fact stood the argument about the risks of disclosure on its head: "During episodes of market stress, a lack of information about a firm's market and credit risk exposures can create an environment in which rumours alone can cause a firm's creditors and counterparties to reduce their dealings with the firm solely to avoid uncertainty. This may impair the firm's market access and funding at the very time that these may be critical to the firm's survival. Moreover, problems encountered by one firm may cause funding or market access difficulties at other firms which, because of a lack of transparency, appear similar to outsiders. As counterparties withdraw from new transactions, market liquidity for some instruments may decline" (BIS, 1994, para. 2.4).

The possible dilemma implicit in these observations cannot be resolved at the level of general statements of good practice. Unsurprisingly, in the *Core Principles* it is acknowledged that "there are certain types of information that should be held confidential by banking supervisors" and that "the types of information considered sensitive vary from country to country" (BCBS, 1997, p. 37). This point (exemplified by evidence discussed below) brings out the Janus-faced attitudes to transparency embodied in actual regulatory regimes.

The problems posed for bank supervision by the increasingly chameleon-like nature of many banks' balance sheets are also extensively alluded to in the statements of BIS-related bodies. Thus, in *Enhancing Bank Transparency* it is acknowledged

that "Many banks now have large-scale international operations and significant participation in securities and/or insurance businesses in addition to traditional banking activities. Their product lines change rapidly and include highly sophisticated transactions, and they have complex legal and managerial structures. These banks present formidable challenges to market participants and supervisors who need to formulate ongoing assessments of banks' activities and risks" (BCBS, 1998a, para. 2). In the Basle Committee's statement entitled *Banks' Interactions with Highly Leveraged Institutions* (a document representing a response by the Committee to concerns expressed about the activities of hedge funds),[10] it is stated that "A complicating factor" (for initiatives to increase transparency regarding exposures to and of highly leveraged institutions (HLIs)) "is that the nature of the activities of an HLI can change significantly over a short period (for instance, the degree of leveraging can increase sharply)" (BCBS, 1999, section 3.3). In the Committee's view this problem nonetheless by no means nullifies the importance of enhanced transparency regarding such HLIs but limits what it can be expected to achieve.

The speed with which balance-sheet information in "the new financial world"[11] becomes out of date has begun substantially to influence financial supervision and statements as to best practice. As the Basle Committee itself has put it: "There have been radical changes in the conceptual approach to banking supervision over recent years. These have been occasioned by the very rapid changes taking place in the financial industry and in the range of activities engaged in by banks in the major financial centres. The net result has been a decline in the reliance on compliance with numerical standards, and a commensurate increase in the emphasis placed on more general concepts such as good governance, sound risk management and effective audit and control procedures. Supervision in the major financial centres now contains relatively more qualitative elements than in the past. That has made it in many ways a more difficult task and one which requires far greater training and experience" (BCBS, 1998b). As is evident from the survey results discussed below, auditing has traditionally played a large role in banking supervision, but its importance and the complexity of the task it must undertake are increasing. Moreover, while supervisors' reliance on numerical data may have diminished, an important part of the shift in supervisory practice is towards according greater importance to vetting financial firms' own systems for evaluating the risks reflected in numerical data generated by their operations. Such increased reliance is occurring at a time when there is still significant variation among firms in the systems they use for this purpose, and when the state of the art regarding these systems is still in a phase of rapid development.[12] These systems are not discussed further here. But they are another force for fluidity in regulatory regimes and for changes in enunciated international banking standards such as those of the EU and the Basle Committee on Banking Supervision.

III. Selected survey results concerning financial reporting, regulation and supervision

In this section there is a review of two surveys of various features of the regimes of financial reporting, regulation and supervision during 1992–1994. The economies covered by the surveys mostly have relatively advanced financial sectors. Although the surveys are not fully up to date, they nonetheless refer to a period well after moves had got under way in industrial countries to strengthen banking regulation as a necessary counterpart to financial liberalization (moves in which multilateral initiatives of the Basle Committee and in the EU played a significant part). The divergence between accepted best practice, on the one hand, and regimes actually in force, on the other, may have narrowed since the period of the surveys (within the EU, for example, partly as a result of national legislation in response to EC directives), but in many areas is likely still to be substantial.[13] The surveys thus illustrate the distance that industrial countries still had to travel to achieve best practice as recently as five years ago; and the road facing developing and transition economies can be expected in the great majority of cases to be longer and more difficult.

Of the two surveys, the one by Ernst and Young (1993) covers several dimensions of financial reporting and its relation to regulation and supervision, while the other by Price Waterhouse is more narrowly focused on banks' provisioning for bad loans (Price Waterhouse, 1994), a subject with a bearing on both their financial reporting and their risk management. The sample in the first survey was larger and covered 23 economies, and included, in addition to 17 industrial countries, Bahrain, Hong Kong (China), Saudi Arabia, Singapore, South Africa and the United Arab Emirates. That in the second survey consisted of 14 industrial countries, the same as in the first survey with the exclusion of Austria, Ireland

and Portugal.[14] With respect to certain features of bank supervision, the surveys were supplemented by information in a report by the ECU Institute on Banking Supervision in the European Community (ECU Institute, 1995).

A. Financial reporting

The Ernst and Young survey exemplified the significant variation among its sample of economies in several features of their regimes for financial reporting. Thus, while annual accounts were an almost universal requirement,[15] only some countries required accounts to be made for a period ending on a specified date in the year, namely Bahrain, Canada, Denmark, France, Italy, Japan, the Netherlands, Portugal, Saudi Arabia, Spain, and United Arab Emirates. At the time of the survey there were still some countries where consolidated accounts were not required by law (although such a requirement is likely to have been introduced in at least some of them since 1992[16]). The countries in question were Bahrain, Luxembourg, Portugal, and even Australia (where nonetheless, despite the absence of a legal requirement, consolidated accounts were produced as a matter of practice).

In the great majority of the countries or territories included in the Ernst and Young survey the format and contents of banks' accounts were prescribed by law,[17] but there were a number where such prescription did not apply to accounting standards or policies, namely Australia, Bahrain, Belgium, Hong Kong (China), Ireland, Singapore, South Africa, the United Arab Emirates and the United Kingdom.[18] In five cases – Australia, Hong Kong (China), Singapore, South Africa and the United Kingdom – the overriding consideration in the preparation of the accounts was presentation of a true and fair view, the bank's directors being left with discretion as to the accounting policies which would best achieve this. Nevertheless, a bank would normally be expected to follow generally accepted accounting principles as codified by a country's accounting body.

As already mentioned, regulatory attitudes towards bank transparency are marked by a certain ambivalence, the benefits of full disclosure to lenders and investors being weighed against the difficulties which it can pose. To a degree in some countries banks are exempted from disclosure under company law regarding certain headings (as compared with non-financial firms). In the Ernst and Young survey such exemption was available to banks in Austria,

Belgium, Hong Kong (China), Ireland, Italy, Singapore and South Africa (as well as to banks in Australia, although here the rights to such exemption were not exercised).[19]

During the Asian financial crisis concentrations of banks' lending to particular sectors (such as property) or in some cases to particular countries were often cited as having made a significant contribution to the proliferation of non-performing assets. Segmental reporting (apparently frequently absent or inadequate in the case of Asian banks) can facilitate the identification of such concentrations through its provision of information on the breakdown of turnover, assets and income by class of business and geographical region.[20] Such reporting was required to be included in the accounts of the majority of countries for which data on the item were made available in the Ernst and Young survey, but there were a number of exceptions, namely Austria, France, Germany, Hong Kong (China), Italy, Portugal, South Africa, Spain and Switzerland (although in these countries too some banks do provide such reports).

B. Auditing, supervisory returns and banking supervision

The extent of auditors' legal responsibilities varied among the economies in the Ernst and Young survey: this variation applied not merely to the examination and verification of banks' accounts narrowly defined but also to their relations with supervisory authorities. The former variation is hardly surprising in view of differences in the historical contexts to which the regulations affecting auditors were a response, but it is the latter which is of particular interest with respect to the relation between procedures for financial reporting, on the one hand, and regulation and supervision, on the other. Indeed, in many countries banks' auditors are no longer only responsible to shareholders but also have an essential role in the process of supervision. For example, in 16 of the 23 economies in the Ernst and Young survey there was direct communication between auditors and supervisory authorities in legally prescribed circumstances.[21] The prescribed circumstances might involve a requirement to report certain matters to the supervisory authorities or might be reflected in a tripartite agreement between the bank, the supervisory authority and the auditor.

In Australia, for example, auditors not only had to give their opinion (under the country's law on corporations) about the trueness and fairness of the banks' accounts and their compliance with reporting standards but also had to provide the Reserve Bank with their opinion on the following matters: the adequacy of internal management systems and controls, the observance of prudential standards, the reliability of statistical data provided by a bank, and its compliance with statutory and regulatory requirements. In Austria auditors had to report to the Ministry of Finance and the central bank facts involving jeopardy to the banks' operation or legal and regulatory violations, as well as to report on compliance with various provisions of the country's law. In Belgium auditors had to report to the Commission on Banking and Finance on banks' regulatory compliance. In Canada, as part of the annual inspection of a bank by the Office of the Superintendent of Financial Institutions (OSFI), a meeting was held with the bank's auditors: the OSFI relied on the auditors' report on annual financial statements and also required them to comment on other matters with a potential for affecting the well-being of the bank. In Denmark the Financial Supervisory Authority (FSA) could order the auditors to provide information concerning a bank's affairs or arrange for an extraordinary audit, and a bank's auditors had the obligation to ensure that the bank informed the FSA of any circumstances vitally affecting continued operation of the bank. In Germany a bank's auditors had extensive reporting obligations regarding legal and regulatory compliance; and they also had to report to the relevant supervisory agency any circumstance endangering the bank's existence or likely to impair its future performance. In Ireland auditors had to report to the central bank circumstances with the potential to affect the bank's ability to meet its obligations to depositors, any breakdown in its financial systems and controls, and inaccuracies in its returns to the central bank. In Luxembourg auditors were responsible to the Luxembourg Monetary Institute for auditing all a bank's activities, including any involvement in money laundering. In the Netherlands the relations between auditors, the central bank and a bank were formalized in a tripartite agreement, and the auditors had a mandatory responsibility to audit every year one of the bank's monthly returns to the central bank. In Singapore auditors were required to comment on the adequacy of loan provisions with a material effect on financial statements. In Spain banks generally requested from their auditors special reports (to be made available also to the central bank) on such matters as auditors' procedures and their tests of the bank's information systems. In Switzerland, in addition to the statutory audit of its accounts, a bank was subject to a wide-ranging special audit which was the primary source of information on its condition for the Federal Banking Commission. The auditors responsible for the special audit also had the task of bringing legal violations and other irregularities to top management's attention and of verifying that appropriate action had been taken, and if this action was considered inadequate, the auditors had to prepare a report for the Federal Banking Commission. In the case of more serious legal violations or irregularities identified the auditors had the obligation of informing the Federal Banking Commission immediately. In the United Kingdom both statutory auditors and "reporting accountants" (appointed by a bank with the approval of the Bank of England) had an important role in bank supervision: at least once a year a "trilateral meeting" was convened as a forum for discussion (between the Bank of England, the bank, and its statutory auditors and reporting accountant) of significant matters arising from the statutory audit, the reporting accountant's reports on the bank's accounting systems, internal controls and prudential returns, and the scope of the reporting accountant's examinations in the next round of reporting.

Another important instrument of bank supervision consisted of banks' periodic returns to the central bank or regulatory authority (prepared in addition to annual accounts). The periodicity of such returns varied, as did the extent to which and the form in which the information contained in them was publicly disclosed (a matter discussed further below). In the great majority of the economies covered by the Ernst and Young survey this periodicity was at least monthly but in some cases greater. In Saudi Arabia, for example, banks submitted bi-weekly, monthly, quarterly and annual returns (the last in addition to their annual accounts). Such returns frequently (but not always) were an input into countries' published official banking statistics.

Whereas the legal authority to conduct on-site supervision was very common, reliance on it as a major component of supervision was much less frequent. Such reliance is a feature of supervision in the United States, one of the countries which did not attribute a legally prescribed role here to banks' auditors.[22] Elsewhere recourse to on-site supervision was more intermittent, such examinations taking place in Ireland, for example, on average about once every three years and in Italy once every five to six years (ECU Institute, 1995, pp. 203, 215).

C.   *Disclosure beyond that in annual accounts*

The information available to banks' lenders and investors generally includes various material additional to their annual accounts. Stock exchanges, for example, often require such information from banks whose securities are listed. Such information was specified as being prescribed in a number of the countries covered by the Ernst and Young survey.[23] As already mentioned, returns to the regulatory authority are an important input into many countries' published official banking statistics. In this form they are typically aggregated. Thus, while such statistics are a source of information about the health of an economy's banking sector (and of subsectors within the sector as a whole) as well as about indicators such as the pace and character of credit growth, they are generally not available in a form designed for possible inferences about the health of particular banks.[24] Even in the United States, where support for disclosure and the market discipline exercised by lenders and investors as a complement to, or even to some extent as a substitute for, bank regulation is particularly strong in some quarters,[25] significant limitations in this area are still a feature of the regulatory regime. The Ernst and Young survey, for example, noted that some of the information in quarterly consolidated Reports of Condition and Income required by the country's regulatory agencies ("call reports"), namely that on loans on which payments are overdue and on highly leveraged transactions, is not available to the public.[26] And other information generated by bank examinations remains confidential (Mayer, 1998, p. 426).

D.   *Provisioning for bad loans*

During the Asian financial crisis the practices of banks in the countries affected regarding the recognition of and provisioning for bad loans have been the focus of much attention. The slowness of such recognition and the resulting shortcomings as to transparency regarding banks' financial strength were believed to have contributed importantly to uncertainties about the scale of the problems facing banking sectors (as did other factors bearing on provisioning, such as ill-defined rules on creditors' rights and difficulties regarding the valuation of collateral).[27]

Practices in this area are the subject of a recent consultative paper of the Basle Committee (BCBS, 1998c). While the coverage of the recommendations in that paper is broad, the recommendations still leave considerable discretion to national authorities as to their detailed application. The review of practices actually in force in the *Price Waterhouse Survey* suggests that considerable discretion was in practice available to banks under the regimes of the 14 industrial countries covered as of March 1994. The extent to which these regimes have been successful would appear to reflect to a significant extent the prevalence of good banking practice rather than the impact of precise regulatory rules.[28]

These points can be illustrated with regard to the issues of the recognition and measurement of impaired loans and the adequacy of specific and general allowances for credit losses.[29] The recommendation of the Basle Committee's paper on the recognition and measurement of impairment is that a bank should identify and recognize impairment when there is a probability that it will not be able to collect, or there is no longer reasonable assurance that it will collect, all the amounts due according to the contractual terms of a loan agreement. Some guidance on the application of this recommendation is provided as follows: "One factor that generally indicates that there has been a deterioration in the credit quality of a loan is that the borrower has defaulted in making interest or principal payments when due on the loan. As a starting point, loans generally should be identified as impaired when payments are contractually a minimum number of days in arrears reflecting domestic payment practices for the type of loan in question (e.g. 30–90 days)".[30] But the need for exceptions to this rule is acknowledged and, as the paper puts it, "Inevitably, bank management has some discretion in determining when reasonable assurance of collecting the contractual amounts no longer exists" (BCBS, 1998c, para. 44), but this discretion should be exercised subject to observance of sound accounting practices and adequate disclosure. The paper recommends that banks measure an impaired loan at its estimated realistic value, in particular attributing fair value to collateral to the extent that the loan is collateral-dependent (where fair value involves valuation on a prudent basis by internal or external qualified professionals and review by management of the assumptions as well as the conclusions of the valuation). "Credit deterioration in individually identified loans should be timely recognized to the greatest extent possible through the establishment of specific allowances or through charge-offs" (ibid., para. 46). "When latent losses are known to exist, but they cannot yet be ascribed to individual loans, general allowances should be established" (ibid., para. 48). Various circumstances

are mentioned as providing guidance concerning the establishment of general provisions such as "past experience and current economic and other relevant conditions, including changes in ... lending policies, nature and volume of the portfolio, volume and severity of recently identified impaired loans and concentrations of credit" (ibid., para. 48), and the paper refers to various methods (including some based on statistical models) in this context.

In the majority of the countries in the *Price Waterhouse Survey* (11 out of 14) a large role in establishing the criteria to be met before the establishment of specific provisions by banks was accorded to management's discretion. Only in Canada, Spain and the United States were official rules specified as applicable: in Canada specific guidance was provided by the OSFI; in Spain rules provided by the central bank applied to different circumstances and categories of borrower;[31] and in the United States, where no regulatory distinction was made between specific and general provisions, banks were required to establish a provision for loan losses in accordance with standards enunciated by the country's accounting bodies.[32] However, the distinction between the two groups of countries in this respect should not be too sharply drawn. In the case of countries not subject to official rules the survey refers nonetheless to accounting standards and industry practice as well as to a measure of official guidance: for the United Kingdom, for example, to a Statement of Recommended Accounting Practice (SORP) of the British Bankers Association; for France to guidance of the French Banking Commission; for Japan to the need for approval by the Ministry of Finance of the level of specific provisions set by management; for Australia, Belgium and Denmark to industry practice; and for Italy to general guidance under current regulation. Regarding the criteria to be met in the establishment of general provisions, official rules were slightly more common: the group of countries where such rules applied also included Denmark (where general provisions were permissible only in very restricted cases), the Netherlands (where an official ceiling for such provisions was in force) and Japan (where general provisions were mandatory but at a level not specified), but not Spain (where management's discretion was permitted).

Managerial discretion also applied in the majority of the countries in the Price Waterhouse survey regarding the levels of specific loan loss provisions and, in most respects to the extent that the exposure was to domestic counterparties, the levels of general loan loss provisions, and regarding the valuation of loan collateral. Only in Japan and Spain were there official rules concerning the level of specific reserves: in the latter these took the form of detailed statutory rules and in the former of ceilings approved by the Ministry of Finance on levels of both "tax-deductible" and "non tax-deductible" provisioning. But once again the survey refers also in this context to accounting standards (in the United Kingdom and the United States), to regulatory guidance (in France and Italy) and to prevalent industry practice (in Australia, Belgium and Denmark).

In the case of general provisions, official rules applied more frequently, most importantly as a result of rules about provisioning for country-risk exposure and about hidden reserves. Thus in Canada minimum provisions had to be established for exposure to countries designated by the OSFI; in Belgium and France there were officially prescribed minimum provisions for exposure to country risk; in Denmark (as already mentioned) the general provisions permitted only in very restricted cases were limited to an amount reflecting recent loss experience; in Germany the adequacy of general provisions had to be certified by a bank's auditor and a ceiling was prescribed for hidden reserves; in Japan rules applied to the amount of the general tax-deductible provision, and other loan-related provisions were permitted with the approval of the Ministry of Finance; in Luxembourg the rates of general provisioning were set by the tax authorities, dividends could be subject to limitation for banks not making adequate provision for exposure to country risk, and there were rules regarding the levels of additional hidden reserves on certain classes of assets; in the Netherlands the central bank provided guidance on the reasonable minimum level for general provisions, on the provision to be made against assets covered by rules concerning country risk, and on the minimum level of a general (hidden) contingency reserve; in Spain, as for specific provisions, detailed statutory rules applied; in Switzerland banks had to make a general provision of a certain percentage for their exposure to countries specified by the Banking Commission, and there were also regulations governing the disclosure of the release of hidden reserves; and in the United States special allowances had to be made for country risk exposures to which the regulatory classification of "value impaired" applied. Even in the United Kingdom, where there was managerial discretion about provisioning for country risk, this discretion was exercised with regard to a "matrix" established by the Bank of England designed to measure the extent of such risk.[33]

Regarding the valuation of loan collateral the survey found that management discretion was very much the rule. Only for Spain and the United States were there references to official rules: in the latter fair value (which is not necessarily defined as market value) was to be used; and in the former there were rules covering the procedures for valuing buildings, the treatment of unquoted shares, the valuation of securities quoted on exchanges at market prices, and the registration of values by the Ministry of Economy. But here again the survey makes frequent references to industry practice (for the United Kingdom, Belgium, Denmark, Italy and the Netherlands), to a major role for consultations with the bank's auditors (for Germany) and to bank-specific consultations with the Ministry of Finance (for Japan).

E.   Some more recent developments

Earlier it was emphasized that since the two surveys discussed in the previous section referred to a period four to six years ago, in a number of respects the situation will have changed regarding both regulation and disclosure. Important influences here will have been the introduction into national legal regimes of provisions reflecting recent EC directives (already mentioned) and recommendations of the Basle Committee.

One area of particular interest in the context of relations between transparency and recent financial innovation is the initiative of the Basle Committee and IOSCO to encourage financial firms to enhance the transparency of their trading and derivatives activities.[34] At the time of the Ernst and Young survey the disclosure rules in force for off-balance-sheet positions in countries' financial reporting were still often at an early stage of development and limited in their coverage of the financial instruments involved. In 15 of the 23 economies included in the survey, for example, the general rule was that trading positions involving off-balance-sheet instruments should be recorded at market value,[35] and in two others (Belgium and Germany) the rule allowed for recording at market value or cost. But even in countries where rules for valuation and disclosure appear to have been relatively full-fledged, it is difficult to infer from descriptions in the survey how successfully these rules were keeping pace with changes in transactional practice on the ground. In some other countries where market value was specified as the valuation rule, the regime for off-balance-sheet positions was clearly rudimentary: in Belgium there were no specific rules, standards or guidelines on the accounting treatment of instruments such as options, futures and swaps; in Hong Kong (China) there were no accounting pronouncements other than with regard to foreign-currency forward contracts, although positions in off-balance-sheet financial instruments taken as part of trading activities were generally accounted for on a mark-to-market basis; and in Saudi Arabia no guidance was available as to the accounting treatment of forward rate agreements, interest rate options, caps and floors, interest rate and currency swaps, and most other derivatives since they were not yet considered to be material for Saudi banks. In Austria accounting for off-balance-sheet instruments had not yet been subject to legislative regulation (although a forthcoming Banking Act was expected to provide some guidance), and as a result practice regarding valuation varied widely.

The scope of the surveys conducted by the Basle Committee and IOSCO is limited to the annual reports of 67 banks and 11 securities firms, selected as the largest institutions involved in the derivatives business in 11 countries (Belgium, Canada, France, Germany, Italy, Japan, the Netherlands, Sweden, Switzerland, the United Kingdom and the United States). The surveys are thus not comparable to the Ernst and Young survey. But they do provide an indication of the scale of recent improvements in the understanding, disclosure and management of risks associated with derivatives activities of major firms, and probably by extension, an indication of the broad direction of change amongst a wider sample of institutions. The conclusion of the two organizations is that "viewed over the 1993–1997 period, the amount, detail and clarity of trading and derivatives-related disclosures in annual reports of banks and securities firms have improved substantially" (BCBS, 1998d, para. 17). This statement can be exemplified with respect to various topics included in the surveys: the proportion of firms that discussed their risk exposure in the context of their overall balance sheets increased from less than one-half in 1993 to 97 per cent in 1997; there were substantial rises in the proportion of firms which described their management of the different major categories of risk – credit, market, liquidity, and operational and legal – although the proportions were still substantially higher in 1997 for the first two categories than for the second two; there was an increase from 33 to 87 per cent in the proportion of firms discussing how market values were estimated; and by 1997, 99 per cent of the firms discussed their accounting policies for derivatives. Nonetheless, the two organizations also opined that "Despite these improvements, there remain signifi-

cant disparities ... as regards the type and usefulness of the information disclosed ... some institutions continue to disclose little, generally, about key aspects of their trading and derivatives activities" (BCBS, 1998d, para. 18).

IV. Concluding remarks

In spite of the time which has elapsed since the date of surveys discussed in the previous section, as already pointed out, they still bring into focus many of the contrasts between evolving concepts about best practice regarding disclosure and banking regulation and supervision, on the one hand, and actual regimes for regulation and supervision, on the other. Moreover, they show how conflicting views about the relative values of disclosure and confidentiality are resolved in the regimes of different countries. The findings of the surveys also amply exemplify the multiple connections between successful financial supervision, on the one hand, and standards and industry practice in the related fields of financial reporting, accounting and auditing, on the other. But on the question of the extent to which disclosure to lenders and investors leads to levels of market discipline which can act not merely as a useful complement to financial supervision but also as at least a partial substitute for it the discussion in this paper points to likely limitations of disclosure's potential in this regard.

The position here would appear to depend on the extent to which a bank's balance sheet consists of marketable assets and liabilities, and on the scope and quality of available information not contained in a bank's published financial reports. Regarding entities still heavily involved in traditional commercial banking (receiving deposits and other repayable funds from the public and granting credits for their own account), long-standing limitations are still relevant to consideration of what disclosure can reasonably be expected to achieve. Such banks' financial reports will continue to contain much useful information for market participants – information whose value can still be enhanced by improvements in accounting standards and changes in regulatory rules about disclosure. Moreover, in such cases aggregated statistics (for which, as mentioned earlier, returns to regulatory authorities are often a major source) will continue to furnish additional important data concerning the position of the banking sector as a whole. But the condition of individual banks will remain difficult for outsiders to gauge on the basis of publicly available information, so that reliance on disclosure as a substitute for important aspects of supervision still seems at most a somewhat remote prospect. These remarks would appear to apply to the great majority of countries, even though securitization and other innovations are making significant inroads in traditional banking in many of them.

In the case of entities whose balance sheets consist to a much greater extent of marketable items the discipline that can be exercised by disclosure is likely to be more important. But this statement is subject to a caveat for lenders and investors similar to that in the remarks of William McDonough cited above (in section II). The marketable items in banks' balance sheets are susceptible to rapid change with the consequence that the information in publicly disclosed financial reports and regulatory returns can rapidly become out of date (not to mention the fact that such information can also be misleading[36]). To some extent financial analysts can compensate the resulting lacunae in their knowledge by reference to continuously available data on the value, for example, of marketable assets on banks' balance sheets.[37] But there are presumably still significant limits to the inferences which can be drawn from such sources, and even in industrial countries with advanced financial sectors the public disclosure of financial firms' balance sheets on a much more frequent basis (say, weekly or even daily) than at present still seems distant (though one needs to avoid dogmatism about any question of the future availability of information in today's world). The growth in the importance of marketable items on banks' balance sheets can be expected to continue to act as a fillip to a shift in the emphasis of financial supervision towards the auditing of firms' internal controls, but until now this has amounted to a change in the qualitative character of such supervision (discussed above in section II) rather than a move in the direction of its replacement.

Notes

1   See especially the reports of the Working Groups of the Group of 22 on the International Financial Architecture, in particular that on transparency and accountability (mimeo), October 1998. In the latter report transparency is defined as "a process by which information about existing conditions, decisions and actions is made accessible, visible and understandable". This paper is concerned with this process as it affects banking supervision and some aspects of the closely related issue of the market discipline on financial firms which can be exercised by lenders and investors.

2   Lack of information about the maturity structure of central banks' forward exchange commitments at the time of the

outbreak of the Asian crisis has been much commented on in this context. Information was also spotty concerning the exposure of banks in certain Asian and Latin American countries to those affected by the crisis in Asia and to the Russian Federation. Moreover, early estimates of the external liabilities of the Republic of Korea in late 1997 (when it was being enveloped by the Asian crisis) were too low by about 25 per cent ($41 billion out of a total of $157 billion) owing to the omission of those of foreign branches of the country's financial firms (JP Morgan, 1998, pp. 11–12). Concerning the substantial overseas network of banking entities from the Republic of Korea which would have been responsible for this borrowing, see Cornford and Brandon (1999).

3   Various possible levels of market efficiency in relation to information are identified by financial economists. The highest level (so-called strong-form efficiency) is that where prices in these markets reflect all the information that can be acquired by analysis of both firms and the economy. If this level applied, the markets would be like an ideal auction house characterized by fair prices and the impossibility of making consistently superior forecasts. A second, lower level of efficiency (semi-strong-form efficiency) is that where prices reflect all published information, and a third (weak-form efficiency) that where they reflect all information contained in past prices (see, for example, Campbell et al., 1997, pp. 20–25). Distinctions based on these levels typically characterize financial economists' empirical investigations of market efficiency. In less narrowly focused contexts, other broader definitions of market efficiency are deployed explicitly and implicitly, and are equally (or even more) important in policy discussion of the subject. Particularly pertinent here is what James Tobin has denoted as "functional efficiency", a concept referring to the broader economic function of the sector supplying financial services, for example the pooling of risks, the facilitation of transactions and payments, and the mobilization of saving for investment as well as their efficient allocation (Tobin, 1984). These other definitions of market efficiency are not so directly linked to information flows as those of financial economists, but such flows are still importantly linked to most aspects of its achievement.

4   The distinction drawn between regulation and supervision in the literature is not completely precise, but generally regulation refers to the establishment of legally enforceable rules and of those enunciated by self-regulatory organizations or "clubs" such as bankers' associations, while supervision refers to implementing, and monitoring compliance with, these rules as well as to tasks associated with the more general oversight of financial firms' behaviour. See, for example, the discussion (where a distinction is drawn between monitoring and supervision) in Goodhart (1998, p. xviii).

5   The improved private-sector transparency for which calls are being made in current discussion of international financial reform is intended to include not only the reporting of financial firms but also that of non-financial entities. Many of the recommendations under this heading (such as those relating to accounting standards and other disclosures required for shares listed on stock exchanges) refer to both. Financial reporting by several economic sectors is characterized by specificities absent elsewhere, but such specificities are especially important for the financial sector and linked in many ways integrally to its regulation and supervision, whose character reflects its central role in economies' functioning and stability. The

discussion here is limited to the transparency issues involving financial firms.

6   Even in the United States, whose banking sector is required to meet relatively high standards of disclosure and where there are growing arguments for increased reliance on disclosure in vetting and disciplining banks, historically "the objective of the bank regulatory agencies has been to preserve the soundness of individual institutions and the integrity of the banking system as a whole. This objective influenced their approach in requiring compliance with disclosure requirements. Generally, the agencies preferred to allow institutions time to resolve financial difficulties. This approach clearly is antithetical to the theory of a marketplace governed by the intense glare of full disclosure" (D'Arista, 1994, p. 340).

7   The character of such misgivings can be illustrated by the following quotation from a recent book about credit risk concerning the likely consequences of the development of a more efficient market for such risk: "But once a large, liquid market for credit has been established, it will become possible to mark loans to market on a direct basis. As record keeping improves, professionals will be able to tap far more reliable data about what happened in the past. Better information will lead to better decision making. But this new-found freedom to trade credit risk will probably lead to greater market volatility: In a world full of portfolio managers chanting the *mantra* of total return, the buy or sell actions started by a few could well turn into stampede" (Caouette et al., 1998, p. 409).

8   As one writer with first-hand experience of bank risk management describes the situation: "For most banks with significant trading operations the composition of their global portfolios does remain broadly similar over the period of one day and quite possibly longer. At the local business unit level the composition of the local portfolio often changes during the day and can look significantly different from one day to the next" (Best, 1998, p. 18).

9   Financial information is material if its omission or misstatement could change or influence the assessment or decision of a user relying on it.

10 The Committee decided to focus its report on financial firms denoted as "highly leveraged institutions", or HLIs, with the three generic characteristics of being subject to very little or no direct regulatory oversight, of having to meet very limited disclosure requirements, and of taking on significant leverage. Hedge funds – which are private investment pools typically following aggressive strategies based on high levels of leverage and remuneration of managers in the form primarily of a percentage of investment profits – are obviously a major subset of HLIs (BCBS, 1999, section 1.1).

11 The phrase is due to Kaufman (1986).

12 For an up-to-date survey of the state of the art see Best (1998).

13 In some of the economies there may also be divergence between the enunciated standards of the regime for accounting and financial reporting and the actual practice of several financial firms, a subject not covered by the surveys.

14 A number of the findings of the surveys are summarized in the annex table.

15 One exemption applying in a number of cases is for newly formed companies.

16 Under the European Community's Bank Accounts Directive of 1986 (86/635/EEC), which includes a requirement for consolidated accounts, deferment of its implementation was permitted only until the financial year 1993.

17 The exceptions were Hong Kong (China) and South Africa.

18 The contents of accounts refer to the items and subjects which they cover, whereas standards or policies refer to the ways in which these are treated, for example the principles governing the numerical measures of accounting items where different alternatives can be envisaged.

19 In Italy banks prepared their accounts in accordance with the Civil Code, which applied to all companies. However, while "the Civil Code prescribes the minimum 9headings which must be included in a balance sheet ... there is a degree of flexibility and banks have expanded and adapted the layout to suit their circumstances" (Ernst and Young, 1993, p. 267). While the full implications of this statement are not completely clear, the possibility of a certain flexibility regarding specific exemptions is suggested.

20 The most recent edition of *Graham and Dodd's Security Analysis* (the evergreen bible of security analysis based on fundamentals) states that amongst recent improvements in disclosure in the United States "segment reporting has proved to be the most valuable" (Cottle et al., 1988, p. 103).

21 Australia, Austria, Bahrain, Belgium, Canada, Denmark, Germany, Hong Kong (China), Ireland, Luxembourg, the Netherlands, Singapore, South Africa, Spain, Switzerland and the United Kingdom.

22 It was a recommended part of United States practice regarding financial reporting that a bank's auditor should consider attending, as an observer and with the approval of the bank, the exit conference of the supervisors and the bank's board of directors or its executive officers (or both). It was also recommended that if the supervisors requested permission to attend the meeting between the auditor and the bank's top management to review the audit report (and if management concurred), the auditor should generally be responsive to such a request.

23 Australia, Austria, Canada, Denmark, France, Ireland, Italy, South Africa, the United Kingdom and the United States. (The absence of a reference to such information in the Ernst and Young survey does not necessarily mean that it was not also required in other countries' stock-exchange regulations.)

24 The same confidentiality often applies to the reports on many subjects (discussed above) by external auditors to regulatory authorities. Many of the matters covered in information exchange between auditors and the OSFI in Canada, for example, are the subject of protocols (Ernst and Young, 1993, p. 119).

25 See Mayer (1998, pp. 425–428). The extent to which disclosure and market discipline can play such roles is discussed further in the concluding part of this paper.

26 Loan information in column A of schedule RC-N, "Past due 30 through 89 days and still accruing", and that in column A of schedule RC-T, "Highly leveraged transactions", were exceptions to the public availability of call reports (Ernst and Young, 1993, p. 550). (The author does not know whether there has subsequently been a relaxation of this rule.)

27 At a conceptual level the connection between loan-loss provisions and financial reporting can be illustrated by the following quotation: "If loans are misclassified or subject to loose classification, loan loss reserves will be inadequate and capital ratios will be overstated. Loan loss reserves are accumulated through provisions, which are deducted from income. If provisions are understated, banks can report higher profits than they have actually earned. Hence, retained earnings, an item in the capital account, will be overstated" (Goodhart et al., 1998, p. 106).

28 The regimes for recognition of loan losses and provisioning in industrial countries have often been wanting (and have

sometimes been subject to relaxations in their stringency) during financial crises in industrial countries. For examples, see the case studies in Sheng (1996).

29   Specific allowances (or provisions) cover likely losses identified on individual loans (or pools of homogeneous loans), while general allowances (or provisions) cover likely losses on loans which have not as yet been specifically identified.

30   See BCBS (1998c, para. 43). Here practices in early 1998 of selected Asian countries regarding the definition of non-performing loans (not necessarily identical to the recognition of loans' impairment) are of some interest. In Malaysia the definition referred to loans three months overdue, and in the Republic of Korea to loans six months overdue (though here the definition was to change to three months overdue). In Thailand a definition of three months overdue was to become effective in 2000, and in Indonesia the same definition was to become effective in 2001 (JP Morgan, 1998a, pp. 8–9).

31   There is a detailed account of the Bank of Spain's rules on loan loss provisions in Annex I of Price Waterhouse (1994).

32   The auditing procedure study of the American Institute of Certified Public Accountants, *Auditing the Allowance for Credit Losses of Banks*, is described in Annex II of Price Waterhouse (1994).

33   In Japan an official ceiling of 30 per cent for the level of provisioning for exposure to country risk had been removed at the date of the Price Waterhouse Survey, but most banks still observed that level (though some had moved to a higher one). In Italy the Association of Italian Banks had issued a circular with a list of countries for which banks were to make provisions of at least 30 per cent against their exposure.

34   This initiative has resulted in a series of four surveys since 1995 of disclosures relating to the trading and derivatives activities of internationally active banks and securities firms. The most recent of these surveys refers to 1997 (BCBS, 1998d).

35   Australia, Canada, Denmark, France, Hong Kong (China), Ireland, Italy, Luxembourg, the Netherlands, Saudi Arabia, Singapore, South Africa, Spain, the United Kingdom and the United States.

36   An interesting and pertinent example of the shortcomings of publicly disclosed data for the United States money-centre banks is furnished by recent research by an analyst at Brown Brothers Harriman into the divergence between their cross-border exposure as disclosed in reports to the Securities and Exchange Commission (SEC), on the one hand, and to the Federal Financial Institutions Examination Council (FFIEC), on the other. Only a little over 50 per cent of the cross-border exposure reported to the FFIEC as of the second quarter of 1998 was included in reports to shareholders available at about the same time. The banks' point of view concerning such disclosures, as reported by *Euromoney*, is instructive and worth quoting at length: "The banks complain that reporting exposures is not an easy task. Each of the reporting agencies plays to a different audience: the FFIEC is primarily concerned with the safety and soundness of the banking system as a whole, the SEC more with the earnings power of the banks. Tax issues, as ever, influence the style and manner in which the figures are reported and, as a finance officer at one of the money-centre banks contends: 'It's not just in emerging markets that there is a problem. Just defining the exposures to commercial real-estate loans is bad enough.' The SEC only requires banks to report exposures once they reach 0.75% of a bank's total assets for a particular country, and only as it stands on the day of reporting" (Currie, 1998).

37   Mayer illustrates the processes involved as follows: "Large commercial loans are already participated out to a number of banks, and these participations trade just like bonds ... at both banks and investment houses. They can be priced, and are, not only by traders but also on the screens of Bloomberg Financial Services" (Mayer, 1998, p. 426).

References

BCBS (1997), *Core Principles for Effective Banking Supervision* (Basle: Basle Committee on Banking Supervision).

BCBS (1998a), *Enhancing Bank Transparency: Public Disclosure and Supervisory Information that Promote Safety and Soundness in Banking Systems* (Basle: Basle Committee on Banking Supervision), September.

BCBS (1998b), *Report on International Developments in Banking Supervision*, Report No. 11 (Basle: Basle Committee on Banking Supervision), October.

BCBS (1998c), "Sound practices for loan accounting, credit risk disclosure and related matters", consultative paper (Basle: Basle Committee on Banking Supervision), October.

BCBS (1998d), *Trading and Derivatives Disclosures of Banks and Securities Firms: Results of the Survey of 1997 Disclosures*, Joint Report (Basle: Basle Committee on Banking Supervision, and the Technical Committee of the International Organization of Securities Commissions [IOSCO]), November.

BCBS (1999), *Banks' Interactions with Highly Leveraged Institutions* (Basle: Basle Committee on Banking Supervision), January.

BEATTIE, V.A., P.D. CASSON, R.S. DALE, G.W. MCKENZIE, C.M.S. SUTCLIFFE, and M.J. TURNER (1995), *Banks and Bad Debts: Accounting for Loan Losses in International Banking* (Chichester: John Wiley).

BEST, P. (1998), *Implementing Value at Risk* (Chichester: John Wiley and Sons).

BIS (1994), "Public disclosure of market and credit risk by financial intermediaries", discussion paper proposed by a Working Group of the Euro-currency Standing Committee of the Central Banks of the Group of Ten countries (Basle: Bank for International Settlements), September.

CAMPBELL, J.Y., A.W. LO, and A.C. MACKINLAY (1997), *The Econometrics of Financial Markets* (Princeton: Princeton University Press).

CAOUETTE, J.B., E.I. ALTMAN, and P. NARAYANAN (1998), *Managing Credit Risk: The Next Great Financial Challenge* (New York: John Wiley).

CORNFORD, A. and J. BRANDON (1999), "The WTO Agreement on Financial Services: Problems of financial globalization in practice", *International Monetary and Financial Issues for the 1990s*, Vol. X, United Nations publication, sales no. E.99.II.D.14 (New York and Geneva).

COTTLE, S., R.F. MURRAY, and F.E. BLOCK (1988), *Graham and Dodd's Security Analysis*, 5th edition (New York: McGraw-Hill Book Company).

CURRIE, A. (1998), "US banks: Transparency begins at home", *Euromoney*, December.

D'ARISTA, J.W. (1994), *The Evolution of U.S. Finance. Volume II: Restructuring Institutions and Markets* (Armonk, N.Y.: M.E. Sharpe).

ECU INSTITUTE (1995), *Banking Supervision in the European Community: Institutional Aspects*, Report of a Working Group of the under the chairmanship of Jean-Victor Louis (Brussels: Editions de l'Université de Bruxelles).

ERNST AND YOUNG (1993), *International Bank Accounting*, 3rd edition (London: Euromoney Publications).

GOODHART, C., P. HARTMANN, D. LLEWELLYN, L. ROJAS-SUAREZ, and S. WEISBROD (1998), *Financial Regulation: Why, How and Where Now?* (London and New York: Routledge).

JP MORGAN (1998a), *Global Data Watch*, 6 February.

JP MORGAN (1998b), *Asian Financial Markets*, 24 April.

KAUFMAN, H. (1986), *Interest Rates, the Markets and the New Financial World* (London: I.B. Tauris).

LEACH, J.A., W.J. McDONOUGH, D.W. MULLINS, and B. QUINN (1993), "Global derivatives: Public sector responses", Occasional Paper No. 44 (Washington, DC: Group of Thirty), pp. 5–16.

MAYER, M. (1998), *The Bankers: The Next Generation* (New York: Truman Talley Books/Plume).

PRICE WATERHOUSE (1994), *Price Waterhouse Survey of Bank Provisioning*, reproduced in Appendix A of Beattie et al. (1995).

SHENG A. (ed.) (1996), *Bank Restructuring: Lessons from the 1980s* (Washington, DC: World Bank).

TOBIN, J. (1984), "On the efficiency of the financial system", Fred Hirsch Memorial Lecture, reprinted in *Lloyds Bank Review*, No. 153, July.

Annex table

FEATURES OF FINANCIAL REPORTING AND SUPERVISION FOR BANKS IN SELECTED ECONOMIES, 1992[a] AND 1994[a]

Key to features

- I. Consolidated accounts required
- II. Accounting standards fixed by law
- III. Exemptions from disclosure obligations for banks
- IV. Direct communication between auditors and supervisors in prescribed circumstances
- V. Segmental reporting required
- VI. Criteria for establishment of specific loan loss provisions
- VII. Criteria for establishment of general loan loss provisions
- VIII. Levels of specific loan loss provisions
- IX. Levels of general loan loss provisions
- X. Valuation of collateral

Economy	I	II	III	IV	V	VI	VII	VIII	IX	X
United States	Yes	Yes	Yes	No	Yes	OR[h]	OR[h]	MD[h]	OR[j]	OR
United Kingdom	Yes	No	No	Yes	Yes	MD	MD	MD	MD	MD
United Arab Emirates	Yes	No	No	No	..	..	..	..	..	..
Switzerland	Yes	Yes	No	Yes	No	MD	MD	MD	OR[jk]	MD
Spain	Yes	Yes	No	No	No	OR	MD	MD	OR[j]	OR
South Africa	Yes	No	Yes	Yes	No	..	..	..	..	..
Singapore	Yes[b]	No	Yes	Yes	Yes	..	..	..	..	..
Saudi Arabia	Yes	Yes	No	No	Yes	..	..	..	..	..
Portugal	No	Yes	No	No	No	..	OR	MD	OR[j]	MD
Netherlands	Yes	Yes	No	Yes	Yes	MD	OR	MD	OR[kl]	MD
Luxembourg	No	No	No	Yes	Yes	MD[g]	MD	MD	OR[kl]	MD
Japan	Yes	Yes	Yes	No	Yes	MD[f]	OR	OR	OR[l]	MD[m]
Italy	Yes	Yes	Yes[c]	No	No	MD[f]	MD	OR	OR[j]	MD
Ireland	Yes	No	Yes	Yes	Yes	..	..	..	..	..
Hong Kong (China)	Yes	Yes	Yes	Yes	No[d]	..	..	..	..	..
Germany	Yes	Yes	No	Yes	No[d]	MD[e]	MD	MD	OR[k]	MD
France	Yes	Yes	No	No	No	MD[e]	MD	MD[i]	OR[j]	MD
Denmark	Yes	Yes	No	Yes	Yes	MD	OR	MD	OR	MD
Canada	Yes	Yes	No	Yes	Yes	MD	OR	MD	OR[j]	MD
Belgium	Yes	No	Yes	Yes	Yes	MD	MD	MD	OR[j]	MD
Bahrain	No	No	..	..	..	..	..	..	..	..
Austria	Yes	Yes	..	Yes	No	..	..	..	..	..
Australia	No	Yes	Yes	Yes	Yes	MD	MD	MD	MD	OR

Source: I, II, III, IV and V: Ernst & Young, *International Bank Accounting, 3rd edition* (London: Euromoney Publications, 1993); VI, VII, VIII, IX and X: *Price Waterhouse Survey of Bank Provisioning*, reproduced as appendix A of V. A. Beattie, P.D. Casson, R.S. Dale, G.W. McKenzie, C.M.S. Sutcliffe and M.J. Turner, *Banks and Bad Debts: Accounting for Loan Losses in International Banking* (Chichester: John Wiley, 1995).

Note: MD: Management's discretion;   OR: Official rules;   .. Not available.

- a   See explanations in text.
- b   Subject to exemptions for non-banking subsidiaries.
- c   Reflecting flexibility regarding presentation of accounts.
- d   Some breakdown of assets and liabilities required.
- e   Subject to some guidelines of the French Banking Commission.
- f   Subject to general regulatory guidance.
- g   Subject to approval of Ministry of Finance.
- h   Without distinction between specific and general loan loss provisions.
- i   Subject to official guidance as to minimum levels for different categories of loan.
- j   For country risk.
- k   Including rules for hidden reserves.
- l   Including rules set by tax authorities.
- m   In consultation with Ministry of Finance.

FOREIGN DIRECT INVESTMENT AND DEVELOPMENT: BALANCING COSTS AND BENEFITS

William Milberg*

Abstract

Inward foreign direct investment (IFDI) is now viewed in many policy circles as an unambiguously positive contributor to economic development, providing a non-volatile source of capital that requires neither a fixed interest payment nor repayment of principal at a specified date. Moreover, IFDI is said to bring technological spillovers that raise efficiency and provide export market access, thus having a net positive impact on the balance of payments. This paper provides a critical survey of the debate over the net benefits of IFDI as a tool for economic development. According to recent empirical studies, there are few cases of successful IFDI-led development. IFDI has usually lagged economic development. Relative to the domestic investment needs of most developing countries, the pool of available foreign direct investment is relatively small. The suppression of labour and environmental standards as a means to attract foreign capital is often ineffective. To capture the potential positive technological spillovers from IFDI requires the attainment of a certain level of absorptive capacity, reflected in infrastructure and human capital. A focus on the expansion of domestic absorptive capacity will spur domestic investment demand which, when sustained over time, is a more reliable determinant of successful growth, development, and even international competitiveness.

* The author is grateful to Yilmaz Akyüz, Gerry Helleiner and Richard Kozul-Wright for comments on a previous draft, to Jan Kregel for general discussion of the topic and to Mahindra Maharaj and Dongyi Liu for excellent research assistance.

I. Introduction

Amidst a financial crisis that began in East Asia in July 1997 and moved to the Russian Federation and then Brazil, there is now considerable doubt, even among heads of the Bretton Woods institutions, about the net benefits of financial liberalization for developing countries.[1] Some of the most respected economists are proposing the use of capital controls to limit the destabilizing effects of volatile international financial flows (Bhagwati, 1998; Krugman, 1998). In the current environment one can expect that foreign direct investment will increasingly be perceived as the main remaining channel for a stabilizing flow of capital from developed to developing countries.

Even before the onset of the global financial crisis, the pendulum of economic opinion had swung to the side of broad support for developing country liberalization of inward foreign direct investment (IFDI).[2] Sir Leon Brittan, Vice-President of the European Commission, sees the liberalization of foreign direct investment as "the next great boost to the world economy ... that could unleash enormous new opportunities for growth and prosperity in developing and developed countries alike" (Brittan, 1995, p. 1). IFDI is now viewed in many policy circles as making an unambiguously positive contribution to economic development, providing a non-volatile source of capital that requires neither a fixed interest payment nor a repayment of principal at a specified date. Moreover, it is said to bring "technological spillovers" that increase efficiency and provide export market access, thus having a net positive impact on the balance of payments, equivalent to the expansion of trade itself. Julius (1990, p. 97), for example, writes that: "As with trade, increased international flows of FDI should be encouraged because they bring both global and national benefits. They stimulate growth through more efficient production and they lower prices through greater competition". And according to a recent OECD study, "Like trade, foreign direct investment acts as a powerful spur to competition and innovation, encouraging domestic firms to reduce costs and enhance their competitiveness" (OECD, 1998, p. 47). Finally, since foreign direct investment (FDI), especially in the manufacturing sector, is often motivated by firms' desire to have an internationally integrated and flexible production process, it is believed that developing countries that fail to attract foreign firms risk being shut out of these growing firm-level, internationally integrated, flexible production "networks", i.e. being left out of the entire process of globalization of production, including international trade. That is, there is a growing perception of IFDI (along with exports) as the key to the door of economic development. In sum, the main features of this view are that IFDI:

- promotes economic growth and development;

- raises employment and wages;

- generates technological spillovers that raise productivity;

- provides export market access;

- leads to improvement in the balance of payments.

The major remaining question, it seems, is how countries should best go about attracting IFDI. While negotiations over a multilateral investment liberalization are temporarily stalled, between 1991 and 1997, over 75 countries unilaterally altered their regulation of IFDI almost always (in 94 per cent of cases) in the direction of more liberal treatment of foreign investment. As of 1997, there were over 1,500 bilateral investment treaties in place (UNCTAD, 1998, p. 57).

While the recent period has provided a healthy response to the dependency rhetoric of the 1960s and 1970s, the analytical pendulum has perhaps swung too far in the other direction, with organizations such as the OECD extolling the virtues of capital account liberalization without fairly assessing its costs.[3] This paper is an attempt to redress that imbalance and provide a critical survey of the debate on the net benefits IFDI as a tool for economic development. It argues that for most countries IFDI should not figure as a central component of any development strategy. Historically, there are very few cases of successful industrialization in which IFDI has been a major driving force. There is a potentially large social cost to the competitive struggle to attract IFDI, and there is very mixed evidence on the degree to which the incentives offered as part of this competition succeed in attracting foreign firms. Thus while policies on IFDI should not be ignored, the policies most effective in "attracting" IFDI are not those relating directly to the foreign sector but those that promote domestic economic growth through investment, infrastructure and human capital development – to raise absorptive capacity – and domestic competition. Finally, the IFDI-based development strategy suffers from a fallacy of composition: if all countries successfully pursue the strategy simultaneously, global excess capacity is likely to develop that will only worsen developing countries' terms of trade.

More specifically, this paper shows that: (i) the hypothesized positive "technological spillover" effects of IFDI have been difficult to verify empirically; (ii) IFDI represents an insignificant share of gross capital formation in most developing countries; (iii) much developing country IFDI represents the acquisition of existing assets as opposed to the creation of new ones; (iv) IFDI has tended to lag behind GNP growth in most developing countries, not to lead the growth process; (v) the competitive struggle among national governments (and sometimes regional governments within countries) to attract IFDI has in general not succeeded in attracting FDI but may have reduced social standards, including the repression of labour compensation, a reduction of labour and environmental standards, and a diminished ability of the State to tax corporate profits and regulate capital generally; (vi) with the development of financial markets and their liberalization in developing countries, IFDI can easily be hedged, which makes it more similar to portfolio capital flows than ever before and thus gives it a potential for instability similar to that of those flows; (vii) IFDI has contributed to growing wage inequality in some developing countries, more than offsetting equalizing Stolper-Samuelson effects; and (viii) IFDI has an ambiguous effect on the host country balance of payments, since the increasing vertical disintegration of production has meant more imports for each dollar of exports at the same time as outflows of profits, interest, dividends, royalties and management fees have been rising.

This paper contains seven sections. Section II provides an overview of trends in developing country FDI. Section III describes the changing relationship between trade and FDI as a result of the growth of firm-based international integration of production. Section IV addresses the issues of capital formation, IFDI's links to finance, and technology spillovers. Section V briefly assesses the effect of IFDI on host country balance of payments, and section VI considers the nexus between growth and IFDI. Section VII concludes with a general discussion of policy.

II. Trends in foreign direct investment[4]

Economic "globalization" may be defined as increase in international capital mobility, the two dimensions of globalization being the globalization of production and of finance.[5] FDI flows and international trade are the central channels for the globalization of production, although, as we shall see below, trade and FDI have a different relation to each other today than they did 25 years ago. FDI is increasingly difficult to distinguish from financial flows. Over the past 25 years, FDI has grown on a global scale at a more rapid rate than trade, and both of these have grown considerably faster than world output (Kozul-Wright and Rowthorn, 1998). Economic theory predicts that, in the absence of market distortions, capital will flow from where its return on investment is lowest (i.e. where capital is most abundant) to where its return is highest (i.e. where it is most scarce), increasing world output and the global efficiency of resource use. Contrary to this prediction, FDI has been increasingly concentrated among developed countries (Brainard, 1993). At the same time, the heightened international mobility of capital, resulting from declining costs of communication and transportation and the development and liberalization of financial markets, has also meant that the international division of labour depends less on comparative advantage and more on firm decisions about the location of production. Location decisions of firms may deviate from those predicted by comparative advantage for a number of reasons. Firms may put national characteristics ahead of relative cost considerations.[6] Also, to the extent that heightened capital mobility has coincided with growing global excess capacity, trade liberalization may not bring the price adjustment necessary to convert a relative productivity advantage to an advantage in terms of absolute money costs. When currency values do not respond to trade imbalances in the expected fashion, then the price adjustment implied by the theory of comparative advantage may also be inoperative.[7]

Over the past 20 years, developing countries have experienced a shift in the composition of inward capital flows. Since the debt crises of the early 1980s reduced both the availability and the appeal of foreign bank loans as a source of capital for developing countries, foreign bank lending to developing countries has declined as a share of total developing country capital inflows, replaced by non-bank financial flows and especially by IFDI.

While the bulk of FDI still takes place among developed countries, developing countries have slowly increased their share of world FDI from 29 per cent to 37 per cent from 1992 to 1997 (table 1). The stock of world FDI that is located in developing countries rose from 23 per cent to 30 per cent between 1980 and 1996 (table 2). But the expansion of FDI to developing countries has not been spread evenly across countries. The increase in the developing country share of the world FDI stock is due

Table 1

FDI INFLOWS, BY HOST REGION AND ECONOMY, 1986–1997

(Percentage of world total)

Region/Economy	1986–1991 (Annual average)	1992	1993	1994	1995	1996	1997
Developed economies	81.34	68.41	63.84	58.23	63.85	57.89	58.21
Western Europe	41.72	48.82	38.55	32.27	37.07	29.61	28.68
European Union	39.66	47.65	37.20	29.46	35.26	27.37	27.01
Other Western Europe	2.06	1.16	1.35	2.81	1.81	2.24	1.67
United States	30.81	10.74	20.01	18.56	17.75	22.65	22.66
Developing economies	18.26	29.06	33.34	39.33	31.86	38.46	37.19
Africa	1.80	1.80	1.68	2.34	1.55	1.43	1.18
Latin America and Caribbean	5.94	10.00	7.92	11.81	9.64	12.96	14.00
Southern Europe	0.05	0.12	0.12	0.17	0.14	0.30	0.20
Asia	10.34	16.86	23.54	24.97	20.35	23.70	21.70
West Asia	0.83	1.03	1.59	0.62	-0.23	0.09	0.47
Central Asia	0.00	0.08	0.19	0.37	0.47	0.62	0.66
South, East and South-East Asia	9.50	15.74	21.76	23.98	20.10	23.00	20.58
Pacific	0.13	0.26	0.07	0.05	0.18	0.06	0.09
Central and Eastern Europe	0.41	2.52	2.80	2.43	4.29	3.66	4.60

Source: UNCTAD (1998), based on annex table B.1.

Table 2

STOCK OF INWARD FDI, BY HOST REGION AND ECONOMY

(Percentage of world total)

Region/Economy	1980	1985	1990	1995	1996	1997
Developed economies	77.5	72.3	79.3	70.6	69.3	68.0
Western Europe	41.4	33.6	44.1	39.1	37.9	36.9
European Union	38.3	31.3	41.5	36.3	35.5	34.6
Other Western Europe	3.1	2.3	2.7	2.8	2.4	2.3
United States	17.3	24.4	22.7	20.5	20.6	20.9
Developing economies	22.5	27.7	20.6	28.1	29.2	30.2
Africa	2.8	3.1	2.2	2.1	1.9	1.9
Latin America and Caribbean	9.9	10.2	7.1	10.2	10.5	10.9
Southern Europe	0.1	0.1	0.1	0.1	0.1	0.1
Asia	9.5	14.3	11.1	15.6	16.5	17.2
West Asia	2.8	5.7	2.8	2.1	1.8	1.7
Central Asia	...	...	0.0	0.1	0.2	0.2
South, East and South-East Asia	6.7	8.6	8.3	13.5	14.5	15.3
Pacific	0.1	0.1	0.1	0.1	0.1	0.1
Central and Eastern Europe	...	...	0.1	1.3	1.5	1.8

Source: UNCTAD (1998), based on annex table B.3.

Table 3

**FDI INFLOWS TO 20 MAIN DESTINATIONS AMONG DEVELOPING AND TRANSITION
ECONOMIES, BY COUNTRY (1996)**

	FDI inflows		
	($ million)	*As percentage of*	
Country/Economy		*FDI inflows to all developing countries*	*World inflows of FDI*
China	40 800	31.4	12.0
Brazil	11 112	8.5	3.3
Singapore	9 440	7.3	2.8
Mexico	8 169	6.3	2.4
Indonesia	6 194	4.8	1.8
Argentina	5 090	3.9	1.5
Malaysia	4 672	3.6	1.4
Poland	4 498	3.4	1.3
Chile	4 092	3.1	1.2
Peru	3 581	2.7	1.1
Colombia	3 322	2.5	1.0
Hong Kong (China)	2 500	1.9	0.7
Russian Federation	2 452	1.9	0.7
India	2 382	1.8	0.7
Republic of Korea	2 325	1.8	0.7
Thailand	2 268	1.8	0.6
Viet Nam	2 156	1.7	0.6
Bermuda	2 100	1.6	0.6
Hungary	1 982	1.5	0.6
Venezuela	1 833	1.4	0.5

Source: UNCTAD (1998), based on annex table B.1.

almost entirely to IFDI to China. In 1996, China accounted for 31.4 per cent of IFDI that flowed to developing countries. China seems to be a popular host of FDI because of both its low labour costs and it enormous domestic market (Feenstra, 1998a). But the skewed distribution of investment among developing countries extends beyond China. The top 10 developing country recipients of IFDI – China, Brazil, Singapore, Mexico, Indonesia, Argentina, Malaysia, Poland, Chile and Peru – accounted for 75 per cent of total IFDI to developing countries (see table 3). This degree of concentration has been largely unchanged for the past 10 years. There has been a shift in the sectoral composition of developing country IFDI, with investment in services now growing more rapidly than investment in manufacturing, which in turn had been growing more rapidly than investment in natural resource development. Two other recent developments are important for developing countries. One has been the shift in Japan's outward FDI orientation: Japanese expansion into the United States market in the late 1980s has been replaced in the 1990s by rapid outward FDI in East and South East Asia.[8] Another dimension of the recent increase in IFDI to developing countries is its highly cyclical nature (World Bank, 1997). Whether these movements in FDI lag or lead movements in GDP is an issue we shall return to below.[9]

III. Market integration and international production

The globalization of production is typically illustrated with reference to the dramatic increase in world trade relative to world GDP. The oft-cited reasons for this increase are, most importantly, the dramatic reduction in the cost of international transportation and communication, the technological revolution in telecommunications and the continued liberalization of international trade, manifested in the many regional agreements and the completion of the Uruguay Round of the GATT.

But a strict focus on the ratio of trade to GDP veils an important underlying change in the structure of trade that has occurred over this period. Most of the global increase in trade has been in intermediate goods, such as automotive components, machinery parts, and legal and financial services. Much of the global integration of production has been within firms. Intra-firm trade now represents 30–50 per cent of the trade volume of the major industrialized countries. Table 4 provides intra-firm trade data for the United States, Japan and Sweden. Subcontracting and inter-firm alliances typically involve arm's-length transactions, and so the intra-firm trade figures understate the degree of increase in the global integration of production.[10] Table 5 gives data on

Table 4

CROSS-BORDER INTRA-FIRM TRADE: UNITED STATES, JAPAN AND SWEDEN, SELECTED YEARS

(Per cent shares in total exports and total imports)

	1977	1982	1983	1989	1992	1993
United States						
Exports	36.0	33.0	34.2	36.0	37.2	36.0
Imports	40.0	37.0	36.8	42.8	42.5	43.0
Japan						
Exports	n.a.	n.a.	22.5	24.5	26.9	25.0
Imports	n.a.	n.a.	15.1	15.3	14.8	14.0
Sweden			1986		1994	
Exports			38.0		38.0	
Imports			3.0		9.0	

Source: UNCTC (1988), UNCTAD (1994, 1996).

Table 5

RATIO OF IMPORTED TO DOMESTIC INPUTS, SELECTED COUNTRIES

(Per cent)

Country	Early 1970s	Mid/Late 1970s	Mid-1980s
Canada	34	37	37
France	21	25	38
Germany	n.a.	21	34
Japan	5	6	7
United Kingdom	26	32	37
United States	7	8	13

Source: Levy (1993), as reported in UNCTAD (1994).

imported input use for France, Germany, Canada, Japan, the United Kingdom and the United States. For almost all industrialized countries (Japan being an important exception) there has been a marked increase in the share of imported to total intermediate inputs used in production. In the United States, for example, the share of imported inputs in total input purchases almost doubled between the early 1970s and the late 1980s.

These trends in foreign outsourcing reflect the increasing ability of firms to profitably break up the production process and locate different parts of it in different countries. Thus there has been a dramatic increase in the ratio of merchandise trade to *value added in industry* (as opposed to GDP) among OECD countries, compared to 1960 and even to 1913 – the end of the last great wave of globalization. As shown in table 6, the increase in trade as a share of value added was considerably more rapid than trade as a share of GDP for five industrialized countries between 1970 and 1990.

A. The globalization of production

The classic examples of the global integration of production are Ford's "world car", with components produced in over 14 countries, and assembly carried out in another three or four locations, or Nike's shoe production, in which the American company employs 50 times more workers in Asia than it does in the United States.[11] But the phenomenon has now spread to many manufacturing and even serv-

Table 6

RATIO OF MERCHANDISE TRADE TO GDP AND INDUSTRY VALUE ADDED

(Per cent)

Country	Ratio of merchandise trade to GDP				Ratio of merchandise trade to industry value added			
	1913	*1970*	*1980*	*1990*	*1913*	*1970*	*1980*	*1990*
France	15.5	11.9	16.7	17.1	23.3	25.7	44.0	53.5
Germany	19.9	16.5	21.6	24.0	29.2	31.3	48.5	57.8
Japan	12.5	8.3	11.8	8.4	23.9	15.7	25.8	18.9
United Kingdom	29.8	16.5	20.3	20.6	76.3	40.7	52.6	62.8
Unites States	6.1	4.1	8.8	8.0	13.2	13.7	30.9	35.8

Source: Feenstra (1998a).

ices sectors. Feenstra (1998b, p. 7) describes the example of the Barbie doll:

> The raw materials for the doll (plastic and hair) are obtained from Taiwan and Japan. Assembly used to be done in those countries, as well as the Philippines, but it has now migrated to lower-cost locations in Indonesia, Malaysia, and China. The molds themselves come from the United States, as do additional paints used in decorating the dolls. Other than labor, China supplies only the cotton cloth used for dresses. Of the $2 export value for the dolls when they leave Hong Kong for the United States, about 35 cents covers Chinese labor, 65 cents covers the cost of materials, and the remainder covers transportation and overhead, including profits earned in Hong Kong. The dolls sell for about $10 in the United States, of which Mattel earns at least $1, and the rest covers transportation, marketing, wholesaling and retailing in the U.S. The majority of value-added is therefore from U.S. activity. The dolls sell worldwide at the rate of two dolls every second, and this product alone accounted for $1.4 billion in sales for Mattel in 1995.

This change in the *structure* of world trade resulting from the international integration of production, more than its growth per se, reflects a shift in the relationship between trade and FDI – from substitutes to complements. Trade and FDI are substitutes when production is carried out in a single location and FDI is market-seeking, and especially when host country markets are protected. When production is internationally integrated, FDI should spur trade – both exports and imports – even when FDI is market-seeking, and certainly when it is motivated by efficiency-seeking.

B. Labour markets and integrated production

The international integration of production by transnational corporations (TNCs) has important implications for labour markets in both developed and developing countries. Developed countries have seen this process reduce labour's bargaining power, either directly or through "threat effects" (Rodrik, 1997). Labour markets today might be viewed as "contestable" in the same way as product markets were in the 1980s. Harrison (1994) argues that the emerging system of globally networked production, with its concomitant increase in foreign outsourcing, reaffirms the dualism of labour markets, increases the demand for contingent work, and increases the inequality of wages and benefits. Feenstra (1998b) attributes almost 30 per cent of the increased wage inequality in the United States (between more and less skilled workers) to foreign outsourcing.

The symmetry of economic theory – following the Stolper-Samuelson theorem – would indicate that rising wage inequality in industrialized countries will be matched by falling wage inequality in developing countries. There is now considerable evidence that over the past 10–15 years many developing countries have experienced a similar rise in the relative wage of skilled workers. In Mexico the ratio of average hourly compensation between skilled and unskilled workers rose by over 25 per cent between 1984 and 1990 (Hanson and Harrison, 1995). Robbins (1996) found a similar pattern in Chile, where between 1980 and 1990 wages of university graduates increased by 56.4 per cent over those of graduates. A study of nine economies – Argentina, Chile, Colombia, Costa Rica, Malaysia, Mexico, Philippines, Taiwan Province of China and Uruguay – found that after netting out labour supply changes, trade liberalization was associated with a rising wage differential between skilled and unskilled workers in all cases except for the second liberalization episode in Argentina (1989–1993), when relative wages were stable.[12] Feenstra and Hanson (1997) argue that it is the increase in FDI and foreign outsourcing by developed country TNCs rather than trade liberalization per se that is responsible for this rising wage inequality in developing countries. Using regional data from Mexico, they find that in regions where FDI is concentrated, over half of the rise in the skilled labour wage share that occurred in the 1980s is associated with foreign outsourcing.

The irony is that precisely at the moment when computerization has led to a revolution in the mechanization of production, the ability to outsource has reasserted the importance of the labour component of production costs. Instead of becoming inconsequential as the result of technological change, labour costs are now an important determinant in the production location decision as firms increasingly "slice up the value chain". According to Krugman (1995, pp. 336–337):

> It is often said that labor costs are now such a low share of total costs that low wages cannot be a significant competitive advantage. But when business people say this, they ... mean that because of the growing vertical disintegration of industry the value added by a given manufacturing facility is likely to be only a small fraction of costs, which are denominated by the cost of intermediate inputs. But this vertical disintegration, or slicing up of the value chain, creates a greater, not a smaller opportunity to relocate production to low-wage locations.

C. *"Low-level" versus "high-level" equilibria*

The simultaneous liberalization of markets and international integration of production by firms have a number of implications for developing countries.

First, important activities of TNCs remain concentrated in home countries – most significantly, most of the research and development effort and of course the decision about the allocation of retained earnings.[13] Second, with a network of affiliates, TNCs may shift production locations in response to changes in costs, including changes in exchange rates. In fact, the increase in global exchange rate volatility is sometimes cited as a cause of location diversification of TNCs, since it allows diversification of costs and revenues (Kregel, 1996; Froot and Stein, 1991). Third, with the location of components of the production process determined centrally, countries may get caught in a "low-level equilibrium trap" (Harrison, 1994) – that is, specializing in low-value-added components of the overall process without the ability to move up to higher-value-added areas of production. The "trap" occurs because the low wages are simply not sufficient to offset low and slow-growing productivity. This successful movement up the "value chain" is one way to characterize the industrialization process in East Asia, beginning with Japan.[14] Amsden (1992, pp. 23–24) argues that TNCs alone are unlikely to foster such a process of developing more sophisticated production linkages from a base of low-skill, labour-intensive manufacturing:

> ... most of the evidence suggests that it does not happen automatically, by dint of free-market forces. If labor-intensive export activity starts a "roll", its momentum is maintained by deliberate government policies. This is partly because many investments linked to labor-intensive activity, say, the manufacture of synthetic fibers for spinning, weaving and apparel manufacture, are not profitable initially at market-determined production costs; and partly because the coordination that is required to realize potential linkages is greater than the market mechanism can, or at least does, provide.

IV. Capital formation, liquidity and technology spillovers

In this section we take up the question of the relation of IFDI to domestic capital formation and technological change. During the 1990s the share of IFDI in gross fixed capital formation rose in every major region in the world, and more in developing countries than in developed ones (table 7). Even sub-Saharan African countries, which have had enormous difficulty in attracting foreign capital, saw IFDI as a share of gross fixed capital formation more than double in the 1990s. Central and Eastern European

Table 7

**FDI INFLOWS AS PERCENTAGE OF GROSS FIXED CAPITAL FORMATION,
BY REGION AND ECONOMY, 1986–1996**

Region/Economy	1986–1991 (Annual average)	1992	1993	1994	1995	1996
Developed economies	3.5	2.6	3.0	2.8	3.9	3.6
Western Europe	5.6	5.3	6.1	5.4	7.2	5.9
European Union	5.7	5.5	6.2	5.2	7.3	5.8
Other Western Europe	4.3	2.5	3.9	8.1	6.2	8.2
United States	6.5	2.4	5.1	4.7	5.8	7.0
Developing economies	3.4	4.2	6.1	7.6	7.4	8.7
Africa	3.9	5.2	6.1	9.5	7.9	7.3
Latin America and Caribbean	5.3	7.6	6.4	8.9	9.8	12.8
Southern Europe	0.4	28.4	8.5	11.1	9.3	19.9
Asia	2.8	3.2	6.0	7.0	6.6	7.4
West Asia	0.8	0.6	2.8	1.2	-0.6	0.2
Central Asia	…	…	…	…	…	…
South, East and South-East Asia	3.6	4.5	6.5	7.9	7.5	8.3
Pacific	20.2	38.2	12.6	9.9	47.9	15.6
Central and Eastern Europe	0.1	1.1	7.4	4.7	10.2	7.5
World	3.6	3.3	4.4	4.5	5.6	5.6

Source: UNCTAD (1998), based on annex table B.5.

countries enjoyed an increase in IFDI from almost nothing to levels approaching 10 per cent of gross fixed capital formation – above the world average. And of course the Chinese boom in IFDI reached a level equal to one-quarter of total domestic investment in 1995. But while the growth in IFDI for developing countries in the 1990s was impressive, for most countries IFDI continues to be a significant but small percentage of gross investment, averaging between 6 and 10 per cent of gross fixed capital formation for developing countries as a whole, with Latin America and developing Europe occasionally moving slightly above this range.

Another feature of the rapid growth of FDI to developing countries in the 1990s is the "boom" in international mergers and acquisitions (M&A). Developing country cross-border M&A sales increased more than fivefold between 1990 and 1997, to over $95 billion in sales (table 8). More than 90 per cent of these M&A investments were in South-East Asia and Latin America. In some cases, privatization has accounted for a large share of FDI inflows – upward

of 25 per cent in some Latin American countries. When FDI is through acquisition of existing assets ("brownfield" as opposed to "greenfield" investment), the demand stimulus from IFDI is less than when it is investment in new productive assets. The extent of technology transfer is also more in question if entirely new productive capacity is not put in place, although in instances of privatization of major sectors, such as telecommunications in South Africa, a major infusion of new technology is typically part of the condition for the sale.

A. Hedging FDI

The increasing importance of M&A sales in capital flows to developing countries represents a blurring in the distinction between portfolio and direct investment. It was emphasized above how this feature of foreign capital inflow is a clear caveat to the view that FDI is preferable to portfolio flows because the former is strictly investment in new pro-

Table 8

CROSS-BORDER M&A SALES, BY REGION/ECONOMY OF SELLER, 1990–1997

($ million)

Region/Economy	1990	1991	1992	1993	1994	1995	1996	1997
Developed economies	132 762	71 439	83 712	97 832	129 123	168 420	186 411	233 768
Western Europe	65 688	39 753	59 248	52 420	60 932	76 295	81 822	138 313
European Union	60 320	38 678	56 906	51 740	58 368	74 812	76 772	133 621
Other Western Europe	5 368	1 075	2 341	680	2 564	1 483	5 050	4 692
United States	54 297	23 815	13 938	34 727	56 372	62 903	70 921	65 151
Developing economies	18 177	10 659	32 174	48 670	60 983	52 746	83 396	95 620
Africa	254	129	422	1 446	2 014	2 475	2 784	2 117
Latin America and Caribbean	8 426	3 898	10 372	13 659	14 831	11 374	22 257	43 809
Southern Europe	108	158	127	1	69	227	...	1 144
Asia	9 386	6 437	21 235	33 542	44 011	38 610	55 538	48 377
West Asia	208	198	4 251	1 289	1 395	2 400	5 528	4 870
Central Asia	...	40	45	1 547	685	859	7 051	5 865
South, East and South-East Asia	9 718	6 198	16 939	30 707	41 932	35 352	42 959	37 643
Pacific	3	37	18	22	58	60	2 817	173
Central and Eastern Europe	8 355	3 038	6 008	15 843	4 904	16 018	4 147	9 883
World	159 959	85 279	121 894	162 344	196 367	237 184	274 611	341 653

Source: UNCTAD (1998), based on annex table B.7.

ductive capacity and the latter merely a "paper" investment. But the blurring of the distinction also relates to the degree of liquidity of the investment. Again, FDI is viewed as more stable because the stock of FDI is considered fixed, i.e. less liquid than a portfolio flow. For a parent TNC, FDI represents two forms of risk: the usual risk associated with any capital investment, and a foreign exchange risk. But to the extent that foreign investors have access to international capital markets, they may seek to hedge this risk by building up domestic liabilities. This "export of capital" to match the FDI "can generate rapid capital outflows" (Claessens et al., 1993, cited in Kregel, 1996). According to Kregel (1996, p. 57), this covering of risk "will produce cross-border flows that put pressure on the foreign exchange market or the domestic money market, which may reinforce other destabilizing elements". This link to the financial market calls into question the view of FDI as inherently more stable than other forms of capital flows. Most of the volatility related to IFDI will not be reflected in the statistics on FDI, and it is difficult to measure the volume of cross-border financial flow generated by these activities of non-financial TNCs.[15]

Another implication of this blurring between direct and portfolio foreign investment is that host country effects of FDI are increasingly a function of the regulations on international financial capital and on the regulation of trade in financial services. Thus, the considerations regarding the need for caution about financial market liberalization are also relevant for FDI, partly by analogy, partly because there is a direct linkage, through the rise in the degree of liquidity of IFDI and the effect of higher world interest rates on developing country IFDI. The high, hurdle rate of return required in order to attract FDI to developing countries is raised even higher as a result of the higher real rates of interest that have accompanied international financial market deregulation.[16]

B. *Technological spillovers*

Quite apart from its contribution to the inherent capital shortage faced by developing countries, IFDI is increasingly supported for its "technological spillovers", including the transfer of technology, the development of managerial and marketing skills and the training of labour. Sometimes included under the rubric of technology spillover is the positive impact of IFDI on domestic competition. According to the OECD (1998, p. 10), "foreign investment … is a major source of technology transfer and managerial skills in host developing countries". The term "spillovers" implies that the beneficial effects of IFDI are contagious in host countries, both within and across industries. One problem in assessing these benefits is that they are difficult to measure, and when case studies have been done, the results have been mixed. One study shows that Venezuelan manufacturing benefited from IFDI in its marketing and after-sales service, but because of a high dependence on imported inputs failed to generated positive spillovers in backward linkages (Aitken and Harrison, 1991). A study of Indonesia found that domestically owned firms located in geographical proximity to TNCs benefited in terms of technology and productivity, but not firms located at a greater distance (reported in WTO, 1998). A study of Japanese outward investment in the electronics sector found that Japanese parent firms "continue to control the core technologies" (Ostry and Harianto, 1995, p. 11). According to Rodrik (1999, p. 37), "the hard evidence is sobering. Systematic studies from countries such as Morocco and Venezuela find little in the way of positive spillovers". Regarding a World Bank example of spillovers provided by the United States firm Singer in Taiwan Province of China, Rodrik comments that "upon closer reading, the spillovers in question turn out to be conventional input-output linkages and labour training. No evidence is presented for the presence of non-pecuniary externalities" (Rodrik, 1999, p. 41).

However, there is some agreement that the ability to capture technological spillovers is a function of absorptive capacity, i.e. infrastructure and education. Thus there is very little evidence of positive spillovers in the least developed economies, but among those higher-income developing economies that have hosted considerable IFDI, such as Mexico, Hong Kong (China), the Philippines and the Czech Republic, some evidence of labour market and technology spillovers has been identified (Blomstrom et al., 1994).[17]

V. Balance-of-payments considerations

The balance-of-payments effects of IFDI have been the subject of heated debate for decades. The relatively large body of empirical research into the effect of IFDI on host developing countries' balance of payments is inconclusive. Moreover, the analysis of the balance-of-payments effects of IFDI is not fruitful unless it considers also the counterfactual of its absence (Helleiner, 1989). Many studies rely on multiple regression analysis, which captures the statistical correlation among variables such as IFDI and net exports, but which is unable to provide evidence of a *causal* relation (Hufbauer et al., 1994). Bosworth and Collins (1999) use regression analysis but estimate separate investment and saving equations for 58 developing countries over the period 1978–1995. They find the effects of IFDI to be strong for both investment and saving and thus to be a complete wash with respect to the current account.

A listing of the balance-of-payments entries affected by IFDI may help clarify the issues of direct/indirect and short-run/long-run effects:

Current account

Exports	(+)
Imports	(-)
Foreign income:	
Profits	(-)
Interest	(-)
Dividends	(-)
Royalties	(-)
Management fees	(-)
Unilateral transfers:	
Wages remitted	(-)

Capital account

Long-term private capital	(+)

With respect to this simple accounting framework, the "disintegration of production" may result in FDI having a more negative effect on host developing countries' balance of payments. While the increasing vertical disintegration of production has meant more imports and exports for each unit of domestic production, profit and royalty outflows have only risen. The situation is worse if the growth in import demand for capital goods and other inputs alone swamps the positive effects of import substitution and export growth. Certainly in the short run, the import demand will be important. But of course in the longer run, as the investment begins to pay off, profit repatriation will increase. If the host country currency devalues relative to the currency of the capital exporter, the situation may be even worse because the host country's foreign debt burden effectively rises. For this reason, foreign affiliates of TNCs may in fact have a more deleterious effect on the balance of payments than firms serving the domestic market that also are engaged in exporting (Kregel, 1994, p. 30).

VI. IFDI and growth: cause or effect?

We turn now to the question of whether IFDI promotes economic growth. To answer this question, we first must ask whether IFDI expands or crowds out domestic investment. If it is the latter, any positive growth effects must come through technology spillovers or other externalities. The evidence on IFDI and domestic capital formation is mixed. Fry et al. (1995) find that when IFDI in developing countries is induced by other capital flows it has no measurable effect on domestic investment. When IFDI is statistically "independent", its effect is strong – a dollar of IFDI brings about 64 cents of gross domestic investment. Bosworth and Collins (1999) estimate an IFDI coefficient of about 0.8 on domestic investment for 58 developing countries over the period 1978–1995. Also, they find that IFDI has an almost identical impact on domestic saving, implying that the growth effects of IFDI are negligible. De Mello (1999, p. 147) reports that FDI was positively associated with income and productivity growth in OECD countries, and negatively associated with growth of both income and productivity growth in non-OECD countries. Fry (1996) finds FDI to be positively correlated with economic growth for a small group of Asian countries (Indonesia, Malaysia, Philippines, Republic of Korea, Singapore and Thailand), but not for a much larger group of developing countries. For this larger group, IFDI was found to reduce the rate of economic growth.

In fact, there is more evidence that the direction of causality is reversed – that is, that economic growth leads to IFDI. In econometric studies, this is captured by the use of lagged values of GNP and GNP growth in estimates of IFDI. A study of IFDI by developing region (for data covering 1972–1988), for example, found that the elasticity of IFDI with respect to lagged GNP growth was 1.62 for Asia, 3.09 for Latin America and 1.60 for Africa (UNCTAD, 1993, table III.6). Another study of United States firm location decisions found domestic market expansion and rapid industrial growth to be the most significant determinants, together with infrastructure development and stable international relations (Wheeler and Mody, 1992).

In the one study that found a positive relation between IFDI and developing country growth rates, the variable was statistically significant in the case of the higher-income group of developing countries, but not for the lower-income group of countries. According to the authors, "from this comparison, one might conclude that there is a threshold level of income below which foreign investment has no significant effect" (Blomstrom et al., 1994, p. 251). This result is not inconsistent with our view of the direction of causality: higher-income developing countries presumably are more likely to have the absorptive capacity to both capture technology spillovers and attract market-seeking IFDI. In this case, IFDI can promote the substitution of domestic production for imports (both directly and indirectly through linkages). Thus the direct pursuit of IFDI is a more reasonable part of a development strategy for middle-income countries, but not for poor countries, which simply lack the absorptive capacity required in order to attract IFDI for any reason other than low wages. The low-wage strategy is rarely effective, for both microeconomic and macroeconomic reasons. At the industry level, incentives have not been especially effective in attracting IFDI, often because low wages are offset by low productivity (Wheeler and Mody, 1992). On the macro side, the low-wage strategy limits income growth and thus prospects for future market-seeking IFDI. Moreover, devaluation that is often required in order to keep real wages low also has the effect of raising the cost of imported inputs.[18]

A. Investment, profits and growth

If exports and IFDI cannot be found to generate economic growth, then what does? Most studies find, not surprisingly, that investment, and particularly fixed investment, is the key variable (DeLong and Summers, 1991);[19] that is developing countries that experience a significant and sustained increase in investment are most likely to see a rise in economic growth. Rodrik (1999) defines an "investment transition" as a "sustained increase in the investment/GDP ratio of five percentage points or more" and finds that "investment transitions are associated with significant increases in economic growth" (Rodrik, 1999, pp. 58–59).

Can IFDI itself generate an investment transition? The answer must be that historically it has not played that role. The investment transitions in the Republic of Korea and Taiwan Province of China, for example, took hold with careful subsidy of the domestic profit rate and performance requirements (Akyüz and Gore, 1996). This combination of carrots and sticks was, if anything, anti-IFDI in its original orientation. IFDI may not crowd out domestic investment, but nor does it appear to have any extraordinary properties above those of domestic investment. In this regard, both proponents of an IFDI-led development strategy and its critics agree, especially for low-income countries, that protection or subsidy for foreign TNCs is unwarranted and may backfire since, as a recent WTO study puts it, "economy-wide distortions offset positive spillover effects" (WTO, 1998; Moran, 1998; Julius, 1990; Rodrik, 1999).

VII. Conclusion

The nature of FDI has changed dramatically in the past 10–15 years. For one, the relation between international trade and FDI has shifted from substitute to complement. No longer is "tariff hopping" the main driving force of market-seeking FDI. The latter is now associated with outsourcing, and a heightened ability to "slice up the value chain". This promotes trade (albeit in intermediate goods) instead of substituting for it. Second, with the development of financial markets and their liberalization, FDI can easily be hedged, making it more similar to portfolio capital flows than ever before and thus having the same potential for instability as those flows. Third, an increasing number of countries, especially developing countries, are competing for IFDI, contributing to a downward harmonization of standards for labour and capital.[20] Given these changes in the nature of FDI, in particular the close links between the latter and both trade and finance, any discussion of trade policy reform and financial market reform must also consider the international regulation of FDI.

As with many aspects of globalization, the new IFDI is not "good" or "bad" for developing countries in an a priori sense. Its effects vary over time, country and industry. IFDI should be understood as a source of capital, technology and market access that must be managed in order to be most effective. While domestic protection for TNC affiliates will promote anti-competitive outcomes, at the same time competition to attract TNCs by offering tax concessions and lax labour standards promote a "low-level equilibrium trap". Such competition has not promoted economic development, but has helped to raise the share of income going to profits in the major industrialized countries (UNCTAD, 1997, pp. 96–97).

Policy makers must realize that the attraction of IFDI is not an end in itself. If sustainable economic growth is the goal, attracting IFDI should not be the centerpiece of most countries' development strategies. According to Rodrik (1999, p. 147):

> Gearing economic policy toward performance in the external sectors of the economy, at the expense of other objectives, amounts to mixing up the ends and the means of economic policy. Furthermore, there is nothing more conducive to trade and DFI than strong economic growth itself. Foreign investors care little about Botswana's huge public sector, and neither are they much deterred by Chinese-style socialism. Policies that are successful in igniting growth are also likely to pay off in terms of "international competitiveness".

Rodrik's remarks are supported by many of the claims made in this paper. First, IFDI has rarely been the driving force for growth; instead, it has lagged, following in the path of stable growth. Second, relative to the domestic investment needs of most developing countries, the pool of available FDI is relatively small. Third, the suppression of labour and environmental standards as a means of attracting foreign capital is often ineffective. Fourth, capturing the potential positive technological spillovers from IFDI requires the attainment of a certain level of absorptive capacity, reflected in infrastructure and human capital. Finally, since there is the possibility of creating additional global excess capacity in the light of weak conditions of effective demand in the world economy, IFDI should not be the centerpiece of any country's development strategy. According to Amsden (1992), policy makers are not the only ones who have blindly promoted the IFDI-led development strategy. Economic theorists have been equally guilty:

> Neo-dependency, flying geese, and product life cycle theories of economic restructuring regard Third World development as a response to investment relocation decisions of the multinationals, but given the insignificance of such investments in the total capital formation of even the most gracious host countries, and given the tendency for such investments to lag rather than lead rapid increases in GNP, this way of viewing industrial development is wagging the dog by the tail (p. 23).

At a time when the great explosion of international portfolio capital flows may finally be coming under control, it is important for both economists and policy makers to think more broadly about how to best manage the globalization of both finance *and* production so that they serve the goal of economic development.

Notes

1 Speeches by British Prime Minister Tony Blair and French Prime Minister Lionel Jospin in the spring of 1998 were highly critical of the current climate of capital market liberalization. For an overview, see Wade and Venerosa (1999).

2 According to Rodrik (1999, p. 37): "The attitude of many developing-country policy makers toward DFI has undergone a remarkable turnaround in the last couple of decades, even more so than in the case of exports. Multinational enterprises used to be seen as the emblem of dependency; they have now become the saviors of development".

3 For example, the title of the OECD study cited above is: *Open Markets Matter: The Benefits of Trade and Investment Liberalisation* (OECD, 1998).

4 This paper deals strictly with inward FDI and leaves aside the issue of outward FDI from developing countries, a topic of obvious growing importance.

5 For an overview of globalization, see Milberg (1998).

6 Jones (1980, p. 258) writes: "Once trade theorists pay proper attention to the significance of these internationally mobile productive factors, the doctrine of comparative advantage must find room as well for the doctrine of 'relative attractiveness' where it is not necessarily the technical requirements of one industry versus another that loom important, it is the overall appraisal of one country versus another as a safe, comfortable, and rewarding location for residence of footloose factors". This view is consistent with Dunning's well-known "eclectic paradigm" (Dunning, 1994).

7 See Milberg (1997) for more on this point.

8 For a discussion of the implications for Japan, see Akyüz (1998).

9 The annex table provides data on the value (in US dollars) of the inward FDI stock for almost all developing countries.

10 Survey results for Mexico in the 1980s showed that 70 per cent of subcontracting was directly or indirectly linked to activities of transnational corporations (Beneria and Roldan, 1987). On the issue of inter-firm alliances, see Cowhey and Aronson (1993).

11 Many of the Asian workers are hired through subcontracting and thus not officially by Nike. See Dicken (1992) for further discussion of these cases.

12 Robbins (1996). Note that this period in Argentina was also the only case in the study in which trade liberalization reduced trade openness (as measured by exports plus imports as a share of GDP). This was largely due to an overvalued exchange rate that dampened exports. Moreover, even this result is overturned when we consider a longer time period: between 1986 and 1994 there was an increase in the return on investment in college education and a decline in the return on investment in less-than-college education. See Pessino (1995) and Amadeo (1995).

13 Moreover, there may be a considerable difference in the management, research and development, and financial strategies of companies of different parent countries (Doremus et al., 1998).

14 See Lee (1995) for an empirical study of the Republic of Korea's success in this regard.

15 A recent study found that between 1992 and 1997 FDI was usually less volatile than portfolio flows, although not in every case, some important exceptions being those of Brazil, Chile and the Republic of Korea. See UNCTAD (1998, p. 15).

16 To the extent that TNCs act as "megacorps" (Eichner, 1976), using FDI to generate future investment funds internally rather than borrow externally, higher interest rates in financial markets would be expected to increase FDI, but not necessarily a reinvestment of profits in host countries.

17 Other spillovers, on wages and export market access, have also been found to be sensitive to absorptive capacity. Aitken, Hanson, and Harrison (1994) found that export market access spilled over to other TNCs in Mexico, but not more generally. And Aitken, Harrison and Lipsey (1995) found that higher wages in United States, Mexican and Venezuelan TNCs spilled outside TNCs only in the case of the United States.

18 This point is developed further in Amsden (1992).

19 Blomstrom et al. (1996) provide evidence that the causality is in fact reversed and that investment is "caused" by prior output growth. Rodrik (1999, p. 65), however, argues that increased profitability will initially spur output and only later investment, thus supporting the view that over time investment drives output.

20 For a review of the evidence, see Milberg and Elmslie (1997). For a discussion of North America, see Crotty et al. (1997).

References

AITKEN, B., G. HANSON, and A. HARRISON (1994), "Spillovers, foreign investment and export behavior", Working Paper No. 4967 (Cambridge, MA: National Bureau of Economic Research), December.

AITKEN, B., and A. HARRISON (1991), "Are there spillovers from foreign direct investment? Evidence from panel data from Venzuela", mimeo (Washington, DC: World Bank).

AITKEN, B., A. HARRISON, and R. LIPSEY (1995), "Wages and foreign ownership: A comparative study of Mexico, Venezuela and the United States", Working Paper No. 5516 (Cambridge, MA: National Bureau of Economic Research).

AKYÜZ, Y. (1998), "New trends in Japanese trade and FDI: Post industrial transformation and policy challenges", in R. Kozul-Wright and R. Rowthorn (eds.), *Transnational Corporations and the Global Economy* (London: Macmillan).

AKYÜZ, Y., and C. GORE (1996), "The investment-profit nexus in East Asian industrialization", *World Development*, Vol. 24, No. 3.

AMADEO, E. (1998), "International trade, outsourcing and labour: A view from the developing countries", in R. Kozul-Wright and R. Rowthorn (eds.), *Transnational Corporations and the Global Economy* (London: Macmillan).

AMSDEN, A. (1992), "A descriptive theory of government intervention in late industrialization", mimeo (New York: New School for Social Research). Published in L. Putterman and D. Rueschemeyer (eds), *The State and the Market in Development* (Boulder, CO: Lynn Reinner).

BENERIA, L., and M. ROLDAN (1987), *The Crossroads of Class and Gender* (Chicago: University of Chicago Press).

BHAGWATI, J. (1998), "The capital myth", *Foreign Affairs*, Vol. 77, No. 3, May–June.

BLOMSTROM, M., R. LIPSEY, and M. ZEJAN (1994), "What explains the growth of developing countries?", in W. Baumol et al. (eds.), *Convergence of Productivity, Cross-National Studies and Historical Evidence* (New York: Oxford University Press).

BLOMSTROM, M., R. LIPSEY, and M. ZEJAN (1996), "Is fixed investment the key to economic growth?", *Quarterly Journal of Economics*, Vol. 111, February, pp. 269–276.

BOSWORTH, B., and S. COLLINS (1999), "Capital flows to developing countries: Implications for saving and investment" (Washington, DC: The Brookings Institution).

BRAINARD, S. (1993), "An empirical assessment of the factor proportions explanation of multinational sales", Working Paper No. 4583 (Cambridge, MA: National Bureau of Economic Research).

BRITTAN, L. (1995), "Investment liberalization: The next great boost to the world economy", *Transnational Corporations*, Vol. 4, No. 1.

CLAESSENS, S. et al. (1993), World Bank Discussion Paper No. 228 (Washington, DC: The World Bank).

COWHEY, P., and J. ARONSON (1993), *Managing the World Economy: The Consequences of Corporate Alliances* (New York: Council on Foreign Relations Press).

CROTTY, J., G. EPSTEIN and P. KELLY (1997), "Multinational corporations, capital mobility and the global neoliberal regime: Effects on northern workers and on growth prospects in the developing world", *Seoul Journal of Economics*, Vol. 10, No. 4, winter, pp. 297–340.

DELONG, B., and L. SUMMERS (1991), "Equipment investment and economic growth", *Quarterly Journal of Economics*, Vol. 106.

DE MELLO, L. (1999), "Foreign direct investment-led growth: Evidence from time series and panel data," *Oxford Economic Papers*, Vol. 51, pp. 133–151.

DICKEN, P. (1992), *Global Shift* (New York: Guilden Press).

DOREMUS, P. et al. (1998), *The Myth of the Global Corporation* (Princeton, NJ: Princeton University Press).

DUNNING, J. (1994), Re-evaluating the benefits of foreign direct investment", *Transnational Corporations*, Vol. 3, No. 1, February, pp. 23–52.

EICHNER, A. (1976), *The Megacorp and Oligopoly* (Cambridge, MA: Cambridge University Press).

FEENSTRA, R. (1998a), "Facts and fallacies about foreign direct investment", mimeo (University of California-Davis), February.

FEENSTRA, R. (1998b), "Integration of trade and disintegration of production in the global economy", *Journal of Economic Perspectives*, autumn.

FEENSTRA, R., and G. HANSON, (1997), "Foreign direct investment and relative wages: Evidence from Mexico's maquiladoras", *Journal of International Economics*, Vol. 42, No. 3/4), May, pp. 371–339.

FROOT, K., and J. STEIN (1991), "Exchange rates and foreign direct investment: An imperfect capital markets approach", *Quarterly Journal of Economics*.

FRY, M. (1996), "How foreign direct investment in Pacific Asia improves the current account", *Birmingham Journal of Asian Economics*, Vol. 7, No. 3.

FRY, M., S. CLAESSENS, P. BURRIDGE, and M. BLANCHET (1995), "Foreign direct investment, other capital flows and current account deficits: What causes what?", Policy Research Working Paper No. 1527 (Washington, DC: The World Bank), October.

HANSON, G., and A. HARRISON (1995), "Trade, technology, wage inequality", Working Paper No. 5110 (Cambridge, MA: National Bureau of Economic Research).

HARRISON, B. (1994), *Lean and Mean: The Changing Landscape of Corporate Power in the Age of Flexibility* (New York: Basic Books).

HELLEINER, G. (1989), "Transnational corporations and direct foreign investment", in H. Chenery and T. Srinivasan (eds.), *Handbook of Development Economics*, Vol. II (Amsterdam: Elsevier Science Publishers).

HUFBAUER, G., D. LAKDAWALLA, and A. MALANI (1994), "Determinants of direct foreign investment and its connection to trade", *UNCTAD Review 1994*, United Nations publication, sales no. E.94.II.D.19 (New York and Geneva).

JONES, R. (1980), "Comparative and Absolute Advantage", *Schweizerische Zeitschrift für Volkswirtschaft und Statistik*, September, pp. 235–260.

JULIUS, D. (1990), *Global Companies and Public Policy* (New York: Council on Foreign Relations for the Royal Institute of International Affairs).

KOZUL-WRIGHT, R., and R. ROWTHORN (eds.) (1998), *Transnational Corporations and the Global Economy* (London: Macmillan).

KREGEL, J. (1994), "Capital flows: Globalization of production and financing development", *UNCTAD Review 1994*, United Nations publication, sales no. E.94.II.D.19 (New York and Geneva).

KREGEL, J. (1996), "Some risks and implications of financial globalization for national policy autonomy", *UNCTAD Review 1996*, United Nations publication, sales no. E.97.II.D.2 (New York and Geneva).

KRUGMAN, P. (1995), "Growth of World Trade: Causes and Consequences", Brookings Papers on Economic Activity (Washington, DC: Brookings Institution).

KRUGMAN, P. (1998), "Saving Asia: the IMF cure has failed. It's time to get radical", *Fortune Magazine*, 7 September.

LEE, J. (1995), "Comparative advantage in manufacturing as a determinant of industrialization: The Korean case", *World Development*, Vol. 23, No. 7.

LEVY, D. (1993), "International production and sourcing: Trends and issues", *Science Technology and Industry Review*, Vol. 13, No. 1, pp. 13–59.

MILBERG, W. (1997), "Globalization and international competitiveness", in P. Davidson and J. Kregel (eds.), *Improving the Global Economy* (Cheltenham, U.K.: Edward Elgar).

MILBERG, W. (1998), "Globalization and its limits", in R. Kozul-Wright and R. Rowthorn (eds.), *Transnational Corporations and the Global Economy* (London: Macmillan).

MILBERG, W., and B. ELMSLIE (1997), "Harder than you think: Free trade and international labor standards", *New Labor Forum*, Vol. 1, No. 1, autumn.

MORAN, T. (1998), *Foreign Direct Investment and Development* (Washington, DC: Institute for International Economics).

OECD (1998), *Open Markets Matter: The Benefits of Trade and Investment Liberalization* (Paris: OECD).

OSTRY, S., and F. HARIANTO (1995), "The changing pattern of Japanese foreign direct investment in the electronics industry in East Asia, *Transnational Corporations*, Vol. 4, No. 1, April, pp. 11–43.

PESSINO, C. (1995), "The labour market during the transition in Argentina", mimeo (Buenos Aires: CEMA).

ROBBINS, D. (1996), "Evidence on trade and wages in the developing world", OECD Development Center Technical Paper No. 119, December.

RODRIK, D. (1997), *Has Globalization Gone Too Far?* (Washington, DC: Institute for International Economics).

RODRIK, D. (1999), *The New Global Economy and Developing Countries: Making Openness Work*, Policy Essay No. 24 (Washington, DC: Overseas Development Council).

ROWTHORN, R., and R. KOZUL-WRIGHT (1998), "Globalization and economic convergence: An assessment", UNCTAD Discussion Paper No. 131 (Geneva: UNCTAD); also in R. Kozul-Wright and R. Rowthorn (eds.), *Transnational Corporations and the Global Economy* (London: Macmillan).

UNCTAD (1993), *Explaining and Forecasting Regional Flows of Foreign Direct Investment* (New York: United Nations).

UNCTAD (1994), *World Investment Report 1994,* United Nations publication, sales no. E.94.II.A.14 (New York and Geneva).

UNCTAD (1996), *World Investment Report 1996*, United Nations publication, sales no. E.96.II.A.14 (New York and Geneva).

UNCTAD (1997), *Trade and Development Report 1997*, United Nations publication, sales no. E.97.II.D.8 (New York and Geneva).

UNCTAD (1998), *World Investment Report 1998*, United Nations publication, sales no. E.98.II.D.5 (New York and Geneva).

UNCTC (1988), *World Investment Report* (New York: United Nations Centre on Transnational Corporations).

WADE, R., and F. VENEROSA (1999), "The gathering world slump and the battle over capital controls", *New Left Review.*

WHEELER, D., and A. MODY (1992), "International investment location decisions: The case of U.S. firms", *Journal of International Economics*, Vol. 33.

WORLD BANK (1997), Global Economic Prospects (Washington, DC).

WTO (1998), "The effects of foreign direct investment on development", Job No. 5229, 30 September (Geneva: World Trade Organization).

STOCK OF INWARD FDI OF DEVELOPING COUNTRIES, 1996

($ million)

Economy	FDI	Economy	FDI
China	172 041	Bolivia	2 063
Brazil	109 951	Slovenia	2 028
Mexico	74 735	Panama	1 729
Singapore	68 062	Uruguay	1 723
Indonesia	56 797	Cyprus	1 713
Malaysia	41 450	Jamaica	1 502
Saudi Arabia	40 035	Namibia	1 492
Argentina	30 414	Botswana	1 442
Bermuda	26 805	United Arab Emirates	1 442
Hong Kong (China)	24 269	Ukraine	1 431
Chile	19 639	Sri Lanka	1 389
Thailand	19 504	Algeria	1 383
Taiwan Province of China	17 600	Liberia	1 377
Nigeria	16 578	Paraguay	1 321
Egypt	14 734	Malta	1 274
Hungary	14 690	Romania	1 243
Republic of Korea	12 491	Syrian Arab Republic	1 119
Poland	11 463	Slovakia	1 109
Colombia	9 305	Cameroon	1 097
Peru	9 058	Myanmar	1 037
Venezuela	8 808	Gabon	1 019
Philippines	8 678	Zambia	996
India	7 948	Croatia	988
Czech Republic	7 061	Ghana	943
Russian Federation	6 468	Côte d'Ivoire	916
Viet Nam	6 252	Azerbaijan	898
Turkey	5 825	Kyrgyzstan	890
Pakistan	5 340	Estonia	886
Tunisia	4 255	Cambodia	849
Trinidad and Tobago	3 954	Congo	742
Ecuador	3 625	Fiji	737
Morocco	3 301	Kenya	702
Costa Rica	3 201	Latvia	679
Angola	2 989	Honduras	657
Cayman Islands	2 642	Lithuania	647
Papua New Guinea	2 564	Jordan	642
Kazakhstan	2 513	Democratic People's Republic of Korea	634
Oman	2 288	Bahrain	606
Dominican Republic	2 279	Bahamas	580
Guatemala	2 267	Saint Lucia	533
Yemen	2 139	Antigua and Barbuda	456

/...

Annex table (continued)

STOCK OF INWARD FDI OF DEVELOPING COUNTRIES, 1996

($ million)

Economy	FDI	Economy	FDI
Guyana	447	Republic of Moldova	137
Bulgaria	446	Kuwait	126
United Republic of Tanzania	444	New Caledonia	120
Senegal	434	Georgia	117
Zimbabwe	420	Gambia	92
Swaziland	407	Mauritania	91
Uganda	393	Mali	90
Lao People's Democratic Republic	373	Central African Republic	81
Nicaragua	355	Brunei Darussalam	71
Chad	335	Maldives	68
Seychelles	334	Burkina Faso	61
Netherlands Antilles	332	Belarus	57
Niger	318	Cuba	57
El Salvador	318	Armenia	55
Uzbekistan	310	Benin	53
Turkmenistan	308	Nepal	49
Democratic Republic of the Congo	293	The former Yugoslav	
Albania	291	Republic of Macedonia	44
Mauritius	285	Tajikistan	41
Malawi	284	Burundi	34
Vanuatu	277	Mongolia	31
Qatar	274	Iran (Islamic Republic of)	31
Togo	272	Cape Verde	30
Aruba	266	Samoa	26
Saint Kitts and Nevis	260	Macau	22
Barbados	238	Comoros	19
Mozambique	231	Djibouti	18
Rwanda	229	Guinea-Bissau	15
Bangladesh	226	Afghanistan	12
Dominica	210	Tonga	8
Saint Vincent and the Grenadines	199	Sudan	7
Lebanon	187	Kiribati	3
Grenada	186	Libyan Arab Jamahiriya	...
Madagascar	179	Sierra Leone	...
Lesotho	178	Somalia	...
Belize	168	Suriname	...
Solomon Islands	161	Virgin Islands	...
Guinea	156	Bosnia and Herzegovina	...
Haiti	146	Yugoslavia	...
Ethiopia	138	Iraq	...

Source: UNCTAD (1998), chapter I.

COUNTRY OWNERSHIP AND DEVELOPMENT COOPERATION: ISSUES AND THE WAY FORWARD

Kwesi Botchwey

Abstract

There is a general consensus among the key actors in development cooperation that national ownership is the most critical condition for successful policy reform and project implementation. The debate on national ownership has recently witnessed a revival against the background of declining flows of official development assistance and the recent crises in the global financial markets.

The literature on the subject bristles with references to the difficulty of defining national ownership, and attempts at definition often quickly turn into a listing of determinants of ownership. But the problem lies not so much with definition as with reconciling the need for national ownership with the role of external intervention through aid flows. At its most fundamental level, ownership is a critical dimension of national sovereignty, and implies a country's leadership in setting development objectives and strategies and in controlling the framework of its relations with external partners. It is distinguished by the authorship of the reform process, the scope of national support behind it, the sustainability of the government's commitment and the intensity of the government's initiatives to promote a national consensus.

A number of evaluations and country case studies reveal many hindrances to national ownership. These include the tremendous asymmetry in the balance of power between donors and aid-receiving countries, the culture of domination and paternalism that in various degrees characterizes donor attitudes, the pursuit of domestic interests by donors, and the sheer complexity of donor procedures and administrative structures which makes coordination of donor activities by countries extremely difficult. As regards the recipient countries themselves, the problems include a failure by many countries to mobilize the technical capacity and domestic political support necessary for the exercise of national leadership. This translates into a loss of leverage by developing countries as a group in the ongoing debate about the future of development cooperation.

The responsibility for asserting national ownership rests squarely with the developing countries themselves and with their collective organizations, including the Intergovernmental Group of Twenty-four. Ownership must begin with the elaboration of a framework for a national development strategy. A second vital step is to develop a reasonably strong body of national consensus behind the national vision.

Ownership of national development policies has become one of the most critical and widely espoused issues in the renewed debate on aid effectiveness and the future of development cooperation. There is general agreement among the key actors – the recipient countries, bilateral donors and the multilateral institutions, particularly the IMF and the World Bank – that ownership is the most decisive condition for successful policy reform and project implementation. This is also the predominant conclusion of academic and other research, much of it based on case studies of country experiences.

Unfortunately, in spite of this general consensus, not much has been achieved. As the recently concluded *External Evaluation of the Enhanced Structural Adjustment Facility* (hereinafter called the *External Evaluation*) noted, "the DAC [Development Assistance Committee] and its members have continued to profess their good intentions, while the recipient countries have, for their part, continued to protest their frustration" (IMF, 1998a, p. 24).

In these circumstances, and against the background of many past shifts in donor sentiment that promised a break with tradition but brought little change, it is tempting to dismiss the talk of ownership as yet another fad in a never-ending, and largely futile, debate. But there is a great deal at stake, especially for the G-24 countries, including even the Group's better-placed members, as recent events in East Asia have shown. The issues raised go to the very heart of the national development process in the developing world. Moreover, the radically changed geopolitical environment in which the aid reform debate is taking place today provides particularly auspicious conditions for making progress. At any rate, it is by no means certain that the failure to swiftly operationalize the consensus on national ownership can be attributed exclusively, or even mainly, to the absence of political will on the part of the providers of official development assistance (ODA).

In these circumstances, it is important to join issues and to thus help to develop a framework for the restoration of country leadership in the formulation and implementation of national development strategies and programmes. This paper aims to contribute to this effort from the perspective of the G-24 group of countries. It is divided into four parts. The first part discusses the context in which the debate on the role of national ownership is taking place, and the dominant forces and factors shaping it. The second part looks at the differing concepts of ownership in the literature and in the official positions and practices of the leading actors, while the third part looks at factors hindering the operationalization of the widely accepted role of national ownership. The last part sets out recommendations for moving matters beyond mere declarations of intent.

I.   The context of the debate

Concerns about national ownership have arisen in the context of a renewed and wide-ranging debate about the role of aid. This larger debate in turn coincides with a sustained fall in net flows of ODA. The numbers are rather confusing and not always comparable, depending as they do, on sources and definitions. But in general, net flows of ODA from the countries that are members of the Development Assistance Committee (DAC), including technical assistance and grants, have fallen to their lowest levels in absolute terms and as a percentage of the aggregate gross national product (GNP) of donors since the target of 0.7 per cent of GNP was set in 1970. Net ODA flows from the DAC countries now hover around 0.25 to 0.3 per cent, compared with the mid-1980s when they equalled 0.35 per cent of average GNP (World Bank, 1998a, p. 50, fig. 1). Moreover, there has been little change in country performance, with the Nordic countries and the Netherlands registering the highest ratios, and the majority of the DAC countries recording declines in their ratios of between 15 and 20 per cent.

The reasons for this sustained decline in ODA levels are much discussed and well known. It is important nevertheless to understand them fully in order to appreciate what space there is for truly making ownership the pivotal factor in development cooperation.

Firstly, there has been a fundamental change in the geopolitical interest mix of the donor countries since the end of the Cold War. Until rather recently, the development needs of the aid-receiving countries did not feature very prominently in the calculations of donors. The most recent cross-country study on aid by Burnside and Dollar (1997–1998) covering a sample of some 41 low-income countries, found that over the period from 1970 to 1993 countries with poor economic policies received as much bilateral aid as those with good policies, i.e. bilateral aid allocations were greatly influenced by donors' political and strategic considerations. The influence of these considerations intensified particularly in the 1970s, when many developed countries, especially the

United States, openly sought to make the granting of aid dependent on the statements and voting record of countries on issues debated in the United Nations and its agencies. The Burnside and Dollar findings coincide with those of many earlier studies: Killick (1991), Krueger et al. (1989), Maizels and Nissanke (1984), and Boone (1996, p. 289 et seq.).

The Burnside and Dollar study also found that in contrast with the record on bilateral aid, allocations of concessional resources and grants by the multilateral institutions went more to countries with good policies, which suggests that political considerations featured less prominently in the lending practices of these bodies. This finding is again corroborated by earlier studies – Maizels and Nissanke (1984) and Trumbull and Wall (1994) – although, even here, it is interesting to note that this is not necessarily true of the late 1960s. Others have suggested that it may be more credible to explain World Bank lending in terms of a mix of considerations, including political factors, than country need and the political environment exclusively (Trumbull and Wall, 1994; Frey and Schneider, 1986).

The influence of these strategic considerations in donor aid allocation decisions has been on the wane in recent times, although their ghosts, now bereft of their Cold War animation, still lurk in the guise of "target countries" and "traditional areas of influence". With the diminished importance of these interests, donors have come to pay greater attention to good policies in aid-receiving countries. Aid coordination groupings such as the Special Programme for Africa (SPA), which determines funding gaps in the countries concerned and provides assessments of their policy environments, enable donors to base their allocation decisions more and more on policies.

The fall in aid flows is also attributable to pressures on national budgets (and therefore also on ODA budgets) in the DAC countries. These pressures, which intensified in the 1980s, generated much anti-aid sentiment, especially in countries where pro-aid sentiment had never been particularly strong in the first place, since cuts in social welfare programmes came to be blamed on charity abroad. In some countries, notably the United States, grossly exaggerated notions of the size of ODA as a percentage of the national budget further soured the public mood. As one *DAC Peer Review of the United States* noted: "the US public does not realize that the United States has by far the lowest level of effort among DAC member countries ... which was 0.12% in 1996" (OECD, 1998a, p. 2). In 1995/96 the United States

contributed \$31 per capita in ODA, compared with \$260 for the four highest-performing DAC members and an average of \$71 for all DAC members.

The growth of anti-aid sentiment was also no doubt fuelled by the triumphal spread of free market ideology in the wake of the spectacular collapse of the Eastern Bloc, which tended to blame the impoverishment of the developing countries on rampant state intervention, and to suggest that the case for ODA was almost entirely vitiated by the ready availability of private capital flows. Although this ultra-liberalism is now slowly giving way to a neo-liberal tendency that recognizes the undue concentration of private capital flows on a few countries, and therefore the need for continuing flows of ODA, a great deal of cynicism still prevails and underscores the importance of the search for new handles for achieving greater aid effectiveness.

The pressure on national budgets in the donor countries is unlikely to ease in the immediate future. In Europe, compliance with the Maastricht target for fiscal deficits will mean continuing fiscal consolidation for most countries, while in Japan the fiscal strains that caused a 10 per cent cut in the aid budget for the fiscal year 1998 are projected to cause further cuts at least through the year 2000.

A third factor driving the renewed focus on national ownership is the widespread disappointment with economic performance in the low-income countries, and the persistence of poverty, particularly in sub-Saharan Africa. Now, in the face of evidence that until relatively recently donors had tended to allocate aid more to advance their strategic interests than to help promote development, a polemical reaction to this talk of "disappointment" might well consist in simply noting that the poor development outcomes were indeed predictable. A less cynical and more appropriate interpretation of the prevailing mood, however, is to see it as signalling a genuine quest for improved outcomes, thanks in part to civil society advocacy in the donor countries.

The ongoing debate on aid effectiveness has been influenced by the foregoing factors. There is a general recognition that the imposition of policies by donor countries and the multilateral institutions which they control as conditions for access to resources usually results in weakened political commitment on the part of political forces and governments in the aid-receiving countries, leading to interruptions in the reform effort and in many cases to the abandonment of the reforms themselves.

The dominant forces shaping the issues and very conduct of the debate on ownership have thus tended to be Bretton Woods institutions and the donors, acting bilaterally as well collectively through the DAC. Although individual ministers and government officials in the recipient countries have been known to complain about the loss of control over their economic development policies,[1] their collective voice has been rather muted in the ongoing discussions. To this day, African countries, for instance, are not represented in the formal meetings of the SPA.

In these circumstances, the definition of concepts and issues, the elaboration of proposals for changes in existing practice, and the very pace of change have been influenced largely by donor-driven initiatives and perspectives.

II. Concepts, determinants and the unfolding practice

Studies on ownership almost invariably begin by noting two seemingly contradictory phenomena, namely a general agreement on the critical importance of ownership to economic reform, side by side with the absence of a rigorous and operationally tangible definition of the concept. Ownership is critical for a number of obvious reasons: it provides the assurance that the country takes responsibility for the implementation and outcome of policies; it ensures that short-term measures are compatible with and do not prejudice long-term development objectives; and, above all, it provides the surest guarantee against policy reversals, thereby ensuring the sustainability of development policies and the benefits they bring. But what it means in practice is by no means as clear-cut. The World Bank's first systematic attempt to define and quantify the determinants of country ownership in its study *Borrower Ownership of Adjustment Programmes and the Political Economy of Reform* (hereinafter called the ownership study) opens with the usual acknowledgement. It notes that "notwithstanding the significance attached to borrower ownership, the notion remains conceptually elusive and insufficiently explored in [the] Bank's policy and practice of adjustment lending" (Johnson and Sulaiman, 1993, p. 2). A paper on ownership sponsored by the Canadian International Development Agency (CIDA) issued about two years after the Bank's study enters the same caveat in almost identical language: "Despite the significance attached to ownership as a factor in the success of development initiatives, neither the concept itself nor its opera-

tional implications are well understood" (Bolger, 1994, p. 1). There is thus very little by way of a systematic definition in the literature, and attempts at definition usually quickly turn into statements of what constitutes empirically verifiable determinants, a task which is no less important but which itself depends on a definition of the concept. The problem clearly does not lie with the peculiar elusiveness of ownership as an etymological category. On the contrary, the persistence of the difficulty attests to the dominance of the donor factor in these discussions. The difficulty lies not so much in defining ownership as such, but in reconciling it with the role of external intervention in the shaping and management of development policy in the aid receiving country. This explains the references in the literature to a "transferring" of ownership to the borrowing country, to "putting the countries in the driver's seat" and to getting the countries to "internalize" negotiated programmes of reform.

At the theoretical and normative level, country ownership is a fundamental aspect of national sovereignty and self-determination. Ownership by a country of its national development policies must imply its leadership in setting objectives and determining strategies and in controlling the framework and management of its relations with external cooperators. In the very nature of things, however, this sovereign right is by no means absolute. It is circumscribed by the workings of the global market for goods and services and by the communications revolution. Moreover, since governments exercise this right on behalf of constituencies on which they depend for their legitimacy and which in the end determine the space for policy reform, national ownership is variable over time and by circumstance. The measurement of the extent or degree of national ownership becomes especially important where difficult policy choices have had to be made in negotiations with external agencies, and when therefore the extent of national support becomes an important indicator of the likelihood of policy sustainability. This explains why there has been so much emphasis in studies by the World Bank and the IMF (and also by donors) on criteria for determining ownership.

The World Bank's ownership study, which was based on a review of performance audit reports and project completion reports on 99 adjustment programmes in 42 countries, proposed a four-dimensional analytical framework, based on the emerging convergence in the literature at the time, each in turn having four sub-categories reflecting degrees of ownership. The four criteria were: (i) the locus of the reform initiative; (ii) the level of intellectual conviction among key policy makers; (iii) expression of political will by the top political leadership; and (iv) efforts towards consensus building among various constituencies (Johnson and Sulaiman, 1993, p. 4). In contrast, the External Evaluation of the Fund's Enhanced Structural Adjustment Facility (ESAF) offered a set of ownership determinants that to some extent overlapped with these, but also added new factors. They included: (i) the authorship of the policy reform programme; (ii) the scope of national support; (iii) the sustainability of the government's commitment; and (iv) the intensity of initiatives by the government to promote a broad national consensus (IMF, 1998a, p. 25).

III. Authorship

In the External Evaluation's analytical framework, authorship refers to the setting of the policy agenda and the initiation of the reform process. It is defined by who sets the agenda and launches the reform path, not who writes the operational programme documents. Consequently, a government lacking the technical capacity to design specific measures or a detailed financial programme, for instance, could engage external experts or even rely on IMF staff to provide this service and still be said to own a programme, if in the end it sets the policy agenda, and negotiates conditions for access to resources which are consistent with its objectives.

IV. Scope of support

This measures the extent of knowledge of and support for the programme within the government as a whole and especially within ministries outside the finance and economics ministries, as well as outside government, particularly amongst groups directly affected by proposed changes in policy, such as manufacturers' associations, chambers of commerce and civil society organizations.

V. Sustainability of government commitment

This indicator tests the consistency with which the government pursues the programme of reform, especially after external resources provided in sup-

port of the programme have been fully disbursed or have ceased. Since the degree of commitment varies over different periods and according to political circumstances, the government's conduct on the eve of democratic elections or in negotiations with trade unions and other labour organizations, for instance, is a reliable gauge of the depth of its commitment and therefore of the chances of the reform effort being sustained.

A number of studies using these definitions, or variants of them, have sought to assess the role of ownership in different policy reform experiences. Those conducted by the World Bank have been aimed principally at establishing the relationship between ownership and successful project or programme implementation (Johnson and Sulaiman, 1993; World Bank, 1990a, 1990b; OECD, 1991). The IMF's latest review of the ESAF, on the other hand, did not seek to establish the relationship between ownership and performance as such. Instead, it sought to examine the factors responsible for the high incidence of interruptions in programme implementation in order to determine whether this could be alleviated by changes in programme design or the frequency of programme monitoring, and in particular whether greater selectivity "would encourage countries to commit themselves more forcefully to appropriate policies". While the approaches and focus of the studies by the two institutions have been different in some respects, they share a common perception of national ownership: it is perceived essentially as the commitment made by the borrowing countries in the context of Bank/Fund programmes. The Bank's borrower ownership study, like earlier reviews, which have pronounced on the issue of ownership, focused directly on ownership of adjustment programmes. Nevertheless, it is interesting also to observe that even within this limited and largely self-serving vision of ownership, the studies have typically established a positive correlation between ownership and programme success (Branson and Jayarajah, 1995).

On the other hand, a number of case studies of donor attitudes to ownership have added different dimensions to the debate on the concept and determinants of ownership and have also highlighted the ambivalence among donors with regard to the very notion of national ownership. A study by CIDA – on Canada's experience with ownership, focusing on the performance of CIDA-supported projects – observes that the Canadian experience demonstrates (i) the significance of different levels of ownership – the national and the local community levels – and (ii) the role of donors in broadening the "ownership base in developing countries" by facilitating the inclusion of stakeholders in project planning and implementation, whom governments, left on their own, would otherwise not include (Bolger, 1994). At the same time, a recent review of the United Republic of Tanzania's relations with donors suggests that many donors tend to see national ownership as meaning the adoption or acceptance by the country of essentially donor-driven initiatives and programmes in practice (see, for example, Helleiner, 1997).

At the level of collective donor assessments, DAC peer reviews of individual country experiences show that although in the wake of the organization's seminal new strategy document, *Shaping the 21ˢᵗ Century: The Contribution of Development Cooperation*, donor countries have begun to adopt formal policy statements heralding a break with the past, acceptance of national ownership remains a major challenge (OECD, 1997).

The IMF's ESAF sets the overall macroeconomic policy framework for bilateral donor aid policies and thus provides a decisive testing ground for country ownership. Accordingly, the findings of the External Evaluation which investigated the record of country ownership in a sampling of countries in sub-Saharan Africa, Asia and Latin America are particularly important. The study concluded that national ownership of IMF-supported programmes was generally weak and that national authorities almost without exception felt they had little control over agenda setting and programme objectives. In addition, it found some correlation between the consistency in programme implementation and high levels national ownership.

VI. Strategic shifts in the aid framework and continuing hindrances to national ownership

The tentativeness and hesitation in the literature regarding the concept and operational determinants of ownership thus reflect the crisis of national ownership, which the country case studies generally illustrate. Among the multilateral institutions and for a majority of donors the emerging consensus is that "partnership" is the most appropriate vehicle for effecting the desired change in donor-recipient country relationships. This shift has taken place in the context of the DAC's call in its development cooperation strategy document (*Shaping the 21ˢᵗ Century*) for an

end to paternalism and the adoption of a partnership model in which "local actors should progressively take the lead while external partners back their efforts to assume greater responsibility for their own development" (DAC, 1996, p. 3). The Swedish framework for a new partnership with Africa sets out a new code of conduct that advocates a radical change in donor attitudes (Government of Sweden, 1998, p. 100).

In the spirit of its new philosophy, the DAC launched in 1997, in consultation with the Government of Mali, a pilot exercise aimed at determining how the principles of partnership aid coordination and local ownership were working in Mali, what improvements could be made and what general lessons could be drawn. The review exercise, which studied evaluation reports and analysed a sample of projects with special innovative features, raised a number of issues which lie at the root of the ownership problem but remain largely unresolved in spite of many attempts at their resolution. The study noted: (a) the fact that Mali had no effective national framework for coordinating aid and for ensuring the consistency of national development strategies; (b) the fact that national development had not always been a major priority with donors; and (c) the sheer multiplicity and complexity of donor administrative structures and procedures and the burden that this places on national capacity. More importantly, it led to the adoption of a number of proposals aimed at enhancing national ownership, including an agreement to waive, on a pilot basis, practices that distorted national procedures and administrative capacity. Prominent among these was the practice among donors of tying procurement to national sources and the insistence on tax exemptions on equipment imports for aid-financed projects (OECD, 1998b, p. 6).

Again, as the Malian exercise and other studies have stressed, the recipient countries themselves must have the political and the technical administrative capacity to take charge. But this will be to no avail if the development cooperation framework does not permit the exercise of leadership. Accordingly, an acknowledgement of the major factors that hinder exercise of national ownership in the existing relations must be the starting point of a solution. They include, in our view the following:

•   The existing framework of donor-country relationships is characterized by tremendous asymmetry in the balance of power. On the one side is the donor wielding the influence that comes not only from the donor's own aid budget but also from its voting power in the multilateral funding agencies. For the G-7 countries this is quite considerable, often giving them leverage in their bilateral relations far beyond what would be reasonably commensurate with the level of their bilateral country aid envelope. On the other side is the recipient country so-called, usually cash-strapped and highly aid-dependent, with all that this means for its fiscal and balance-of-payments situation. The most dramatic demonstration of this preponderant donor leverage is the fact that most donor delegations, regardless of the ranking of their members, would usually insist on and be granted an audience with Ministers or even heads of State.

- Donors still suffer in varying degrees from a culture of domination and paternalism, together with unremitting suspicion and mistrust of the integrity of local procedures and initiatives. In particular, in the area of project management, donor agencies are often compelled by domestic legislative and administrative requirements to adopt accounting procedures that inhibit the exercise of local responsibility. As one study put it: "Most donors still operate on the basis of a 'transaction' accountability – that is, an elaborate system of controlling the inputs and outputs of the aid planning and delivery system to ensure efficiency and effectiveness. One result of this is an inexorable pressure on donors to lower risk and uncertainty by managing (i.e. controlling) as many project initiatives as possible".

- Behind the veil of a generalized affirmation of multilateralism donor, aid practices are still driven to a significant extent by the pursuit of domestic interests – usually contracts and markets for donor country suppliers and consultants – in ways that inhibit the exercise of national ownership either directly by overriding local government policy, or indirectly by discouraging the development and use of national capacity in the recipient country. The pursuit of bilateral donor interests is in turn often carried out directly through tied aid or indirectly through pressure on the local authorities to favour donor suppliers and contractors on pain of reduced future aid flows. In addition to imposing a cost on the recipient country of tied aid in reduced value for money, the World Bank has estimated that tied aid reduces the value of aid by about 25 per cent (World Bank/OECD, 1999, p. 28) – this practice excludes or discourages sub-

contracting to local sources and the use of local expertise. In Africa alone, some $4 billion in aid funds go to support about 100,000 expatriates annually (World Bank, 1998b, p. 24).

In spite of the progress made in recent times in aid coordination, the frequency of donor programming and evaluation missions and the sheer complexity of donor procedures and administrative structures still constitute a significant burden on national capacity, making it difficult for the national authorities to prepare adequately for discussions with visiting donor missions and to coordinate aid-supported programmes. One study has estimated that in the United Republic of Tanzania, for instance, a conservative estimate of 600 projects calls for 2,400 quarterly reports to be submitted to oversight missions in different donor capitals, and over 1,000 consultancy missions to appraise, monitor, coordinate and evaluate project activities. Each mission will in turn request meetings with key ministry officials and produce a report which government must comment on (World Bank/OECD, 1999, p. 28). At a more global level, these constraints make it difficult for the countries to develop and maintain a focus on an endogenous national development framework in their relations with donors even where they have the capacity to do so. Significantly, the Mali review noted that "the complexity of donor procedures and proliferation of aid-driven parallel administrative structures have made national management difficult with negative consequences for the returns to public investment" (OECD, 1998b, p. 4).

The hindrances are not confined to the bilateral donors; they exist at the level of the recipient countries as well. They include:

- There is a failure on the part of many countries to mobilize the technical capacity (or develop it where it does not exist) and the domestic political support necessary for the exercise of national leadership in relations with donors. To be sure, this has to do in part with the distractions and disincentives of aid dependence. But in the final analysis it is the result of the dynamics of the domestic political situation. In many parts of the developing world, a significant number of trained personnel have been exiled by political instability or marginalized from the national development process through the politics of exclusion. At the same time wrong economic policies have badly eroded public sector employment incentives.

• Where domestic political processes are not democratic and participatory, governments are unable to create the necessary political space for national consensus-building. In such circumstances they would more readily succumb to donor dictates in the hope of obtaining resources to prop up parasitic state structures and the privileges that go with them.

• At the collective level, the loss of leverage by the developing countries as a group in the conduct of development cooperation and in the ongoing debate about its redesigning is in many respects the result of the fragmentation of the group's institutional and consultative arrangements.

In the overall relations between developing countries and donors the central problem of ownership is how to operationalize the notion of ownership in such a way as to achieve a balance between the now universally agreed need for national leadership in setting development strategies and implementing them on the one hand, and the legitimate concern of donors regarding accountability for the use of aid resources on the other hand.

There is, however, a third arena – and perhaps in the final analysis the most decisive one – for the determination of the role of national ownership in the system of development cooperation, namely the relations of aid-receiving countries with the Bretton Woods institutions, especially the IMF, to the extent that these relations perform a de facto certification role not only for official development assistance but also for private capital flows. The External Evaluation of the ESAF reported, perhaps predictably, that conditionality constituted the greatest source of tension in IMF/country relations, noting that "The persistent concerns about the loss of ownership come from the feeling that governments are left no choices in negotiations", and that these concerns reflect a general view in the client countries that "the negotiation process tends to be one-sided, and produces agreement mostly through a convergence around [IMF] staff positions" (IMF, 1998a, p. 5 et seq.). These observations sum up the crux of the matter. The problem, as the study correctly noted, is not that *any* conditions for access to IMF and World Bank resources are inherently irreconcilable with national ownership. These resources must after all be revolved and must thus be provided in circumstances that ensure a reasonable prospect of their being repaid. Rather, the problem lies with conditionalities that result from a negotiation process which does not

permit a fair consideration of preferred national choices of a reform path or of a particular sequencing of corrective measures. Indeed, the overwhelming conclusion of most studies on the subject is that such conditionalities seldom succeed in inducing countries to sustain policy reforms. The IMF itself, in a published but unfortunately as yet little known acknowledgement of the problem, has proposed, in line with the recommendations of the external evaluation, that it afford greater flexibility to missions to allow greater scope for a consideration of alternative policy mixes (IMF, 1998b, p. 7).

VII. The emerging consensus and the way forward

After years of discussion involving academic researchers, donor governments and agencies and the multilateral institutions, there appears to be a consensus on the elements of a new development cooperation framework based on *partnership* – a relationship based, in the colourful language of the DAC, on "more ownership and less donorship", or, in a now familiar and rather unfortunate jargon, "putting the countries in the driver's seat" – and *selectivity,* that is the concentration of concessional resources on a select number of countries based on *performance*. A recent policy study by the Overseas Development Council (ODC, 1999) summarizes the distinguishing features of the new framework as follows:

• Country aid allocations would be determined by a differentiation among countries based on policy performance, with countries grouped into (i) performers, (ii) reformers, (iii) post-crisis countries, and (iv) non-performers;

• Aid to poor performers would be limited and would, moreover, be concentrated on poverty alleviation and support for institution building;

• Performance criteria would include macroeconomic policies as well as poverty alleviation and governance policies;

• Each donor would decide on the different weights to be attached to the different performance criteria;

• Performance criteria and the different weights given to them by the different agencies, the classification of countries according to these weights, and the reasons for and analysis on which such classification was based would be made public.

In this scheme of things, the issue of ownership is by and large moot for the countries in the category of performers that would set their own policy framework, public investment programmes and budgets, and receive aid in support of their policies as so defined. The issue is not quite so clear for countries in the next two categories; and the last group of countries receive no aid at all, save for possible humanitarian assistance. Although the World Bank, the regional development banks, notably the African Development Bank, and most donor agencies have begun to adopt their own interpretations of the partnership concept, the neat classification set out above is nowhere near a systematic and uniform interpretation or application. Moreover, it is by no means clear that the problems of national ownership would be resolved by the wholesale adoption of the scheme. Indeed, if the operation of the World Bank's current practice in country assessment is any guide, it is clear that what these latest rumblings portend is a unilateral application of country classification criteria whose logic and analytical details are kept from the general public and the countries themselves! More importantly, a performance-based aid selectivity framework that does not include the role of the IMF is unlikely to succeed, given the primary certification role that both donors and the market accord the institution in matters of macroeconomic policy.

VIII. The way forward

In discussing the importance of ownership in aid relations and the need to establish a new operational framework for its realization, one must recognize the differentiation among the developing countries and the relative importance of the problem to different groups. Two factors underpin this differentiation, namely dependence on aid, and access to private capital flows.

From its peak in the good years from 1984 to 1991 when it exceeded private flows, ODA declined to less than 25 per cent of private flows in 1996 and 1997, despite the East Asian crisis which led to a 25 per cent fall in private flows in 1997 compared with 1996. In spite of this decline in absolute ODA levels and in their relative importance in global capital flows, aid dependence in the low-income groups, especially in sub-Saharan Africa, remains high. The

20 most highly aid-dependent countries with an average GNP per capita of some $350 received (on average) over the period 1993 to 1996 ODA equivalent to 31 per cent of their GNP compared with the 58 countries with the least aid dependence which had an average ODA to GNP ratio of 1.2 per cent (World Bank/OECD, 1999, p. 8). Obviously, the issue of donor intrusiveness and the loss of national control over the development process have greater significance for the aid-dependent countries than for the others, especially as these also happen to be the ones with the least access to private capital flows.

Apart from the growing commitment among donors both bilaterally and collectively through the DAC to a changed cooperation framework that respects the primary role of national ownership, there are important changes in policy and attitudes in the Bretton Woods institutions that do not by any means suggest that the past is entirely buried, but at least create favourable conditions for moving matters forward.

At the World Bank, the Partnership Group, in a paper issued in May 1998, proposed a new partnership framework in which the key development actors on the basis of "shared objectives and comparative advantages" act in support of the country's own development strategy, and an aid coordination process led by the country again in the overall framework of its development programme (World Bank, 1998c). In an even more important signal, the Bank's President, in his address to the 1998 Annual Meetings, called for a new partnership "led by governments and parliaments of the countries", whereby the Bank and donors "must learn to be better team players capable of letting go" (Wolfensohn, 1998). In an even more recent proposal for a Comprehensive Development Framework, he again stresses the need for the countries to "determine goals and phasing, timing and sequencing of programmes" (Wolfensohn, 1999, p. 9).

At the IMF a recent paper issued in response to a request by the Executive Board, following its consideration of the report on the External Evaluation, makes a number of proposals for fostering national ownership. They include proposals to give IMF missions greater flexibility to enable them to agree on programmes that have greater national support and ownership. In particular, the paper recommends that "more attention be paid to considering alternative policy mixes that would be consistent with appropriate programme objectives". It also acknowledges the need to guard against the risk of agreements reached in this way being significantly altered at headquarters.

In the final analysis, however, the responsibility for asserting national ownership rests squarely with the countries themselves and with their collective organizations, including the G-24.

IX. Initiatives by the country

At the country level, ownership must begin with the elaboration of a national development framework that sets out the country's long-term strategies and the means of achieving them. Particularly for the low-income countries with a high incidence of aid dependence, such a strategy must have as its overriding objective an end to aid dependence through accelerated export-led growth financed by optimal levels of domestic resource mobilization and supplemented by increasing flows of foreign private capital.

While national capacity to formulate development strategies obviously differs from country to country, it is difficult to imagine a country today that does not possess the expertise among its nationals at home or abroad to undertake the task. It is not as if this involves the technology of space rocketry. The talk of capacity constraints in sub-Saharan Africa especially is greatly exaggerated in the fast-growing literature on capacity building and often serves to provide a pretext for the engagement of foreign expertise. At any rate, a country that determines – and this is conceivable particularly in a post-conflict situation – that it does not have the expertise in-house can engage the services of independent consultants to assist.

A second vital step is for the country to develop a reasonably strong body of national consensus behind the national vision. Recent country experiences suggest that once these conditions have been met, and that once a national development framework has been formulated and a reasonable degree of national consensus mobilized behind it, the country's leadership in relations with development cooperation partners can be significantly enhanced.[2] Now, although it is obviously for each country to determine what political processes it would employ in mobilizing the necessary degree of political support for a national programme, a number of devices have proved particularly helpful in countries that have achieved relative success in sustaining

reform efforts with a high degree of national ownership. These include:

- The formation of economic management teams (EMTs) made up of ministers and senior officials from the technical and economics ministries, as well as of senior cabinet members and political leaders, to take charge of the management of the reform effort and the coordination of the roles of different ministries and departments, so that the programme is not, in reality or perception, the preserve or burden of the Minister of Finance;[3]

- The involvement of all ministries and key government departments, as well as the legislature and representatives of the private sector, in the preparation of the strategy document;

- The holding of national conferences with the widest possible participation, at which the national strategy document is subjected to frank and open debate;

- Greater transparency in the conduct of negotiations with donors and particularly with the World Bank, the regional development banks and the IMF.

These initiatives at the individual country level are unlikely to succeed in bringing about a systemic change in the practice and culture of development cooperation without the leverage of developing country group solidarity. Indeed, one of the most remarkable features of the current uni-polar international system is the fragmentation in the collective voice of the developing countries as a group, compared with the situation in the 1980s. While this has to do, obviously, with the tremendous economic disparity that has developed within this large grouping since the 1980s, it also has to do with a failure to focus on the great body of common interests that lie beneath the growing diversity. For the low-income countries especially, this has important implications, and even for the middle-income countries these considerations are not entirely irrelevant.

The vast majority of countries involved in these aid relations are particularly vulnerable in their individual capacities. They have neither the leverage of market size nor geopolitical value. While their collective external debt amounts to a substantial sum, individually they have little debtor leverage and pose no systemic threat. Their relatively high levels of aid dependence and limited access to private capital markets add to their vulnerability. For these countries especially, but not exclusively, a rejuvenation of the political solidarity of the developing country movement can be helpful in bringing about the desired changes in the system of development cooperation. In this regard, they can benefit a great deal from better dissemination of G-24 technical papers, and from better coordination of the Group's political and technical work with the G-77 and the relevant UN agencies.

The country initiatives must in turn be supported by changes in the overall framework of development cooperation that more than acknowledge by word the primacy of national leadership. In particular, this requires that:

- The aid coordination discussions, consultations, country pilot studies and evaluations be brought to some conclusion so that the process itself does not become another tract in an aid-effectiveness debate that proceeds interminably while business goes on as usual. An important step in this regard would be to coordinate the aid coordination discussions and processes themselves, preferably through the World Bank's Operations Evaluation Department, so as to facilitate a conclusion free from undue bilateral pressures. Aid coordination initiatives and studies are currently taking in too many different places, to say nothing about their cost (World Bank/OECD, 1999, p. 28). The conclusion of these ongoing aid coordination processes would enable agreed changes to be implemented uniformly, enabling national development programmes to become the starting point of development cooperation.

- For the World Bank and other regional banks and for the IMF, a clear break with the past must mean the adoption of the country's own national development framework as the primary policy document, with the country strategy Paper (CAS) serving as a supplementary document in the case of the Bank, and the national document serving as the country's policy framework paper in the case of the IMF.

Conclusion

The longer-term objective interest of the low-income countries that for now are so heavily dependent on aid is to follow policies that enable them to accelerate their growth through enhanced

competitiveness for the export of manufactured goods and services. But given the extreme capital scarcity in these countries and the constraints on domestic resource mobilization which they face, their development efforts can be helped a great deal in the short term by enhanced and better-targeted ODA through its direct supplementation of their domestic resources, and the catalytic effect it has on private capital flows. Even for countries with little or no dependence on aid, the issue of national ownership is not entirely irrelevant. The recent events in East Asia show that there can be a sudden reversal of fortune and that national ownership can become critical in deciding the form and content of internationally supported bail-out operations. National ownership in the development cooperation framework is important for securing a consistent focus on strategic long-term development objectives and for guaranteeing the sustainability of the national development effort in these countries. In the final analysis, therefore, it the most important precondition for aid effectiveness.

Notes

1　Based on interviews conducted by the author in the course of the External Evaluation of the ESAF (August 1997).

2　Eritrea and Ethiopia have been resolute in their commitment to objectives and targets set out in their own programmes. From the author's interviews with Country Directors in the World Bank, it appears that they are succeeding in getting the Bank and donors to adopt these national programmes as the overriding policy framework document.

3　Ministers of Finance are often slow to accept the role of such management teams, perceiving them as encroachments on their domain. But without such collective machinery, perfectly well-conceived programmes are often resisted by other ministers out of a sense of rivalry with the Ministry of Finance, which they perceive as possessing too much power and as conspiring with the IMF, especially against the national interest.

References

BOLGER, J. (1994), "Ownership: The concept and CIDA's experience", paper prepared for CIDA Policy Branch and presented at the European Centre for Development Policy Management (ECDPM) Roundtable on Partnership in Development Cooperation: Combining Recipient Responsibility with Donor Accountability, Maastricht, July.

BOONE, P. (1996), "Politics and the effectiveness of aid", *European Economic Review*, Vol. 40; cited in *Global Development Finance* (Washington, DC: World Bank, 1982), p. 52.

BRANSON, W., and C. JAYARAJAH (1995), *Structural and Sectoral Adjustment: World Bank Experience, 1980–1992,*

World Bank/OECD Study (Washington, DC: World Bank).

BURNSIDE, C., and D. DOLLAR (1997), "Aid spurs growth: In a sound policy environment", *Finance and Development*, Vol. 34, No. 4, pp. 4–7.

BURNSIDE, C., and D. DOLLAR (1998), *Assessing Aid* (New York; Oxford University Press), pp. 47 et seq.

DAC (1996), *Shaping the 21ˢᵗ Century: The Contribution of Development Cooperative*, Report adopted at the 34ᵗʰ High Level Meeting of the Development Assistance Committee, Paris, May 1996.

FREY, B., and F. SCHNEIDER (1986), "Competing models of international lending activity", *Journal of Development Economics*, Vol. 20, March, pp. 225–245.

GOVERNMENT OF SWEDEN (1998), *Africa on the Move: Revitalizing Swedish Policy Towards Africa for the 21ˢᵗ Century* (Stockholm).

HELLEINER, G.K. (1997), "Eternal conditionality, local ownership and development", cited in IMF (1998a).

IMF (1998a), *The External Evaluation of the Enhanced Structural Adjustment Facility* (ESAF), Report by a Group of Independent Experts (Washington, DC: International Monetary Fund).

IMF (1998b), "Distilling the lessons from the ESAF reviews", mimeo (Washington, DC), July.

IMF (1997), "The ESAF at ten years: Economic adjustment and reform in low-income countries", IMF Occasional Paper No. 156 (Washington, DC).

JOHNSON, J.H., and S.W. SULAIMAN (1993), "Borrower ownership of adjustment programs and the political economy of reform", World Bank Discussion Paper No. 199 (Washington, DC: World Bank).

KILLICK, T. (1991), "The development effectiveness of aid to Africa", Policy Research Working Paper No. 646 (Washington, DC: World Bank).

KRUEGER, A., C. MICHALOPOULOS, and V. RUTTAN (1989), *Aid and Development* (Baltimore, MD: Johns Hopkins University Press).

MAIZELS, A., and M. NISSANKE (1984), "Motivations for aid to developing countries", *World Development*, Vol. 12, No. 9.

ODC (1999), "Supporting effective aid: A framework for future concessional funding of multilateral development banks", ODC Policy Essay No. 23 (Washington, DC: Overseas Development Council), pp. 29–40.

OECD (1991), *Annual Review of Evaluation Results*, Report No. 9870 (Paris), 30 August.

OECD (1997), *Development Co-operation Report* (Paris).

OECD (1998a), *OECD News Release: DAC Peer Review of the United States* (Paris), 9 April.

OECD (1998b), *Review of the International Aid System in Mali: Progress Report and Most Recent Developments*, DCD/DAC (98) (Paris), Vol. 16.

TRUMBULL, W., and H. WALL (1994), "Estimating aid: Allocation criteria with panel data", *Economic Journal*, Vol. 104, pp. 876–882.

WOLFENSOHN, J.D. (1998), "Address to the Annual Meetings", mimeo (Washington, DC: The World Bank), 6 October.

WOLFENSOHN, J.D. (1999), "A proposal for a comprehensive development framework", discussion paper, mimeo (Washington, DC: World Bank), January.

WORLD BANK (1990a), *Adjustment Lending: An Evaluation of 10 Years of Experience* (Washington, DC).

WORLD BANK (1990b), *Adjustment Policies for Sustainable Growth* (Washington, DC).

WORLD BANK (1998a), *Global Development Finance* (Washington, DC).

WORLD BANK (1998b), "The challenge of globalization for Africa", paper for Dakar Leaders Forum, World Bank, Africa Region (Washington, DC), June.

WORLD BANK (1998c), "Partnership for development: PROSED actions for the World Bank: A discussion paper", mimeo (Washington, DC).

WORLD BANK/OED (1999), "Aid coordination and the role of the World Bank", *OED Review (Phase 1)*, mimeo (Washington, DC).

SOCIAL FUNDS IN STABILIZATION AND ADJUSTMENT PROGRAMMES

Giovanni Andrea Cornia*

Abstract

Social Fund is a broad term which refers to a variety of programmes – Social Emergency Funds, Social Investment Funds and Social Action Programmes – that evolved during the last ten years at the initiative of the Bretton Woods Institutions to offset the increase in poverty induced by adjustment. Social Funds have distinguished themselves from traditional programmes because: they had a strong short-term anti-cyclical character; they were mostly multisectoral; they emphasized employment generation and human capital formation rather than food subsidies and social insurance; they were run by temporary autonomous bodies rather than governments; they focused mainly on the social groups affected by adjustment; they were relatively costly in per-capita terms; and they counted on greater visibility and external support than normal government programmes.

However, Social Funds played a minor role in reducing poverty, reversing adverse shifts in income distribution and creating employment. In most cases, the number of jobs created was less than one per cent of total employment. This was due partly to limited funding, poor targeting and inadequate sequencing, as Social Funds were generally introduced after years of crisis and adjustment.

Despite years of social expenditure cuts, even moderate-sized Social Funds could have brought about important welfare gains had their expenditure been allocated to the poorest groups and to high-efficiency programmes. Social Funds rarely focused on activities with the highest social rates of return but rather on activities that required little programme preparation and had large demonstration effects. One of the causes of this phenomenon was their "demand-driven" nature, as many projects were selected among the proposals submitted by municipalities and non-governmental organizations. There was a tendency to short-circuit the poorest parts of the population who have a very limited capacity to articulate their demands and mobilize counterpart funds. Many Social Funds were formulated with the political objective to reduce domestic opposition to the adjustment process, and in particular of mollifying the influential groups affected by adjustment.

Greater impact on poverty would have required much larger resources, more permanent relief structures, improved planning and targeting and, especially, better coordination and sequencing with the fiscal cuts entailed by macroeconomic adjustment, a fact underscored once more by the recent Indonesian experience. Yet, while Social Funds have significant shortcomings, and while their effectiveness maybe questioned in strong states, they could still fulfill important functions in weaker states and emergency situations.

---

*   I should like to thank Sampsa Kiiski for the compilation of tables 2 and 3, Szuszanna Oinas for her excellent assistance in the search of the literature, and Ke-Young Chu for sharing drafts of his ongoing research in this area. I would also like to express my gratitude to Tony Addison, Ke-Young Chu, Gerry Helleiner, Sampsa Kiiski, Mansoob Murshed, Sanjay Reddy and the participants in the Technical Working Group Meeting of the G-24 (Colombo, 2–4 March 1999) for extensive and very useful comments on an earlier draft of this paper. All remaining inaccuracies are obviously my own.

I. Introduction and historical context

From the political-economic perspective, the 1980s and 1990s can certainly be described as "decades of policy reform". The widespread balance-of-payments crises of 1981–1984, the debt crisis of the mid-1980s, the simultaneous shift of the World Bank to structural adjustment lending, and the wave of stabilization, restructuring and privatization programmes introduced in the former socialist economies of Europe were the main factors leading to a rapid increase in stabilization and structural adjustment programmes. A rough idea of the intensity of this effort at policy reform can be had from the number of adjustment programmes carried out with the assistance of the Bretton Woods institutions (BWIs) during this period: while in the 1970s the number of countries initiating programmes with the support of the IMF averaged about 10 per year, it increased from 19 to 33 between 1980 and 1985 (Cornia et al., 1987, p. 49). As a result, in the 1980s the Latin American countries undertook an average of six adjustment programmes with the assistance of the BWI, while Jamaica, Mexico and Costa Rica undertook between 9 and 14 each. Likewise, in the 1980s the African nations initiated an average of seven adjustment programmes, with Senegal, Kenya, Mauritius and Côte d'Ivoire undertaking between 12 and 15 (Jespersen, 1992, table 1.2). The effort at policy reform continued unabated in the 1990s with the onset of the transition to the market economy and, more recently, with the eruption of the "Asian crisis".

The poverty, distributive and growth impact of these reform programmes has been and remains the object of continuous debate. This debate has led to a gradual evolution in the policy stance of the World Bank and, more recently, of the International Monetary Fund (IMF). During the first half of the 1980s, adjustment concentrated mainly on restoring macroeconomic balance, as the BWIs expected that this would lead to a rapid resumption of growth, and that the interests of the poor were best served by the restoration of macroeconomic balance. It soon became apparent, however, that the resumption of growth would take longer than initially expected, that adjustment caused at least a temporary increase in poverty and that, in the interim, measures were needed to offset the social costs imposed by adjustment on vulnerable groups and enhance the political viability of the reforms (World Bank, 1986). In 1990, the World Bank (1990, p. 23) publicly acknowledged the need to develop special Social Funds (SFs) which were to accompany an unaltered approach to adjustment, focusing on rapid macroeconomic stabilization and price reform. Indeed, starting in 1987, a few developing countries had begun introducing semi-autonomous and fast-disbursing SFs aimed at compensating the "adjustment poor" by means of anticyclical income maintenance and social expenditure programmes (with the persistence of economic stagnation, some of these programmes lost their anticyclical nature and became semi-permanent). This is the phase which saw the development of the first sizeable Social Emergency Funds (SEFs) in Ghana and Bolivia. At a later stage, the distinction between "adjustment poor" and "chronic poor" started to be deliberately blurred and the scope of SFs was gradually enlarged so as to address also the problems of the "chronic poor", who despite the adjustment reforms were still being bypassed by growth and welfare programmes.

In a third phase, the SFs increasingly shifted from "compensatory" to "promotive" measures. They sought, in other words, to incorporate the poor into the production process by increasing their human and physical assets. During this period SEFs evolved into Social Investment Funds (SIFs), which effected by and large a programmatic shift from income maintenance to community-based provision of social services.

It is difficult to assess the precise number of SFs introduced in the wake of, or (less frequently) concurrently with, adjustment programmes. The literature in this area indicates that almost every country in Africa and Latin America has since the late 1980s launched SFs of some kind (UNCTAD, 1994; Glaessner et al., 1994; Marc et al., 1995; Reddy, 1998; Bigio, 1998). In addition, most transitional economies were engaged in a deep revision of their social insurance systems and introduced unemployment insurance and social assistance. SFs were less frequent, though activities in this area were initiated in some of the poorest countries.

The impact of the SFs is difficult to assess, not least because during their comparatively brief existence their objectives, main activities, target population, funding patterns, administrative mechanisms and institutional set-up have continuously evolved. Also, their impact has varied in relation to the strength of the social protection arrangements inherited from the pre-adjustment/transition era, and to the social impact of adjustment policies themselves, which in turn have enjoyed varying degrees of success in different country settings. Even well-designed, well-funded and well-implemented SFs could not, in the end, compensate for the negative impact of major crises stemming from ill-designed development or adjustment policies.

Despite these methodological difficulties, this paper argues that, notwithstanding the visibility and high level support they enjoyed, most SFs – particularly those of the first generation Social Emergency Funds (SEFs) and those developed in sub-Saharan Africa – aroused misplaced expectations but played a minor role in reducing the number of unemployed and "adjustment poor", let alone "chronic poor". This was due partly to their very limited funding and partly to their poor targeting. In addition, while SEFs were generally implemented more flexibly and rapidly than state welfare programmes, if account is taken of their higher unit costs per capita, their economic efficiency has not generally been greater than that of ordinary social programmes (Stewart and van der Geest, 1995). Owing to their limited duration and their more general inability to foster innovation in parallel branches of government, they have also not been able to foster the adoption of more flexible and decentralized approaches to the delivery of social services in social ministries. Finally, the emphasis placed during the last decade on short-term SFs may have also diverted the attention of policy-makers from the extension and reform of existing formal social security arrangements, thus diverting attention and resources from building capacity in the core social ministries.

Second- and third-generation SFs have been less affected by some of these problems. The emphasis of SIFs on community participation and a multiplicity of private, NGO, and local/central government providers may have promoted social objectives in national development, helped in mobilizing additional energies and resources from the communities, and helped in extending health and education services in areas not reached by governments. Also in this case, however, it is too soon to conclude that the approach to the provision of low-cost basic services followed by third-generation SIFs has been shown to be consistently superior – even in countries with weak public institutions – to the standard state-centred approach.

All-in-all, SFs are no panacea. Sustainable poverty reduction requires a complementary macroeconomic policy which takes into consideration its social impact, greater long-term investments in social capital, and the development of permanent social security systems which, while drawing on communities, the private sector and local administrations,

are part of a nationwide framework. Indeed, unsurprisingly, the new SFs have worked better where such an institutional framework already existed. This conclusion emphasizes the urgency of building, in normal times, permanent and cost-effective social security systems, including the formal type, and, as the South Indian experience shows, including in low-income agrarian settings.

II. Social protection systems in the pre-adjustment era

A. *Main formal and informal programmes*

Prior to the introduction of SFs, many developing countries had built a variety of social safety nets comprising food subsidies, direct nutrition interventions, employment-based schemes and, in a few cases, targeted social assistance transfers. Many middle-income countries had also introduced social insurance programmes which protected – to various degrees and with widely different coverage – against the risks of unemployment, old-age, injury, sickness, maternity and widowhood. Finally, in all countries traditional family- or community-based mechanisms provided, in normal times, relief from some of the worst forms of poverty or contingent risks (Ahmad et al., 1991). Though these programmes constituted efficient social protection systems in several countries which, regardless of their income level, had made social security a priority, most SFs did not derive inspiration from these prior experiences. The main features of the pre-adjustment social protection arrangements are therefore reviewed hereafter with the purpose of providing a background against which the SFs introduced over the last 10 years can be assessed.

1. Informal social security arrangements

In most developing and some transition economies, such as those of the Caucasus and Central Asia, the extended family and the community played an important role in social insurance, income redistribution and poverty alleviation (see the chapters by Agarwal and Platteau in Ahmad et al., 1991). The extended family was the main source of support for the elderly and poorer relatives. Community-level food security arrangements for the needy were common (often reflecting religious norms) and represented an efficient social assistance mechanism.

Meanwhile, labour exchanges (ensuring that basic tasks were carried out during one's sickness) provided some form of informal insurance. In normal times, these arrangements worked relatively well. In particular, they are less affected than formal schemes by informational and adverse selection problems.

2. Formal, insurance-based social security programmes

These programmes existed in all European socialist economies, several countries of Latin America and a few countries of South-East and East Asia (table 1). They were mainly fashioned on those of the industrialized countries and provided insurance against the risks of unemployment, sickness, invalidity, old age and occupational injury. Already in 1975–1980 in the Southern Cone, Costa Rica and Cuba, they absorbed between 5 and 11 per cent of GDP (table 1) and covered over two thirds of the active population (Mesa Lago, 1991). In Mexico, Paraguay and most Andean countries, coverage rates ranged between 18 and 50 per cent, and in Central America between 2 and 19 per cent. In turn, most (middle-income) socialist economies had achieved universal coverage for most risks, with the exception of unemployment and poverty, i.e. scourges that socialism was supposed to have eradicated (table 1).

In contrast, in most "Asian tigers" (except Malaysia) social insurance programmes were well below the level predicted by their GDP per capita, urbanization rate and development of the formal sector (table 1). The Republic of Korea only recently introduced unemployment insurance, which is still virtually absent in Indonesia and Thailand. In the latter, for instance, the Social Security Fund provides some health, disability and maternity benefits only to employees of large firms. This "institutional underdevelopment" can be explained by the low unemployment which was experienced over three decades of fast growth, but which proved very costly during the crisis of 1997–1999 (see below).

Several factors rendered the Western model of social security of little applicability to low-income countries with a small formal sector and a large share of the workforce in agriculture. To begin with, the causes of poverty in these countries were (and remain) different from those in the industrialized countries, and were unlikely to be removed by insurance-based interventions. Secondly, private markets for risk insurance were underdeveloped. Thirdly, insurance-based schemes covered only civil servants and the industrial "labour elite", and bypassed the

self-employed and those employed in casual jobs. Finally, they entailed unit costs per capita which prevented their extension on a non-contributory basis because of the problems encountered in mobilizing adequate revenue for this purpose. The dominant view was therefore that without drastic modifications, Western-style insurance-based systems could not have protected much of the population of low-income countries from the economic shocks resulting from the adoption of stabilization and structural adjustment programmes.

However, already in the pre-adjustment era, there were examples of formal arrangements in low-income rural settings that had overcome the limitations of the "Western social insurance model" and had developed a low-cost, non-contributory state-funded scheme providing coverage against key risks of immiseration. Indeed, also in low-income countries, contingent poverty arising from circumstances such as old age, sickness, disability, injury and widowhood is a main factor in chronic poverty that cannot be tackled by measures increasing access to assets or employment. The Kerala (India) non-contributory pension scheme, for instance, covers almost all the elderly poor, while some form of social assistance is available to half of the workers in the unorganized sector (Guhan, 1995). The Tamil Nadu programme, in turn, includes social pensions for old age, agricultural labourers, widows and the physically handicapped, as well as survivor benefits, maternity assistance and accident relief. All the households below the poverty line are eligible – except in the case of pensions, where the means-testing is more stringent. An estimated 17 per cent of poor households in Tamil Nadu are covered by this programme, and nearly 60 per cent of the beneficiaries are women. A detailed evaluation suggested that the targeting efficiency of the programme was high, moral hazard did not pose a problem (because of benefit level and design) and overheads were low (3–5 per cent). On all counts, contingency-related social assistance had much better cost-benefit ratios than many other safety nets, including self-targeted employment programmes (Guhan, 1995). Guhan (1992) estimated that the extension of such a minimum social assistance package to all poor households of India with these characteristics would cost only 0.3 per cent of GDP.

3. Employment-based safety nets

Where unemployment insurance was not available or too costly, several countries developed em-

Table 1

EXPENDITURE ON SOCIAL INSURANCE PROGRAMMES IN SELECTED COUNTRIES, 1975 AND 1989

	Total social expenditure			Pensions	Other social insurance[a]	Family allowance	Progr. for civil servants	Public assistance[b]
	1975	1989	1989					
	(Per cent of GDP)		*($ per capita)*	*(Shares of 1989 total expenditure)*				
Burkina Faso	1.1	0.8	2.0	42.2	37.5	20.3	-	-
Kenya	0.7	1.1	3.8	41.0	16.4	-	41.4	1.2
Senegal	1.2	1.0	7.4	-	9.3	24.1	66.6	-
Bangladesh	0.0	0.0	-	-	-	-	-	-
India	1.5	0.3	1.0	78.9	21.1	-	-	-
Sri Lanka	0.8	2.3	8.6	13.2	0.1	-	79.2	7.5
Thailand	0.0	0.0	0.2	-	100.0	-	-	-
Philippines	0.8	0.9	5.8	44.8	17.3	-	37.9	-
Malaysia	1.6	2.8	60.0	58.5	2.3	-	39.2	-
Brazil	5.7	5.4	41.4	77.0	13.9	1.3	7.8	-
Mexico	2.7	2.9	66.6	19.6	49.1	5.5	25.8	-
Argentina	6.5	3.9	94.8	80.1	2.1	17.8	-	-
Costa Rica	4.2	7.4	124.6	24.4	-	75.6	-	-
Chile	11.2	11.8	207.2	67.9	28.0	4.1	-	-
Poland	15.0	9.9	156.0[c]	65.7	8.1	21.5	2.4	2.3
Bulgaria	12.9	15.2	311.6	56.0	33.0	11.0	-	-
USSR	13.6	10.8	401.6	80.1	17.7	2.2	-	-
Czechoslovakia	17.2	21.8	594.0	58.1	20.6	18.2	-	3.1
Memo items:								
United States	11.7	12.2	2535.0	38.9	23.6	-	13.5	24.0
W. Europe[d]	20.6	22.6	4056.5	40.8	31.4	5.6	9.3	12.9
Nordic countries[e]	19.8	26.7	6175.8	38.2	31.0	6.6	2.4	21.8

Source: Calculations by the author, based on ILO (1996).

a Insurance expenditure against sickness, maternity, injury and unemployment.
b Includes payments to war victims.
c 1988.
d Unweighted average of France, Germany, Italy and the United Kingdom.
e Unweighted average of Denmark, Finland, Norway and Sweden.

ployment-based safety nets. For people of working age, several arguments justify the adoption of public work schemes over other transfer programmes. To start with, public work programmes not only permit the achievement of specific poverty alleviation objectives over the short run, but also contribute to the growth of productivity and poverty alleviation over the long term by speeding up capital formation, particularly if this benefits mostly the poor. In addition, they are less affected by the labour supply and adverse selection problems associated with direct transfer programmes. Four of the best known pre-adjustment public work schemes are briefly reviewed below.

The Maharastra Employment Guarantee Scheme (MEGS) was launched on occasion of the crop failure of 1972–1973 during which cereal production per capita had fallen to 49 per cent of its 1967–1968 level (Drèze, 1990). In 1983, the programme was replicated nationwide and was later merged in the *Jawahar Rozgar Yojana,* possibly the largest employment programme of this type in the world (Stewart and van der Geest, 1995). During 1972–1973, MEGS created one billion person-days of employment (corresponding to year-round full-employment for almost five million people), with 20 per cent of the rural population of several districts taking part in the programme (Drèze, 1990). As Drèze notes (p. 89), "Even though real wages were very meagre, the contribution of relief works to total village income in 1972–1973 was often enormous". With the recovery of the rural economy, the programme was scaled back in subsequent years, but during 1988–1993 it still created 80 to 120 million days of employment per year, thus helping to avert the most acute forms of transitory and chronic poverty (Guhan, 1995). During this period, MEGS relied on important domestic resources (equal to 10 per cent of the state development expenditure) and absorbed around 3 per cent of the rural workforce.

Chile's Minimum Employment Programme (PEM) was instituted in 1975 in the face of a major recession. In 1976 it already covered 5.2 per cent of the labour force and reached its peak during the 1982–1983 recession when the Occupational Scheme for Heads of Households (POJH) was also introduced. In 1983, no less than 13 per cent of the labour force (or 40 per cent of the jobless) participated in one or other of these two programmes (Raczynski, 1988; World Bank, 1990) at a total budgetary cost equal to 1.4 per cent of GDP. Both programmes were well targeted and appear to have played an important role in family survival despite the low value of the subsidy they provided.

Costa Rica's multisectoral FODESAF was introduced in 1975, well before the onset of the crisis, to develop "supply-driven" programmes in a variety of areas (mortgage subsidies, water supply schemes, school feeding programmes, and so on), benefiting exclusively the poorest of the poor. Since its beginning, the programme was executed by the ordinary administration and received by law 5 per cent of the wage bill in both the private and the public sectors as well as 20 per cent of the sale tax on most consumer goods. Altogether FODESAF absorbed substantial domestic resources ($123 million a year), and in the 1980s accounted for 5.0–7.8 per cent of government expenditure. With the exception of mortgage subsidies, the programme was highly progressive in reaching the poor, and provided an average subsidy per capita of about $80 to those below the poverty line.

Public works-based safety nets proved successful also in African countries such as Botswana and Cape Verde. In Botswana, the Government adopted extensive measures to combat the collapse of diamond exports in 1981–1982 and the droughts of 1981–1982 and 1985–1986 (Quinn et al., 1988). The Government's response focused on supplementary feeding, nutritional treatment of malnourished children and a Labour-Based Relief Programme (LBRP). The latter comprised a series of labour-intensive projects such as the building or rehabilitation of roads, dams, livestock wells and pit latrines. At two thirds of the national minimum, the LBRP wage was considerably higher than the opportunity cost of labour in a drought year, and thus attracted a considerable supply of able-bodied workers, women in particular. At its peak, in 1985/86 the LBRP provided 74,000 workplaces, a number almost equivalent to the jobs lost in the rural economy. In 1985 the LBRP alone replaced 35 per cent of the income lost by households. The total cost of the relief programme in the peak year was 2 per cent of GDP. If food aid is factored in, the total value of the Drought Relief Programme doubled.

4.   Consumer subsidies

Prior to the introduction of adjustment and transition programmes, many developing and all socialist economies relied on a variety of subsidy schemes aimed at guaranteeing access to food, fuel and other basic items. In urban South Asia the subsidy took the form of targeted rations sold to low-income people in "fair price" shops. Generalized wheat or tortilla subsidies were available in Brazil, Egypt, Morocco and Mexico. In Sri Lanka the programme distributed food stamps to about half the population, mostly low-income groups. Generalized food subsidies for grains, cooking oil and sugar were the most common. In 1980, they absorbed between 0.5 per cent of GDP (in India) and 3.1 per cent (in Sri Lanka), with an average of about 1 per cent (Pinstrup Andersen, 1987). In the extreme case of Egypt, food subsidies absorbed 7.2 per cent of GDP.

The literature has emphasized that even generalized food subsidies do help the poor: indeed, while the non-poor capture a larger share of the total subsidy, the transfer represents a greater share of the initial income of the poor than of that of the non-poor. In spite of this, these programmes were costly and poorly targeted, had a low transfer efficiency and caused large distortions in relative prices. Food subsidies targeted by broad criteria (inferior commodities, poor areas, schoolchildren, nursing mothers and so on) and direct nutritional interventions constituted, in contrast, cost-effective transfers that, once in place, could be expanded to protect the poor during periods of economic downturn or sharp price adjustments (Chu and Gupta, 1998, ch. 2).

B. Strengths and weaknesses of pre-transition safety nets

In the countries clearly committed to social development, the good performance of the safety nets described above depended crucially on their ability to expand coverage rapidly and at acceptable costs during periods of increasing stress; this, in turn, was due in large part to their *permanent institutional structure* (a stable core of experienced staff, established working procedures, clear eligibility and project selection criteria, a portfolio of projects, evaluation approaches and so on). Secondly, it depended on an adequate allocation of resources (between 2 and 4 per cent of GDP per year, excluding insurance-based programmes). These were mainly provided from domestic sources, thus reflecting a genuine commitment to the objectives which the programmes were established to achieve. Thirdly, most activities were executed in a supply-driven manner, though the areas hit in particularly severe ways were often given priority in execution. Though with considerable variation from one programme to the other (and with the limitations discussed below for generalized food subsidies), these programmes were fairly well targeted, and their transfer efficiency was acceptable or good.

However, these social protection systems faced considerable problems, including in those countries committed to fighting poverty. To start with, community-based safety nets worked relatively well during normal times but had a modest protective capacity during periods of acute stress, particularly in the case of co-variant risks among members of the same community. In addition, it is likely that informal mechanisms have eroded with the spread of urbanization (although, as in Zimbabwe, sophisticated forms of two-way urban-rural transfers have developed). Second, in countries with low coverage, social insurance systems could expand only in line with the development of the formal sector, and were thus unable to protect large sections of the population during crisis periods. Other non-contributory programmes (food coupons, income transfer to the poor, etc.) were, in turn, often unable to increase their coverage rapidly because of red tape, bureaucratic inertia (because of the low salaries of most civil servants) and limited political will. Thirdly, the adjustment crises of the 1980s and 1990s were of a *multifaceted nature*, i.e. they simultaneously pushed up unemployment, triggered sharp rises in the prices of food and other basic items, reduced access to public health and education, rendered them more costly, worsened their quality, and so on. These crises required multisectoral responses and the coordinated interventions of various ministries, which in many cases operated with unclear mandates, showed little inclination to cooperate and suffered from severe donor-induced fragmentation of social programmes. Finally, a few of the pre-existing subsidies, such as the generalized food subsidies, were largely captured by the middle class. Their mis-targeting and the large budgetary outlays they entailed impeded the expansion of such programmes in periods of spreading crises.

III. The Social Funds introduced during the adjustment-transition period

A. Types and distinguishing features of the Social Funds

"Social Funds" is a broad term which refers to a variety of programmes that have gradually evolved during the 1980s and 1990s in Latin America and Africa. In Eastern Europe the social cost of the transition was instead addressed through the establishment of state-sponsored social assistance offices, unemployment insurance and active labour market policies (Elster et al., 1998, ch. 6). At a later stage, SFs were launched, or are being developed, in the low-income transition countries of the Balkans, Caucasus and Central Asia (Bigio, 1998). SFs can broadly be classified as follows (though the dividing lines are not always clear).

1. Social Emergency Funds

Social Emergency Funds (SEFs), such as the *Fondo de Emergencia Social* of Bolivia and Ghana's PAMSCAD, were the first to be introduced in the wake of mounting criticism about the "social cost of adjustment". In general, SEFs were transitory and countercyclical programmes targeted on the adjustment poor and, in some cases, the non-poor affected by adjustment. Their dominant goal was to transfer resources to these groups during the implementation of adjustment programmes, which they were meant to support. This was to be achieved through multisectoral programmes comprising employment generation (e.g. labour-intensive public work schemes), support to social services (e.g. through the distribution of medicines) and other emergency measures. SEFs were managed through a variety of non-traditional mechanisms – mainly autonomous or semi-autonomous bodies drawing on the private sector and civil society – independent from the public administration. To a considerable extent, they were funded externally (table 2) and were implemented (with glaring exceptions, such as PAMSCAD) fairly rapidly. Most of them were demand-driven, i.e. projects were initiated at the request of local communities, municipalities, private firms and NGOs.

2. Social Investment Funds

As economic recovery took hold, SEFs were to be replaced by Social Investment Funds (SIFs), which were designed to accelerate economic growth through the development of human capital and other measures enhancing the access of the poor to productive activities. As in the case of SEFs, SIFs were mainly demand-driven and multisectoral. And also in this case, their administration was to bypass normal management and budgetary channels, particularly by relying on non-governmental organizations and private entities that were to be established to run the funds, and to avoid the wastage and delays typical of the public administration. SIFs operated over a longer-term horizon (some of them were given a permanent status) and aimed at the alleviation of

poverty by means of activities aiming at expanding the supply and utilization of services in the fields of health, education, training, and water and sanitation. While they were often launched in the wake, or shortly after the completion, of adjustment programmes, their activities extended beyond this phase. In addition, these programmes were funded with domestic resources to a greater extent than the SEFs (table 2).

3. Social Action Programmes

A third, less frequent, type of SF consisted of Action Programmes. Social Action Programmes (SoAPs), however, are generally very flexible and less easy to characterize neatly. They are of a multisectoral nature, include both protective and promotive measures, and are predominantly supply-driven. They are administered by line ministries and are therefore fully part of a country's institutional development machinery. While they are often part of a stabilization or structural adjustment programme, they tend to focus on both the "adjustment poor" and the "chronic poor". This type of SF has never been prevalent, though one can cite important exceptions, such as Ghana's PAMSCAD and Pakistan's SoAP.

All-in-all, SFs (especially SEFs and SIFs) distinguished themselves from traditional social programmes because they had a strong *short-term* anticyclical component; were mostly *multisectoral* (as opposed to the "vertical programmes" of line ministries); emphasized *employment generation* through public works and *human capital formation* (and less so food subsidies, and the expansion of social insurance and assistance); often exhibited *high cost per capita* for both wage and non-wage items, though this was less the case for SIFs (see on this the literature reviewed in Stewart and van der Geest, 1995); focused mainly on the *social groups affected by adjustment* and not on the structural poor; and counted on much *greater external support* than the usual government programmes, and mostly relied on *demand-driven* (as opposed to state-initiated) schemes; and were run by temporary *autonomous bodies* with the administrative flexibility needed to ensure fast programme implementation. In this regard, the SFs were thought to be an effective way to earmark resources directly for the social sector, safeguard them from a possible political highjacking and avoid a slow and inefficient budgetary process.

Table 2

SIZE OF SOCIAL FUNDS AND TOTAL SOCIAL EXPENDITURE IN SELECTED COUNTRIES IN LATIN AMERICA AND AFRICA

Country	Name of SF, years	Total amount of SF in $ million	Percentage of external funds[a]	SF per programme year, as per cent of GDP[b]	SF per programme year, as per cent of SE[c]	Social expenditure as a percentage of GDP before SF[d]	/ during SF[e]	Real social expenditure per head in national currency[f] before SF[d]	/ during SF[e]
Latin America									
Bolivia	FSE, 1986–1991	191	85	0.72	11.0	6.2[g]	6.6	96	98
Bolivia	FIS, 1990–1994	96	69	0.38	4.5	6.3	8.7	92	136
Chile	FOSIS, 1990–1994	77	43	0.04	0.3	13.1	13.1	52 500	62 300
Ecuador	Several, 1983–1990	180	n.a.	0.20	3.8	5.9	5.2	12 300	10 300
El Salvador	FIS, 1990–1993	67	67	0.31	9.3	3.7	3.4	158	156
Mexico	PRONASOL, 1989–1993	2 500	0	0.17	2.7	5.1	6.5	126	171
Nicaragua	FISE, 1990–1994	93	n.a.	...	...	n.a.	16.9	...	...
Panama	FISE, 1990–1993	32	62	0.10	0.6	16.5	16.1	349	396
Africa									
Cameroon	SDA, 1991–1995	49	78	0.11	1.8	6.0	7.7	18 100	19 100
Egypt	SFD, 1991–1995	613	n.a.	0.36	2.7	12.8	13.7	144	159
Ghana	PAMSCAD, 1987–1992	80	94	0.22	3.8	5.3	6.4	2 850	3 650
Madagascar	SIRP, 1989–1993	41	88	0.28	7.5	3.5	3.8	8 930	9 310
Zambia	SRP, 1989–1993	49	94	0.28	5.7	5.4	4.9	166	140
Zambia	MPI, 1991–1995	20	n.a.	0.12	2.2	4.8	6.5	142	151

Source: UNCTAD (1994), Glaessner et al. (1994), Marc et al. (1995), Reddy (1998) and IMF, *Government Finance Statistics* (1998).

a   Share of SFs funded with foreign, NGOs' and other resources.
b   Total value of SF, divided by the number of years of operation, in per cent of the average yearly GDP during the period.
c   Total value of SF, divided by the number of years of operation, in per cent of the average yearly social expenditure (SE) during the period. Social expenditure includes health, education, social security, housing and other amenities.
d   Average over the two years preceding the establishment of SFs.
e   Unweighted average during the programme years.
f   At 1987 prices.
g   1983–1984.

B. *Rationale for the introduction of Social Funds*

An assessment of the performance of SFs requires an understanding of the explicit or implicit motivations which led to their establishment. These can be summarized as follows.

1. *Compensating the new poor (and "non-poor affected") for the "social cost of adjustment"*

In the mid to late 1980s, the BWIs and governments of adjusting countries started recognizing that the recovery to be triggered by adjustment would be preceded by a period of recession and increasing poverty. SFs had therefore to be introduced to compensate for this temporary increase in poverty. As noted by UNCTAD (1994, p. 7), "Two-thirds of the laws enacting ... [safety nets] in Latin America as well as those in Egypt and Ghana explicitly referred to social costs of economic reforms as a major reason to adopt emergency measures".

2. *Compensating the poor for the "costs of non-adjustment"*

Some World Bank analyses (e.g. Marc et al., 1995) have suggested that SFs were introduced to avoid a further fall in the living conditions of the poor following years of economic mismanagement. However, the information available about the timing of the introduction of the SFs invariably shows that those started after structural adjustment had been in operation for a few or several years, pointing also in this way to the limited ability of the macroeconomists and social sector economists of the World Bank to work effectively together. Very seldom did genuine preoccupations about increasing poverty lead to the launch of externally supported SFs in non-adjusting countries.

3. *Political economic factors*

Political reasons were often the most salient ones, as adjustment entailed unpopular corrective measures or was not likely to benefit the poor over the short term (or at all, as in economies with highly concentrated export sectors and land distribution). Without SFs, the reforms could have thus been opposed because of the asymmetric distribution of their costs and benefits. This was particularly the case when the interests of politically vocal groups work-

ing in the non-traded sector (traders, civil servants and so on) were affected. As vividly noted in Marc et al. (1995, p. 19) with reference to Guinea:

> Despite the government's commitment to sustain the implementation of a SoAP, the economic recovery programme is not likely to benefit, in the near term, the most vulnerable groups ... If unaddressed, these issues could generate considerable opposition to reforms and put the whole adjustment process at risk.

A less cynical version of this argument is that if a government was not able to generate enough popular support for the economic reforms, it would not have been able to sustain any adjustment programme, without which the poor would have suffered even more because of a likely return to unsound macro policies.

4. *Surrogatory approach and institutional innovation*

After years of economic decline and stringent structural adjustment, national bureaucracies were no longer able to respond to crisis situations and implement swiftly targeted actions in a multisectoral and coordinated way. In addition, in some areas affected by adjustment, where compensatory programmes were needed, the state administration was absent or deficient especially at the local level. And even in normal times, most branches of the public administration suffered from low efficiency and inertia, and were unable to develop autonomously "new approaches to the delivery of social services" drawing on local governments, civil society and the private sector. Another quote from Marc et al. (1995, p. 20), taken from the World Bank's Zambia Social Recovery Project, illustrates this point:

> Several constraints make it difficult for traditional projects to provide immediate responses to pressing social problems. Further, the crisis has decimated many structures and systems that will otherwise provide social services and employment opportunities for these vulnerable groups. The traditional public sector entities' capacity is stretched to the limits ...

5. *Removal of structural causes of poverty*

As noted, SIFs focused on long-term poverty alleviation measures. In many developing countries, poverty is visibly related to lack of human capital (especially health and education) among large sections of the population. By itself, "neutral growth" will not increase access to these services (especially in remote areas), because of the limited priority, budgetary funds and administrative resources assigned to these activities. SIFs tried, therefore, to fill, if only in part, some of these gaps.

C. Scale of the intervention

1. Number and types of Social Funds

It is practically impossible to provide a full account of the SFs introduced from 1986 to date, as in some countries programmes have been of limited financing and duration, and as data for the economies in transition and the safety nets recently launched in South-East and East Asia remain scant. Be that as it may, it appears that SFs have been extremely common in Latin America, very common in sub-Saharan Africa, and rare, but becoming more common in South Asia, South-East Asia and the low-income economies in transition.

In sub-Saharan Africa, at least 31 medium and small SFs, typically spread over three to five years, have been planned and implemented in 26 countries since 1987–1988 (Marc et al., 1995; Reddy, 1998). In Latin America 21 (and probably more) programmes have been launched since 1986 in 20 countries (Glaessner et al., 1994; Reddy, 1998): their number rose exponentially over time (from one in 1987, to five in 1990, to ten in 1992) following the political success of the 1986 Bolivian SEF (Wurgarft, 1992). SFs are fairly new in the economies in transition: the microcredit component of the Albanian Poverty Alleviation Programme was the first in the region followed by that of Armenia. In 1998, various types of SFs were in operation or in preparation also in Georgia, the Republic of Moldova, Romania, Tajikistan and Uzbekistan (Bigio, 1998). SFs were implemented also in Cambodia, India, Mongolia, Pakistan and Sri Lanka, as well as in Egypt, Jordan and Tunisia (Reddy, 1998; Chu and Gupta, 1998). Chu (1998) reports that various types of safety nets were created in 1998 in the Republic of Korea, Thailand and Indonesia.

All-in-all, more than 70 countries introduced some kind of SFs, with several countries (Bolivia, Egypt, Senegal, Peru, and so on) launching more than one, thus underscoring the importance attached to these arrangements by national authorities, the BWIs and UNDP. The distribution of SFs by type indicates that SEFs and SoAPs dominate, especially in Africa,

and that SIFs are common only in a few Latin American countries (Reddy, 1998). Recently there has been, however, a clear shift to community-based SIFs focusing on the creation of social infrastructure: for instance, out of a portfolio of 1,500 projects for a total commitment of $120 billion, the World Bank supported in 1997 over 50 such funds with a total commitment of $1.3 billion (Bigio, 1998).

2. Volume and sources of funding

While there is sufficient information on allocations to SFs, less is known about real programme expenditures. These, furthermore, have frequently been staggered over longer periods than planned, possibly "diluting" the impact of SFs. This said, it appears that the total resources allocated by donors and national institutions to SFs have varied substantially. In Africa, SFs relied on resources varying between $6 million and $25 million, though actual disbursements were often lower (Marc et al., 1995, annex 1, table A.5). In Latin America, SFs absorbed greater external and domestic resources, ranging from $40 million to an exceptional $2.5 billion in the case of Mexico's Pronasol (table 2). Even in this region, however, the scope of SFs remained small. In the words of Morley (1998, p. 46) "Only one fund in the region, Nicaragua, spends as much as 1 per cent in its GDP ...". The information on South-East and East Asia suggests much higher amounts for 1998 (see below), though it is unclear over how many years will these be disbursed.

Because of the little time available when they were set up, and because of the scepticism that sometimes accompanied them (Hutchful, 1994), in low- to medium-income countries, especially in Africa, 78–94 per cent of SF resources were provided by international donors (particularly by the World Bank) in the form of budgetary support. An important part of the external support was in the form of concessional lending, though it could be argued that countries should borrow for programmes in this area only on a temporary basis and where programmes are clearly targeted on the poor. In middle-income countries, in contrast, SFs were funded to a greater extent with domestic resources, either from national budgets or from capital freed up through debt-for-development swaps. In second-generation SIFs and SoAPs, a greater share of total programme costs was funded from local budgets or community contributions.

Regional differences persist when standardizing SF expenditures by GDP or total social expenditure. While Africa's SFs absorbed on average between 0.1 and 0.3 per cent of their GDP *per programme year* (for, typically, 4–5 years), in Latin America this ratio was, especially among low-income countries, between 0.4 and 1.0 per cent (table 2). In 1998, the Indonesian Government allocated no less than 7.5 per cent of GDP (6 per cent to subsidize rice, soybeans, sugar, fuel, drugs and other basic items, and 1.5 per cent for public works schemes) as part of an IMF stabilization programme. The Government of the Republic of Korea, in turn, assigned 2.5 per cent of GDP, mainly for an extension of the eligibility and duration of the recently created unemployment insurance and social assistance. In Thailand in 1998, allocations for public works, job-creation programmes, training and broadening access to health and education reached 5.7 per cent of GDP (Chu, 1998).

In terms of total social expenditure (which includes the outlays through SFs and other extrabudgetary mechanisms), allocations to SFs in Africa have ranged between 1.7 and 7.4 per cent *for every year of the SF programme*. In Latin America, the same figure was 2.3 and 13.7 per cent, with the exception of small "demonstration programmes" such as those of Chile and Panama. The point to be noted here (compare third and fifth columns in table 2) is that during the SFs years, social expenditure (as a percentage of GDP or on a per capita basis) declined in four cases (Panama, Ecuador, El Salvador and Zambia) out of the 12 in table 2, rose by an amount less than, or equal to, the expenditure on SFs in two (Bolivia and Madagascar, where some kind of diversion from the regular social expenditure to SF might have occurred), and rose in the remaining six.

These figures would suggest that in half of the cases considered in table 2, SFs have been accompanied by an overall rise in social expenditure in relation to the two years preceding their launch. This result, however, is mainly due to the choice of the baseline, i.e. the relatively depressed years of 1987–1989. When the comparison is made in relation to the pre-crisis/adjustment years (broadly 1979–1981; the crisis hit the hardest in 1982–1984 and the rise in the number of adjustment programmes followed suit), it appears that the SFs have not been capable of offsetting the fall in social expenditure/GDP ratios and in social expenditure per capita which occurred between 1979–1981 and 1987–1989 (table 3 and chart 1). Indeed, in 10 cases out of the 14 included in table 3, the additional outlays on SFs and the autonomous recovery of social expenditure during these years less than compensated the initial fall in social expenditure or were not able to stop its declining trend, despite the fact that the needs of the populations were often heightened by large falls in income per capita.

IV. Assessment of the impact of social funds

A. *Macro impact on employment creation, poverty alleviation and access to services*

In only a few cases (e.g. countries such as Peru, Bolivia and Mexico which absorbed substantial resources) have SFs had a temporary and localized effect in containing the drop in the population's standard of living. Even in the case of large programmes, the impact on employment and incomes was generally negligible. In commenting on the impact of SFs sponsored by the Inter-American Development Bank, Morley (1998, p. 46) argues that, while these were at times useful in providing simple low-cost social infrastructure to communities that never had access to them before, their employment and income effect was very modest. In his words:

> ... only the first emergency fund of Bolivia added more than 1 per cent per year to the total number of jobs in the economy ... and three added more than 0.5 per cent ... In other words, the funds did not have a major impact on the supply of jobs ... Most of the jobs created were temporary ... and for unskilled labour at wages equal or below the minimum wage in the region, not an above-poverty wage.

Stewart and van der Geest (1995) confirm that SFs generally played a minor role in increasing employment and incomes among the poor, and in offsetting the adverse shifts in income distribution induced by the adjustment programmes. In their view, this was partly due to their limited coverage and partly to poor targeting. As they note (p. 21), "this double failure was even true of the 'star' performer, Bolivia, which had substantially more resources devoted to it than later schemes such as those of Honduras and Senegal".

Indeed, the adjustment-related SFs have not been large, effective and *timely* enough to offset the deterioration imposed by years of economic decline and adjustment, especially in countries such as Ecuador, Venezuela and Zambia, which in the 1980s registered declines of GDP in 15–35 per cent and

Table 3

SOCIAL EXPENDITURE IN SELECTED COUNTRIES IN LATIN AMERICA AND AFRICA BEFORE AND DURING THE IMPLEMENTATION OF SOCIAL FUNDS

Country SFs and years	Social expenditure in per cent of GDP			Social expenditure per capita		
	Pre-crisis and adjustment[a]	*Two years prior SF[a]*	*During SF[a]*	*Pre-crisis and adjustment[b]*	*Two years before SF[b]*	*During SF[b]*
Latin America						
Bolivia FSE, 1986–1991	6.0 (1978–1980)	6.2 (1983–1984)	6.6 (1986–1991)	111 (1978–1980)	96 (1983–1984)	98 (1986–1991)
Bolivia FIS, 1990–1994	6.0 (1978–1980)	6.3 (1988–1989)	8.7 (1990–1994)	111 (1978–1980)	92 (1983–1984)	136 (1990–1994)
Chile FOSIS, 1990–1994	19.3 (1980–1982)	13.1 (1988–1989)	13.1 (1990–1994)	65800 (1980–1982)	52500 (1988–1989)	62300 (1990–1994)
Ecuador Several, 1983–1990	5.9 (1980–1982)	5.7 (1981–1982)	5.2 (1983–1990)	12300 (1980–1982)	12000 (1981–1982)	10300 (1983–1990)
El Salvador FIS, 1990–1993	6.1 (1980–1982)	3.7 (1988–1989)	3.4 (1990–1993)	284 (1980–1982)	158 (1988–1989)	156 (1990–1993)
Mexico PRONASOL, 1989–1993	7.5 (1980–1982)	5.1 (1987–1988)	6.5 (1989–1993)	208 (1980–1982)	126 (1987–1988)	171 (1989–1993)
Panama FSE, 1990–1993	14.8 (1985–1987)	16.5 (1988–1989)	16.1 (1990–1993)	377 (1985–1987)	349 (1988–1989)	396 (1990–1993)
Africa						
Cameroon SDA, 1991–1995	6.8 (1985–1987)	6.0 (1989–1990)	7.7 (1991–1995)	25700 (1985–1987)	18100 (1989–1990)	19100 (1991–1995)
Egypt SFD, 1991–1994	16.7 (1981–1983)	12.8 (1989–1990)	13.7 (1991–1994)	156 (1981–1983)	144 (1989–1990)	159 (1991–1994)
Ghana PAMSCAD, 1987–1992	6.4 (1977–1978)	5.3 (1985–1986)	6.4 (1987–1992)	4130 (1977–1978)	2850 (1985–1986)	3650 (1987–1992)
Madagascar SIRP, 1989–1993	...	3.5 (1988)	3.8 (1989–1993)	...	8930 (1988)	9310 (1989–1993)
Zambia SRP, 1989–1993	9.5 (1976–1982)	5.4 (1987–1988)	4.9 (1989–1993)	358 (1976–1982)	166 (1987–1988)	140 (1989–1993)
Zambia MPI, 1991–1995	9.5 (1976–1982)	4.8 (1989–1990)	5.8 (1991–1995)	358 (1976–1982)	142 (1989–1990)	151 (1991–1995)

Source: Calculation by the author, based on IMF, *Government Finance Statistics* (1987, 1991, 1997); IMF, *International Financial Statistics* (1997); World Bank (1998).

a Percentages.

b Social expenditure per capita in constant 1987 local currency units.

large cuts in social spending. In sub-Saharan Africa, resource limitation was a key factor: many SFs could count on only $10 to $20 million (Marc et al., 1995, annex 1, table A.2) – a modest amount, even in very small economies. As noted in section II, pre-adjustment programmes such as MEGS, PEM-POHJ, LBRP and FODESAF, as well as insurance-based and food subsidies schemes, relied on substantially larger resources than those allocated recently to SFs in most African and Latin American countries.

SIFs and SoAPs often showed design improvements over SEFs, but also suffered from under-funding (table 2), and the resources allocated

Chart 1

SOCIAL EXPENDITURE IN REAL GDP IN SELECTED COUNTRIES SINCE 1976

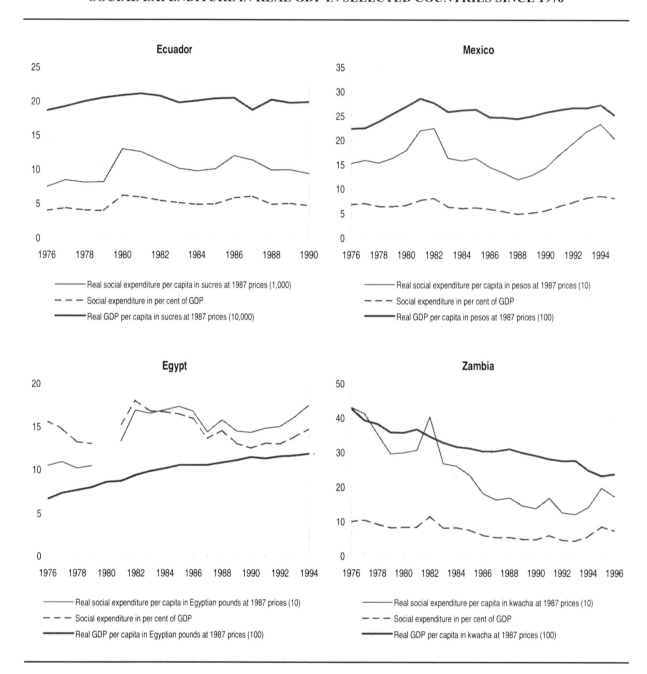

Source: IMF, *International Financial Statistics* (various issues); and IMF, *Government Finance Statistics* (various issues).

to them were not such as to warrant a perceptible impact outside some limited areas. In addition, while SIFs-SoAPs reflected a more genuine concern for the plight of the poor, were better coordinated with the adjustment programmes and were often institutionalized within the national bureaucracies, they were not able to alter the orthodox position on key adjustment decisions such as the extent of deflation, the speed of removal of subsidies, interest rate increases, and the extent of the devaluation and liberalization of portfolio flows, i.e. decisions which are now being criticized for their potential impact on growth, poverty and distribution. Despite growing evidence of the social impact of adjustment and mounting theoretical criticism, the basic adjustment paradigm has remained unchanged (Stiglitz, 1998a).

Greater impact on poverty would have thus required much larger resources, better forward planning (a portfolio of project investments, well-tested administrative mechanisms and an early identification of funding sources) and, especially, greater attention to the poverty impact of the fiscal contraction entailed by macroeconomic adjustment, and the extent-sequencing of cuts in food subsidies. In Indonesia, for instance, an initial drastic reduction in public expenditure was replaced – when its nutritional and poverty impact became evident – by a much more flexible policy "tolerating" a fiscal deficit of 10 per cent of GDP so as to accommodate food subsidies to the tune of 6 per cent of GDP. Almost always, *ex ante* macro policy decisions have had a greater impact on employment, incomes and poverty than *ex post* SFs. The question then is whether alternative macro policies can be followed. A recent external evaluation of IMF-sponsored ESAFs concluded for instance that there is room for manoeuvre and that:

> ... the traditional Fund concern with fiscal deficits needs modification. While the Fund is correct to emphasize that domestic deficit financing should always be avoided, the attempt to reduce current account and aid-exclusive fiscal deficits further (or indeed to run a surplus) has no bearing upon the control of inflation, while it is damaging for growth [and poverty alleviation] (IMF, 1998, p. 31).

B. Impact on income distribution

In the 1960s and 1970s, the IMF's main distributive preoccupation concerned the impact of stabilization on the rural-urban income gap. As for the size distribution of income, the Fund's view was that while stabilization necessarily had distributional repercussion, "domestic political considerations will largely determine who bears the burden of reducing and restructuring aggregate demand" (Johnson and Salop, 1980, p. 23); that stabilization may entail changes in factor payments that were undesirable from an egalitarian perspective, and that "real wage rates may have to fall and real profit rates increase so as to encourage increased foreign capital inflow" (ibid).

The theoretical debate of the 1990s about the distributive impact of adjustment points to different outcomes depending on initial conditions in terms of institutions, human and physical infrastructure; size, export-orientation and labour-intensity of the tradable sector; and policy mixes (Kanbur, 1998). Empirical evidence, however, shows that income inequality increased in the 1980s and 1990s in about two thirds of the developed, developing and transitional countries with data spanning at least these two decades, and that this increase is explained in part by the polices introduced over this period (UNCTAD, 1997; Cornia, 1999). Adjustment policies affect inequality in at least two ways. First, the over-deflation and recessions which often characterize them tend to depress the wage share in total income (IMF, 1998). In industrialized countries, recessions have a greater impact on profits than on wages because of the stickiness of the latter, and because well-developed social safety nets cushion most of the loss of wage income. In contrast, in developing countries – where wages are downwardly flexible and social safety nets much weaker – the labour share in total income falls and income concentration rises. Second, even with a robust recovery of output over the medium term, distribution may deteriorate because of the impact of structural reforms promoting greater wage flexibility, reduced regulation, erosion of the minimum wage, reduced unionization, reduced tax progressivity and privatization (Tanzi, 1996; Cornia, 1999). As Tanzi (1996, p. 11) notes, "There is a real possibility that the implementation of (structural) reform measures has negative effects on employment and income distribution".

Within this context, given their minuscule size, the impact of SFs on the nationwide distribution of income has certainly been negligible, with the possible exception of the new East Asian SFs. At the local level, changes in inequality might have been, in principle, more perceptible, although SFs were instituted for the purpose of reducing the number of "adjustment poor", and distributive objectives were not dominant. By increasing the share of labour income in the local economy, however, SFs – and especially SIFs – may contribute to a lasting improvement in local-level distribution. Much depends, however, on the precision of the targeting of the subsidies they provide, and on who will benefit over the longer term from the assets created by the public works scheme components of the SFs.

C. Microeconomic efficiency and sustainability

The unit costs of goods and services produced by the first wave of SFs (mostly foreign-sponsored – see table 2) were as high or higher than those provided by the ordinary public administration. Wages and salaries in SEFs – as in the Bolivian programme

– were generally much higher than those paid in the civil service (which were generally very low), while the expensive cost pattern of (foreign-funded) investment in administrative infrastructure (vehicles, computers and so on) could not be easily replicated at the national level (UNCTAD, 1994; Stewart and van der Geest, 1995). The SEFs, in other words, gained in flexibility and rapidity of execution, but could not be sustained or replicated on a national scale. This contrasts, for instance, with the low-cost, high-efficiency approaches promoted by UNICEF since the 1980s in the field of basic services (Cornia, 1989).

In particular, the performance of SEFs with public works schemes was mixed. Partly because of their recent creation, in only a few cases were these programmes able to create durable assets. Indeed, the success of such schemes depends on the existence of a well-analysed portfolio of projects which promise a satisfactory return on investments, entail a modest cost per job created, have a wage bill to total programme expenditure ratio above 0.7, offer wages which will not attract workers already employed but which nonetheless can ensure the livelihoods of hired workers, and can be financed by the government budget, foreign grants and fees for the use of the newly created infrastructure. Most SEFs were unable to satisfy most of these criteria, especially those relating to unit costs, wage rates and targeting.

The problems of the financial and institutional sustainability of SEFs were lessened with the introduction of SIFs and SoAPs. These programmes generally relied on greater domestic commitment and funding, were open-ended, and were better integrated with the national administrations. In addition, they focused on activities (creating human capital and social infrastructure in areas not reached by government services) which have a longer-lasting effect on poverty alleviation and inequality than short-term income maintenance programmes. Finally, they adopted a community-based development philosophy, in which village organizations cooperate with local government, the private sector and foreign donors in the choice, design and implementation of projects (schools, health clinics, roads) responsive to their immediate needs. As long advocated by UNICEF and other institutions (Cornia, 1989, p. 183):

> .... greater reliance on community participation and social mobilization in the design, delivery and monitoring of these activities has ensured, in the first instance, a greater internalization of the programmes' benefits by the poor. Secondly, the introduction of less skill-

intensive approaches leads to substantial cost containment ... Thirdly, community participation facilitates the mobilization of additional resources such as labour and locally available materials which have a low opportunity cost but intrinsic productive value.

However, as noted by Stiglitz (1998b), while the participatory, low-cost approach has some intrinsic advantages, especially in emergency situations, the jury is still out as regards its general applicability and effectiveness. So far, it has taken hold in only a relatively small number of countries and communities. Within these, problems of potential capture by local interest groups can be a problem. In addition, this policy of "let one thousand flowers bloom" is potentially fraught with coordination problems, and can work effectively only within a solid regulatory framework with strong accountability mechanisms put into place (Mwabu et al., 1999). For instance, recent theoretical literature in the field of asymmetric information and incomplete contracting (Hart et al., 1996) would suggest that social services whose delivery is easily standardized and quality easily monitored (e.g. in the case of a tube well installation) could be more easily contracted out to the private sector than activities (such as those in the health sector) where requirement changes and standard of service are difficult to observe. Finally, SIFs and SoAPs are not viable in all types of countries, such as those where cost-effective social institutions for the delivery of social services and income maintenance already exist. In countries where those institutions exist but are not functioning effectively, attention would be better focused on their improvement rather than on the creation of new SFs.

D. *Institutional and design problems*

Like most other public policies and programmes, SFs have not escaped a number of design problems which, in some cases, call into question their logic and existence.

1. *Sequencing of SFs*

The first generation of "compensatory" SFs was established a few years after the introduction of stabilization and adjustment programmes. While a large increase in the number of the latter occurred right at the beginning of the 1980s and lasted the whole decade, the number of SFs started to rise only in the late 1980s and early 1990s. In addition, several of the initial SFs, such as PAMSCAD, needed a period of several years after their approval before they started operating effectively (Hutchful, 1994). A delay between macroeconomic stabilization and the introduction of SFs was also observed with regard to the IMF-led adjustment programmes introduced over the last two years in South-East Asia. As already noted in an earlier evaluation of the World Bank's lending to the social sector sponsored by the G-24 (Emmerij, 1995), macroeconomic stability and concern for growth continue to take precedence over social sector concerns. Because of such delays, the ability of SFs to shelter the poor from the costs of adjustment is therefore reduced, as SFs often started operating when substantial increases in poverty and unemployment and falls in access to social services had already occurred, thus highlighting their "curative" rather than "preventive" function.

2. Congruence with macroeconomic objectives

Even a cursory review of SFs points to contradictions between their targets and the macroeconomic objectives of adjustment. Except in those cases in which new outlays on SFs are financed through equivalent declines in "less-efficient" ordinary expenditure (the data in table 2, however, show little evidence of such a "substitution effect"), the increase in public spending implicit in SEF-SIFs contradicts the expenditure reduction drive of most adjustment programmes. Large SFs financed with domestic resources (such as Mexico's PRONASOL, or those being implemented in South-East Asia) may enlarge fiscal deficits and increase the size of the public debt, just after drastic expenditure compressions have occurred. Their effects on the balance of payments and the price level depend on the import content of the demand of the poor, on whether food and other basics are imported, and on whether the economy operates within its production possibility frontier. In addition, as noted by Stewart and van der Geest (1995), SFs increase the supply of non-tradeable goods (e.g. public infrastructure) right when structural adjustment attempts to shift resources towards the tradeable sector (however, in many developing countries affected by surplus labour an increase in social infrastructure achieved without diverting resources, labour in particular, from the traded goods sector would not be harmful). Finally, those SFs which encompass sizeable food-for-work programmes can have a negative effect on local food prices and production, thus possibly increasing poverty among the rural poor. One wonders, therefore,

about the wisdom of large expenditure cuts, when these are followed shortly thereafter by expenditure increases.

3. Demand-driven versus supply-driven approaches

One of the innovations introduced by all SFs was to target the programmes exclusively on those communities which explicitly asked to take part into them. In fact, many of the projects financed by SEFs and SIFs alike were selected from the proposals submitted by municipalities, NGOs and other entities. While this approach may lead to the selection of projects better responding to the needs of the populations affected, it often tends to short-circuit the very poor, who have a limited capacity to organize and articulate their demands effectively and to mobilize the counterpart funds needed for project implementation (Hutchful, 1994). In this way, SFs do not reach the poorest of the poor, who are unable to express their needs, acquire a sense of ownership of the projects or to marshal the required participation. A demand-driven approach needs to be complemented therefore by supply-driven interventions, as well as efforts at social outreach, focused on the poorest areas and groups. An explicit gender focus may often be required in these complementary supply-driven programmes, as a strong gender bias often prevents women's groups from bidding successfully for demand-driven programmes. For instance, in the supposedly successful Bolivian SEF, only 1 per cent of the programme participants were women (Stewart and van der Geest, 1995).

4. Limited institutional innovation in the delivery of social services

SFs were mainly administered by autonomous bodies, as it was felt that cumbersome government procedures were ill-suited for dealing with emergency situations. A potential long-term benefit of SFs was therefore the transfer of institutional and managerial innovation to a sclerotic public administration; this could have helped to lessen the usual efficiency problems of state-run social programmes over the long term. SEFs adopted more flexible recruitment procedures and pay scales and less unwieldy approaches to project design and cost planning, and relied frequently on subcontractors and a multiplicity of public, private and non-profit welfare providers. As noted, these attempts were in line with recent efforts to develop more flexible approaches to the delivery of social services (Mwabu et al., 1999). However, the "short termism" of many SEFs was an obstacle to the transfer of this innovative approach: most of them were of a highly temporary nature, implemented by bodies not only extraneous to but also disconnected from line ministries, while the institutional arrangements adopted for their administration were discontinued at the end of their operation.

Only more recently have SIFs started to be gradually integrated into, or at least coordinated with, government programmes, and in only a few cases were the relationships established with local governments and communities maintained by the successor development administration. Even in these cases, however, the relative independence of SFs (which focus on the creation of physical infrastructure) can create conflicts with the line ministries (which have to ensure the current running of the facilities thus created and might be faced with hard choices when having to allocate scarce recurrent budgets between core social programmes and SFs). While it is too soon to conclude whether this approach is workable over the longer term, there is a suggestion that the benefits of the decentralized, multi-provider, community-based approach accrue more easily where state organizations provide a clear planning framework and adequate supervision.

5.   Unclear relation with pre-existing social security arrangements

A country's ability to manage social costs during crises crucially depends on the existence of well-established institutions. While better than nothing, ad hoc SFs hastily developed during social emergencies lacked the structures (staff, rules and procedures) to start operating efficiently and on a scale to provide effective protection at affordable costs. A brief comparison illustrates this point.

During the period 1989–1992 the Czech Republic, Slovenia, Hungary and Poland experienced a contraction in real wages of 15–25 per cent, unemployment surges of up to 14 per cent and a jump in the price of basic commodities. While childcare deteriorated and poverty rates increased somewhat, a much greater crisis was averted, thanks to reliance on the (reformed) social security system inherited from the socialist era and to the rapid establishment of unemployment insurance and social assistance. In these countries, SFs played a limited role (UNICEF-ICDC, 1995). In contrast, despite the rapid establishment of SFs, the Asian economies affected by the 1997–1999 financial meltdown incurred higher social costs (including sharp rises in uncompensated unemployment, malnutrition and mortality) than would have been predicted from their income levels and the state of their public finances. By 1998 unemployment affected 15 million people in Indonesia, 1.6 million in the Republic of Korea and over 2.5 million in Thailand (Chu, 1998) and contributed to a rapid spread of poverty which could not be offset through community-based interventions and useful but limited-impact SFs. The main problem in this case was the weakness of the social security systems, especially in the field of unemployment compensation and social assistance (table 1). The "institutional underdevelopment" which gradually evolved over time in the areas of social insurance and assistance in those countries proved very detrimental when the 1997 crisis erupted.

This comparison underscores the fact that the preservation and reform of existing social security arrangements (by reducing costs, expanding coverage, reforming benefit generosity and duration, and introducing benefits for new risks), and their extension during normal times, are more efficient and equitable in containing the costs of severe crises than hastily arranged, temporary SFs in both middle-income countries and low-income countries with strong public administrations. Improving these arrangements should thus form the basis of the recommendations of the IMF, World Bank and ILO in normal times. In this regard, it is possible that the emphasis placed during the last 10–12 years on the creation of high-visibility, short-term SFs – even in countries with formal social security systems – diverted resources and attention from their strengthening. As noted in section II, such arrangements need not to be very expensive and could be funded in part with savings on other expenditures, such as generalized food subsidies.

E.   Allocative and targeting gains

As shown in table 3, the resources mobilized by the SFs were generally a fraction of those available in, or retrenched from, social budgets at the time of the crises and adjustment programmes which preceded the launch of the SFs. The partial replacement of prior cuts would not have been a cause for concern, had the efficiency and targeting of the new SFs been substantially greater than those of the retrenched programmes. Indeed, the vast literature produced by, among others, UNICEF and the World Bank has long argued that welfare gains can be achieved in a period of declining budgets if public expenditure is reallocated to the poorest groups or to low-cost, high-efficiency programmes such as immunization programmes, rural education, and so on.

There is, however, little evidence that the introduction of SFs led to allocative or targeting gains. Although SFs resources were, as a rule, disbursed faster and more flexibly than in most public programmes, they were seldom allocated on a priority basis to activities which had the highest social rates of return (such as primary education, vaccination programmes and female literacy), but rather to activities which were quick-disbursing, required little programme preparation and had considerable demonstration effects.

As for their targeting, though the stated objective of SEFs was to *compensate* the "new poor", or the "poor getting poorer" because of adjustment (i.e. groups [ii] and [iii] in table 4), the evidence on the *targeting* of SFs is mixed. The percentage of poor among the beneficiaries of the SFs varied substantially. SFs with some objective criteria (poor areas, female-headed households, and so on) have reached the poor more effectively. Programme leakage, for instance, has been low in the Zambia PUSH programme focusing on female-headed households. This has not been the case, however, where such an approach was not followed or where self-selection mechanisms (e.g. appropriately low wages in public works programmes) were not in operation. The Bolivian SEF (which paid wages well above the minimum wage) is a good case in point. Although this programme benefited 1.2 million people (or 14 per cent of the population), it did not reach the poorest. Stewart and van der Geest (1995) found, for instance, that only 13.5 per cent of SEF workers were drawn from the bottom two deciles of the population, but that 63 per cent belonged to the third and fourth income deciles. In addition, only 1 per cent of the beneficiaries were women.

Targeting imbalances by region were observed also in the case of PAMSCAD, where 78 per cent of the civil servants redeployed as part of the programme were above the poverty line. The redeployment of civil servants, furthermore, absorbed many more funds than the programmes for nutrition, women, water wells, etc. (Hutchful, 1994; UNCTAD, 1994). And in the Honduran SIF according to Reddy (1998, p. 49), "municipalities with a higher poverty incidence received only 5.40 US$ per head, whereas those with lowest incidence received 56.40 US$.

Both Senegal's DIRE and AGETIP ... were also significantly urban-biased". Some of these programmes were explicitly meant to pacify those vocal groups (such as retrenched middle civil servants) which, though not poor, had been affected by adjustment (group [vi] in table 4) and could have opposed the overall adjustment programme.

The targeting precision of adjustment-related SFs has been considerably lower than that of the pre-adjustment, employment-based safety nets illustrated in section II (Maharastra's EGS, Chile's PEM-POJH and Botswana's LBRP). In addition, such programmes were better funded and could therefore cover a much greater share of the poor than the adjustment-related SFs, which thus excluded many poor from their programmes.

One of the causes of the relatively poor targeting of SFs was their "demand-driven" nature. As noted, this approach often bypassed the poorest, who had a limited capacity to organize and articulate their demands effectively and, in some cases, to mobilize the counterpart funds needed for project implementation. Another cause was that the wages paid in public works schemes were above the national average and in this way attracted people who were already employed.

Some recent literature argues that while ineffective in creating employment and income for the "new poor", the new wave of community-based SIFs has been relatively successful in providing social services to the "old poor" living in areas not reached by public services, i.e. to group (i) in table 4. Morley (1998, p. 47) argues that "The funds deliver government services to poor communities that never had them before ... and they build simple social infrastructure quite efficiently at low cost. They improve the living conditions of the poor even if the measured incomes of the poor do not go up very much".

F. *Political economic considerations*

As noted in section III, many SFs (such as the Egyptian and Ghanian ones) were formulated with clear and dominant political objectives at the forefront, including the desire to reduce domestic opposition to the adjustment process. This was achieved by compensating the economic losses of influential groups of non-poor (such as the upper layer of the bureaucracy and university students) who, though not poor or severely impoverished, could have disrupted

Table 4

POVERTY TRANSITION MATRIX BETWEEN BEFORE AND AFTER ADJUSTMENT

Before adjustment \ After adjustment	*Poor*	*Non-poor*
Poor	(i) unaffected "structural poor", without: • human capital (low-skilled underemployed) • land and credit • access to market (lack of infrastructure) • public services (health/education/water/R&D) (ii) poor "getting poorer" • urban poor in the NT sector hit by T-NT terms of trade changes • landless rural workers and food-deficient farmers	(iv) former poor exiting poverty • small-scale market producers of tradables (if T-NT terms of trade are effectively modified) • newly employed workers in T sector
Non-poor	(iii) non-poor "getting poor" • low-income workers in the NT sector (hit by T-NT terms of trade changes) • low-income employees in the T sector if wage/employment increases are less than the increase in prices of traded wage goods • people surviving on transfers	(v) non-poor getting richer • medium- and large-scale entrepreneurs of T goods • people with rare types of human capital (vi) impoverished but not poor • upper layers of the bureaucracy • medium-high-income people in the NT sector

Source: Author's compilation.

Note: "T" and "NT" refer to the traded-goods sector and the non-traded-goods sectors, respectively.

the orderly implementation of the adjustment process. For these reasons, SFs were highly publicized, had considerable visibility and, as argued by some critics, focused more on "face saving" rather than on giving a "human face" to the adjustment process (Hutchful, 1994). According to others (Graham, 1993), SFs were "instruments to build new coalitions" in favour of structural adjustment. The composition of such coalitions varied from one country to another and included different mixes of "new poor", "old poor" and "non-poor".

In addition, though SFs have been managed according to transparent management criteria, they have not been immune to political interference and were frequently manipulated, for instance to give preference to friends and those who favoured the adjustment process (Graham, 1993). Indeed, SFs have created a new coalition of stakeholders who have sufficient personal incentives to support the adjustment process. This coalition includes the poor – old and new – benefiting from compensatory programmes, as well as the NGOs, local governments and other constituents of the civil society, which act as SF's intermediaries and acquire, in this way, greater weight when dealing with the central government.

In many cases, SEFs benefited from limited political commitment by the national authorities. In Ghana, the Government accepted the launch of the once path-breaking PAMSCAD only grudgingly, and on the condition that it would not entail additional aid, cause no diversion from ongoing projects and not impose unsustainable future recurrent costs on the public administration (Hutchful, 1994). The same author notes that "Ghanaian officials did not take the programme seriously, and among the public there was the perception that PAMSCAD was a 'cheap' palliative intended largely for demonstration effects".

V. Policy recommendations

In the light of the record reviewed in this paper, we recommend that further efforts to address poverty and distributional concerns in future adjustment programmes take into consideration the following points.

(i) Sustainable poverty reduction requires a series of measures, including a macroeconomic policy attentive to its social impact, sustained investments in social programmes, and the develop-

ment of permanent social safety nets which, while drawing on all components of society, are well integrated in a nationwide social protection and development framework.

(ii) Adjustment programmes should strive to avoid too large initial social expenditure cuts and foster a greater congruence between the objectives of macroeconomic stability and social protection. The experience reviewed in this paper is that large initial cuts in social expenditure were only in part reversed by the launch, years later, of SFs. The BWIs are not immune from criticism in this regard. As already noted in an earlier evaluation of the World Bank's policy on poverty alleviation prepared for the G-24 (Emmerij, 1995), the Bank's strong rhetoric on poverty alleviation was not able to sufficiently change its internal organization to meet this new challenge, mobilize adequate domestic and international funds or to alter the orthodox position on key adjustment decisions (such as the extent of budgetary contraction, speed of removal of subsidies, surge in interest rates, and so on), which have been shown to have a large and immediate social impact.

(iii) It is essential and urgent to overhaul and develop *during normal times* permanent and cost-effective social security systems, including those of the social insurance type, and, as the Indian experience shows, including in low-income rural settings. Reformed, cost-efficient permanent social arrangements are likely to be more efficient in containing the social costs of severe crises than hastily arranged, temporary SFs. Creating permanent, and yet flexible and cost-effective, social safety nets (including against natural disasters such as droughts and floods) should thus be a priority of the IMF, World Bank and ILO. Ad hoc SFs should be established mainly in the case of unpredictable contingencies, or whenever a too rapid expansion of existing social institutions and arrangements would risk crippling their overall functioning.

(iv) During periods of crisis and adjustment, the anticyclical components of the social safety nets need to be allocated adequate domestic (and, if needed, external) resources. While the specific funding level and activity mix of these anti-cyclical components depend on the intensity of the crisis and on the population groups affected, it will be virtually impossible to achieve nationwide social protection objectives with the level of resources allocated to SFs during the last 10 years.

(v) The sequencing and administration of SFs also require attention. Anticyclical safety nets need in fact to be introduced concurrently with adjustment programmes or prior to their launch because of the time it takes to set them up) – and not years after these have been in operation – as the increases in poverty and unemployment which may occur immediately after adjustment could became permanent, deeply rooted and difficult to deal with. One way to minimize response times is to entrust the responsibility for these interventions to permanent institutional structures which can count on well-tested response procedures and infrastructure. While such infrastructure should be scaled back during normal years, it should not be closed or wound down. Indeed, during normal years, the SFs (e.g. an employment fund) could accumulate resources which could later help in setting up employment schemes during years of recession. In this way, these arrangements would facilitate an inter-temporal redistribution of resources which could help to sustain living standards during difficult years.

(vi) Finally, the targeting of the social protection programmes should also be considered. First of all, targeting should aim not only at reducing programme leakage (i.e. the inclusion of non-poor in programme activities) but also at minimizing the exclusion of deserving poor from those activities. Second, in this regard, the priority assigned to demand-driven programmes should be combined with complementary efforts aimed at reaching in a state-initiated mode, supported by adequate social outreach, those regions where the poorest of the poor, unable to express their needs and marshal even minimal resources, live.

References

AHMAD, E., J. DRÈZE, J. HILLS, and A. SEN (1991), *Social Security in Developing Countries*, WIDER Studies in Development Economics (Oxford: Oxford University Press).

BIGIO, A.G. (1998), *Social Funds and Reaching the Poor*, EDI Learning Resource Series (Washington, DC: World Bank).

CHU, K.-Y. (1998), "Social safety nets for Asian economies in crisis", mimeo (Washington, DC: IMF).

CHU, K.-Y., and S. GUPTA (1998), *Social Safety Nets: Issues and Recent Experience* (Washington, DC: IMF).

CORNIA, G.A. (1989), "Investing in human resources: Health, nutrition and development for the 1990s", *Journal of Development Planning*, Vol. 19 (New York: United Nations).

CORNIA, G.A. (1999), "Liberalization, globalization and income distribution trends", UNU/WIDER Working Papers No. 153 (Helsinki: United Nations University/World Institute for Development Economics).

CORNIA, G.A., R. JOLLY, and F. STEWART (1987), *Adjustment with a Human Face: Protecting the Vulnerable and Promoting Growth* (Oxford: Clarendon Press).

DRÈZE, J. (1990), "Famine prevention in India", in Jean Drèze and Amartya Sen (eds.), *The Political Economy of Hunger*, Vol. II, WIDER Studies in Development Economics (Oxford: Oxford University Press).

ELSTER, J., C. OFFE, and U.K. PREUSS (1998), *Institutional Design in Post-Communist Societies* (Cambridge, UK: Cambridge University Press).

EMMERIJ, L. (1995), "A critical review of the World Bank's approach to social-sector lending and poverty alleviation", in UNCTAD, *International Monetary and Financial Issues for the 1990s*, Vol. V (New York and Geneva: United Nations).

GLAESSNER, P.J., KYE Woo Lee, A.M. SANT'ANNA, and J.-J. DE SAINT-ANTOINE (1994), "Poverty alleviation and social investment funds: The Latin American experience", World Bank Discussion Paper No. 261 (Washington, DC: World Bank).

GRAHAM, C. (1993), "Market transition and the poor: New coalitions for economic reform", mimeo (Washington, DC: Brookings Institution).

GUHAN, S. (1992), "Social security for the unorganized poor: A feasible blueprint for India", discussion paper (Bombay: United Nations Development Programme and India Gandhi Institute of Development Research).

GUHAN, S. (1995), "Social security options for developing countries", in J. Figueredo and Z. Shaheed (eds.), *Reducing Poverty through Labour Market Policies: A Contribution to the World Summit for Social Development* (Geneva: International Institute for Labour Studies).

HART, O., A. SHLEIFER, and R.-W. VISHNY (1996), "The Proper scope of government: Theory and an application to prisons" (Harvard, MA: Economic Research).

HUTCHFUL, E. (1994), "Smoke and mirrors": The World Bank's social dimension adjustment (SDA) Programme", *Review of African Political Economy*, Vol. 62, pp. 569–584.

ILO (1996), *The Cost of Social Security: Fourteenth International Enquiry, 1987–1989* (Geneva: International Labour Office).

IMF (1998), "External evaluation of the ESAF", report by a group of independent experts (Washington, DC: International Monetary Fund).

IMF-GFS (various issues), *Government Finance Statistics* (Washington, DC).

IMF-IFS (various issues), *International Financial Statistics* (Washington, DC).

JESPERSEN, E. (1992), "External shocks, adjustment policies and economic and social performance", in G.A. Cornia, R. van der Hoeven and T. Mkandawire (eds.), *Africa's Recovery in the 1990s: From Stagnation and Adjustment to Human Development* (Basingstoke, UK: Macmillan).

JOHNSON, O., and J. SALOP (1980), "Distributional aspects of stabilization programs in developing countries", IMF Staff Papers (Washington, DC: IMF).

KANBUR, R. (1998), "The implications of adjustment programmes for poverty: Conceptual issues and analytical framework", in Ke-Young Chu and S. Gupta (eds.), *Social Safety Nets: Issues and Recent Experiences* (Washington, DC: IMF).

MARC, A., C. GRAHAM, M. SCHACTER, and M. SCHMIDT (1995), "Social action programmes and social funds: A review of adjustment and implementation in sub-Saharan Africa", World Bank Discussion Paper No. 275 (Washington, DC: World Bank).

MESA LAGO, C. (1991), "Social security in Latin America and the Caribbean: A comparative assessment", in E. Ahmad, J. Drèze, J. Hills and A. Sen (eds.), *Social Security in Developing Countries*, Social Security in Developing Countries, WIDER Studies in Development Economics (Oxford: Oxford University Press).

MORLEY, S. (1998), "The Inter-American Development Bank's study of social study", in A.G. Bigio (ed.), *Social Funds and Reaching the Poor*, EDI Learning Resource Series (Washington, DC: World Bank).

MWABU, G., C. UGAZ, and G. WHITE (1999), *New Patterns of Social Provision in Low Income Countries*, forthcoming.

PINSTRUP ANDERSEN, P. (1987), *Consumer Oriented Food Subsidies: Costs, Benefits and Policy Options* (Baltimore, MD: Johns Hopkins University Press).

QUINN, V., M. COHEN, J. MASON, and B.N. KGOSIDiNTSI (1988), "Crisis-proofing the economy: The response of Botswana to economic recession and drought", in G.A. Cornia, R. Jolly and F. Stewart (eds.), *Adjustment with a Human Face: Ten Country Case Studies* (Oxford: Oxford University Press).

RACZYNSKI, D. (1988), "Social policy, poverty, and Vulnerable Groups: Children in Chile", in G.A. Cornia, R. Jolly and F. Stewart (eds.), *Adjustment with a Human Face: Ten Country Case Studies* (Oxford: Oxford University Press).

REDDY, S. (1998), "Social Funds in developing countries: Recent experiences and lessons", UNICEF Staff Working Paper No. EPP-EVL-98-002 (New York: UNICEF).

STEWART, F., and W. VAN DER GEEST (1995), "Adjustment and Social Funds: Political panacea or effective poverty reduction?", Employment Paper No 2 (Geneva: ILO, Employment Department).

STIGLITZ, J. (1998a), "Broader goals and more instruments: Towards the post-Washington consensus", 1998 WIDER Annual Lecture (Helsinki: United Nations University/ World Institute for Development Economics Research).

STIGLITZ, J. (1998b), "Keynote address", in A.G. Bigio (ed.), *Social Funds and Reaching the Poor*, EDI Learning Resource Series (Washington, DC: World Bank).

TANZI, V. (1996), "Fiscal policy and income distribution", paper delivered at the seminar "International Experience and Policy", Santiago, Chile, 12–13 July 1996, mimeo.

UNCTAD (1994), "Recent developments in Social Funds and safety nets", paper submitted to the Standing Committee on Poverty Alleviation in Geneva, 24 January.

UNCTAD (1997), *Trade and Development Report 1997*, United Nations publication, sales No. E.97.II.D.8 (New York and Geneva).

UNICEF-ICDC (1995), *Poverty, Children and Policy: Responses for a Brighter Future*, Economies in Transition Studies, Regional Monitoring Report No. 3 (Florence, Italy: UNICEF-International Child Development Centre).

WORLD BANK (1986), "Financing adjustment with growth in sub-Saharan Africa, 1986–1990" (Washington, DC: World Bank).

WORLD BANK (1990), *World Development Report 1990 – Poverty* (New York: Oxford University Press for the World Bank).

WORLD BANK (1998), *World Development Indicators* (Washington, DC: World Bank).

WURGARFT, J. (1992), "Social Investment Funds and economic restructuring in Latin America", *International Labour Review*, Vol. 131, No. 1.

STRENGTHENING DEVELOPING COUNTRIES IN THE WTO

Bhagirath Lal Das

Abstract

This paper tries to explore the reasons for the weak participation of developing countries in GATT/WTO, ways to strengthen their participation, and the need for effective support in this process. The continuing weakness of developing countries in the WTO is of particular concern owing to the expanding coverage of the WTO, the deeper and wider implications of its agreements, and the greater vulnerability of developing countries.

The GATT and the WTO have provided both opportunities and challenges, and some developing countries, particularly in East and South-East Asia and, to a lesser extent, Latin America, have been able to take advantage of the GATT in expanding their exports. However, a large number of developing countries did not derive much benefit from GATT because of their continuing weakness in production and supply, and even those countries with sufficient production and supply capacity have faced the severe import restrictions of developed countries in some of the most important sectors. Developing countries have also experienced new types of restrictions, particularly in the form of anti-dumping action and import restraint. They receive less than equal treatment in several areas, and have made significant concessions to developed countries without obtaining concessions in return. Moreover, the recommendations of the panels and the Appellate Body tend to be adverse to the interests of developing countries, and there are several loopholes and traps in the agreements which are detrimental to the developing countries. Clearly, there is some flaw in the strategy and operation of the developing countries in the WTO.

One of the reasons for the ineffective role of the developing countries in the WTO lies in the decision-making process in that institution, despite the fact that the number of the developing countries is nearly four times as large as that of the developed countries in this forum, which has the system of one country, one vote. A majority of developing countries does not have the opportunity to participate in the actual negotiations, which take place in small groups behind the scene. Thus, the developing countries have a grim prospect in the WTO. They must gear themselves up fully to meet the tasks ahead involved in the implementation of existing WTO agreements, the review of some of the provisions of these agreements, and further negotiations, including in several new areas such as environment, investment, competition, government procurement, trade facilitation and electronic commerce. Developing countries should individually strengthen their decision-making machinery in respect of the issues handled in the WTO, and as a group they need to strengthen cooperation and coordination. But they also need considerable assistance from outside, ideally in the form of a support programme with the participation of the main international agencies operating in the relevant areas.

I. Introduction

Developing countries have never had a decisive role in the GATT/WTO system, but their weakness may be much more damaging now than ever before because of three newly emerging factors. First, the WTO is spreading its coverage to more and more new areas. Second, the impact of WTO agreements and their operation is much wider and deeper for the economies of the countries, particularly the developing ones. Third, and perhaps most important, the economies of the developing countries are much more vulnerable now than before because of both their own weakness and their exposure to an uncertain external environment.

Previously, the principal impact of GATT rules was on a country's imports and exports; but now the WTO agreements have much wider implications for a country's economy. The disciplines on services and intellectual property rights (IPRs), which are the new additions to the system as a result of the Uruguay Round of multilateral trade negotiations (MTNs), have a significant impact on the production process, technological development, financial institutions and the insurance sector, inflow and outflow of funds from the so-called invisible account, and vital modern infrastructure, such as telecommunications. The new agreements in the areas of information technology goods and electronic commerce will have a considerable impact on revenue resources, as will be explained below. There are also more recent pressures to include still other new areas, such as the protection of investors' rights, and the social clause, which will both deepen and widen the national impact of WTO activities. For example, the proposals on investment, if finally carried through, will have a profound impact on the balance-of-payments situation as well as on the sectoral and regional balance of investments in a country.

With so much at stake, one would expect the developing countries to strengthen their capacity in respect of the WTO negotiations. Indeed, some of them are now better prepared. The concluding phase of the Uruguay Round did bring about some awareness in a number of developing countries as to the implications of the negotiations. In some of the developing countries there were extensive national debates on the various issues. But even for those few developing countries that are better prepared now than before the level of preparation is far below what is needed. And, even now, the vast majority of other developing countries have hardly any preparation.

The WTO, in which developing countries are numerous and where the voting pattern is based on one country one vote, provides a good setting for the developing countries to be effective. They can in fact turn it into an institution to serve their interests and make it an example of an international or multilateral institution working for their benefit. But unfortunately they have not been able to take initiatives, nor have they succeeded in defending themselves effectively in this institution.

This paper is intended to explore the reasons for the weak participation of developing countries in GATT/WTO; ways to strengthen their participation and the need for effective support in this process. All this is discussed in the context of the opportunities for developing countries and the challenges confronting them in the GATT/WTO system.

II. Opportunities, challenges and response

A. *Opportunities and response*

Though the main negotiations on the text which finally emerged as the GATT took place principally between the United States and the United Kingdom in the 1940s, several developing countries formally participated in those negotiations and joined the GATT right in the beginning. As the agreement is based on the principle of reciprocity in the exchange of concessions, it is naturally more appropriate for participation by countries at similar levels of economic development. To make it more relevant for developing countries, the principle of reciprocity was not rigidly followed in the case of concessions expected from them, while they received the benefit of concessions made by others through the operation of the most favoured nation (MFN) treatment clause, which ensures total non-discrimination among the members in respect of enjoyment of benefits.

There were other advantages to joining the agreement. It obviated the need for entering into a series of bilateral agreements with various countries and renewing them from time to time. Also it provided some protection to the weak trading partners through a multilateral dispute settlement system, which precluded unilateral actions.

By the early 1960s it was felt that the special and differential treatment granted to developing countries needed more positive and constructive policies and actions on the part of developed countries. These were included in Part IV of the GATT. The practice of non-reciprocity was given formal recognition through an explicit commitment by the developed countries in Part IV to the effect that they do not expect reciprocity from the developing countries. Later, a decision (1979) of the Tokyo Round, commonly called the Enabling Clause, made it possible to grant special tariff concessions to developing countries without going through the elaborate process of waiver of the MFN treatment clause.

Most of the developing countries have not been able to take full advantage of the opportunities provided by GATT/WTO because of their undeveloped supply capacity. But some of them did improve their supply capacity and expanded their trade, taking advantage of the opportunities available in other countries. Their industrial production and export grew fast. Some of the Latin American countries have been in this group, though not on a sustained basis. Several South-East Asian and East Asian economies utilized the opportunities on a more stable basis, resulting in faster growth of industrial production and exports. They were able to take advantage of the market opportunities in developed countries in expanding their own economies at a fast rate. But a large number of developing countries have not benefited significantly from the trading system encompassed by the GATT/WTO, nor has it brought about any significant improvement in their income and wealth.

B. Past challenges

Even the limited benefits to a few selected countries in Latin America and Asia have not been without severe handicaps. Any rapid expansion of exports in a sector has invariably generated protectionist tendencies, policies and measures in the developed countries. All this has curtailed the opportunities available to the developing countries. Such tendencies manifested themselves in the form of special trade regimes in some sectors, restraints on import and export activities outside the framework of GATT, enthusiastic use of anti-dumping investigations and duties and the current trend of using environmental concerns for restraining imports. Further innovative methods of trade restrictions in the form of linking trade to labour standards are in the pipeline. It is useful to briefly revisit these stages of the GATT in order to anticipate the problems ahead.

As soon as developing countries started having a good growth rate in the export of textiles, the industries in developed countries felt the pressure of competition. Instead of letting the market operate freely in this sector, the developed countries sponsored a separate regime, called the International Arrangement in the Trade of Textiles, commonly known as the Multi-Fibre Arrangement (MFA), in derogation of the normal GATT rules. Severe restraint on the export of textiles from developing countries imposed under this special regime limited their industrial growth.

Later, restraints were imposed in some other sectors as well. For example, the major developed countries imposed quantitative limits to the export of jute products and leather products, which were mainly exported by the developing countries. Further, a few developing countries with the capacity to export steel were also affected by special restrictions in that sector.

What is important to note is that the major developed countries did not hesitate to bypass or circumvent the normal GATT disciplines in sectors of particular importance to the developing countries when developing-country exports in these sectors were perceived to cause problems for their domestic industry. The normal principle of free and liberal trade was totally forgotten; and this has a lesson for the future.

Obviously it was all done under pressure from the domestic industry, and there is no reason to believe that the developed countries are in any better position now to resist similar pressures. Herein lies the fear that they may again resort to import-restrictive measures in sectors where they face serious competition from the developing world.

Besides, further new methods have been used lately to restrain imports from the developing countries. Their imports have often been subjected to anti-dumping investigations and anti-dumping duties. Even when the investigations have not resulted in the imposition of duties, the trade has been disrupted by the uncertainty caused by the initiation of the investigation. And more recently, trade-restrictive measures in some sectors have been imposed by some major developed countries, relying on the general exceptions clause (Article XX of GATT 1994) on the grounds of protecting the environment.

C. *Emerging challenges*

These trends have added to the strains of developing countries in expanding the prospect for their exports. The situation appears particularly serious when viewed in the context of the current determined efforts of the major developed countries to expand the opportunities of their economic operators in developing countries. The WTO is being used as an important instrument for this purpose, as the developed countries have found it to be especially effective in pursuing their objectives. In particular, the possibility of retaliation through the integrated dispute settlement mechanism makes enforcement of the obligations of developing countries quite effective.

This is probably one reason why the major developed countries should try to broaden WTO coverage to include new areas, some of which are quite unrelated to the traditional areas of GATT, i.e. trade in goods. Services and intellectual property rights entered the WTO in the Uruguay Round. Efforts are under way to expand the coverage of environment and introduce investment into this forum. It is an example of the persistence and tenacity of the developed countries that the area of investment, which was put forward in GATT during preparations for the 1982 Ministerial Meeting and some time thereafter, without much success, is still being pursued vigorously. The issue of competition is being pushed in order to ensure free operation of developed-country firms in developing-country markets. In some traditional areas too developed countries are making efforts to expand the market access of their goods. One important example is government procurement, where the exercise has started with transparency.

All these trends present new challenges to developing countries. There are four factors in particular which make their recent and current burden in the WTO heavier than a decade ago. First, the subjects and pattern of negotiations have become much more complex. For example, the negotiations on the liberalization of financial services or in the various areas of IPRs are really very intricate. Directly participating in the dispute settlement process either as a complainant or as a defendant is also quite complicated, because of the intricacies of the legal interpretation, which now is routinely a part of the panel or appeal process in disputes.

Second, the role of the developing countries in WTO negotiations has changed significantly. Earlier, they were negotiating mostly for special concessions and relaxations from the developed countries, whereas now the negotiations are more about extracting concessions from them. It is a much more difficult exercise, as the expectations of the demanders must be balanced against minimum commitments from one's own side.

Third, the developed countries have started taking up these negotiations with a new determination to expand the access of their economic entities in developing countries. Their attitude and approach appear to have changed in recent years. The old concept of enlightened self-interest in seeing of their own long-term prospects in harmony with the development of developing countries has been replaced by expectations of immediate gains of expansion of current opportunities in the developing countries, irrespective of its effect on those economies.

Fourth, the developed countries, particularly the major ones, are more coordinated in their objectives and methods in the WTO, whereas the developing countries have been losing whatever solidarity they had in the past. Furthermore, the developed countries have a great deal of self-confidence. They feel they can solve their economic problems by proper coordination of policies among themselves; and they do not see a need for support from developing countries in this regard. This has naturally reduced their sensitivity to the problems of the latter.

III. Manifestation of weakness of developing countries

Amidst all these challenges in the WTO, the developing countries are naturally in a very weak position. This weakness is manifested in various ways, some of which can be easily identified. For example: (a) the developing countries have been getting less than equal treatment in several areas; (b) they have been making significant concessions to major developed countries without getting much in return; (c) wood several important provisions of special and differential (S&D) treatment of developing countries have not been properly implemented; (d) the areas of interest to developing countries have been consistently ignored and not attended to; (e) in the dispute settlement process important interpretations are emerging, which have the potential to constrain their production and export prospects; (f) big loopholes and traps have been left in some agreements which risk having an adverse impact on the developing countries. All this needs to be elaborated upon and clarified by means of examples.

A.   *Less than equal treatment*

Often there is a call from developing countries to be given special and differential treatment in GATT/WTO; but one seldom considers the instances of less than equal treatment meted out to them over a long period, particularly since the Uruguay Round agreements came into force. Some examples are given below.

• The ultimate means of enforcement of rights and obligations in the WTO is retaliation, which is almost totally impractical for developing countries. Although the recommendations and findings of the dispute panels are normally accepted and implemented by the countries concerned, in really sensitive cases a country may hesitate to do so, and then the only option is to retaliate. But developing countries may find this ultimate weapon difficult to use, for both economic and political reasons. Hence, they have an innate handicap in ensuring the implementation of the findings and recommendations, particularly in difficult cases, which leads to a basic weakness in enforcing their rights.

• There is also the serious problem of cost once the stage of recommendations and findings in the dispute settlement process has been reached. This process is so complex and costly that developing countries have to think very seriously before they initiate it. A developed country can start it with much greater ease than developing countries. Similarly, the developing countries face a serious handicap in defending themselves in a case in the WTO because of the cost involved. They are very poorly placed in the WTO in respect of enforcing their rights and ensuring observance of obligations by other countries .

• There is a similar problem in respect of subsidies and dumping. The complexity of countermeasures against subsidies and dumping makes these contingency provisions less useful for the developing countries. At the same time, the cost of defending themselves against such measures exposes them to unfair risks of victimization.

• Certain products which are mainly of export interest to developed countries have been rushed through for agreements on zero tariff. There are two specific examples. At the 1996 WTO Ministerial Meeting in Singapore a proposal was suddenly put forward by major developed countries, and subsequently approved, for an agreement that information technology goods would have zero duty. Then, at the 1998 WTO Ministerial Meeting in Geneva, there was a provisional agreement on standstill in respect of duties on electronic commerce, which practically means zero duty. Products of export interest to developing countries have never received such prompt and decisive consideration in the GATT/WTO system.

• Services sectors of interest mainly to developed countries have been similarly rushed through in the negotiations to culminate in agreements. Specific examples are the agreements on financial services and telecommunication services. The sectors of interest to developing countries, meanwhile, have been no meaningful progress.

• Individuals from developing countries are subject to more restrictions on doing business than individuals from developed countries, and are thus additionally handicapped with regard to exporting goods and services.

• International technical standards and rules of origin are being formulated which will have important implications for the market access of goods, but the developing countries barely have the resources and capacity to participate in the process.

• In the agricultural sector, the subsidies used mainly by some developed countries (contained in annex II to the Agreement on Agriculture) – e.g. those for research and development, crop insurance, resource retirement programmes – have been made immune to any countermeasure, whereas those used generally by developing countries (some of them included in Article 6.2 of the Agreement on Agriculture) – e.g. land improvement subsidies and input subsidies – do not have such immunity.

• In respect of subsidies on non-agricultural products, those used mainly by developed countries – e.g. on research and development, regional development and environmental standards – have been made non-actionable; whereas those used by developing countries for the expansion and diversification of their industries do not receive such favourable treatment.

- In the textiles sector, as mentioned earlier, developed countries have followed the practice of "less than equal treatment" of developing countries for more than three decades. A special multilateral trading regime was introduced in this sector in the early 1970s, in derogation of the normal GATT rules, and has continued to apply for nearly three decades.

- As mentioned earlier, some other products of interest to developing countries, such as leather and jute, have been subjected to special restraints on import in developed countries.

B. Major concessions by developing countries without anything in return

The above illustrations of less than equal treatment are also examples of the major concessions given by developing countries to the developed countries without insisting on or obtaining any commensurate concessions in return. Usually this softness has been displayed by the developing countries with three considerations. First, they have agreed to some of these measures in a spirit of cooperation, for example in the areas of textiles, leather and jute, as the developed countries needed support for their adjustment process in those sectors. Second, in some cases which were more prevalent during the Uruguay Round, they agreed to concessions under intense pressure from major developed countries. The inclusion of services and IPRs in the WTO agreements, and the agreements on financial services and telecommunications services are some important examples. Third, more recently there has been a tendency among the developing countries to be over enthusiastically accommodating. They have agreed to proposals without having or asking for adequate time to examine the implications properly. The agreements on zero duty on information technology goods and electronic commerce are the main examples.

In the negotiations on international trade, it is not wrong to make concessions per se, because the exercise of negotiations is meant to be one of give-and-take. What is totally wrong is to make concessions without getting anything in return. And this is precisely what has happened lately in the GATT/WTO negotiations. When developing countries agreed to let services and intellectual property be governed by WTO agreements, they made a significant concession to the developed countries, which were the sole winners from these concessions. Similarly, when they

agreed to have agreements on liberalization in financial services and telecommunications services, it was again a major concession. The agreements on zero duty on information technology goods and electronic commerce have been yet other significant concessions. And there has been no commensurate counter-concession offered or given by the developed countries, which have been the main beneficiaries of developing-country concessions.

Under a rational negotiation strategy, the developing countries should have asked for and insisted on some important concessions in the areas of their own interest. Hardly any developed country ever makes a concession in the multilateral forum without obtaining something in return. But with the developing countries the case has been quite the converse, as they have repeatedly been making concessions but received none in return.

C. Special and differential treatment not implemented

Special and differential (S&D) treatment provisions are contained in Part IV of GATT 1994 and in the various Uruguay Round agreements. Those contained in Part IV of GATT 1994 – in Articles XXXVI, XXXVII and XXXVIII – are very significant. In these provisions the developed countries have undertaken a commitment to "accord high priority to the reduction and elimination of barriers to products currently or potentially of particular export interest to less-developed contracting parties, including customs duties and other restrictions which differentiate unreasonably between such products in their primary and in their processed forms". They are further committed to "refrain from introducing, or increasing the incidence of, customs duties or non-tariff import barriers on the products currently or potentially of particular export interest to less-developed contracting parties". The developed countries have also to "give active consideration to the adoption of other measures designed to provide greater scope for the development of imports from less-developed contracting parties". These "other measures" may include "steps to promote domestic structural changes, to encourage the consumption of particular products, or to introduce measures of trade promotion". (In GATT "less-developed contracting parties" means the developing countries.)

Of course, these commitments are not of a contractual nature, in the sense that there can be no retaliation for their non-fulfilment. While that does not mean that these commitments do not have to be implemented, the fact is that these provisions have never been taken seriously by the developed countries, and the developing countries have not been able to have them implemented.

In the new WTO agreements there are very few elements of S&D treatment in the nature of the actions of developed countries and expectations from developing countries. One example of the former is in Article 66 of the TRIPs Agreement, which makes it obligatory for developed countries to "provide incentives to enterprises and institutions in their territories for the purpose of promoting and encouraging technology transfer to least-developed country Members in order to enable them to create a sound and viable technological base". And an example of the latter is the provisions of Article XIX of the General Agreement on Trade in Services (GATS), which requires "appropriate flexibility for individual developing country Members for opening fewer sectors, liberalizing fewer types of transactions, progressively extending market access in line with their development situation…".

Developing countries have not been able to persuade developed countries to implement these provisions sincerely.

D. *Areas of interest to developing countries*

The subjects of interest to developing countries have hardly ever occupied the centre stage in the GATT/WTO. There have been repeated attempts by developing countries to focus attention on these issues, but they have not succeeded. Some important examples are given below.

Tariffs in the developed countries on products of special export interest to developing countries continue to remain high. Quantitative restraints on imports in several sectors of interest to them were in place for a long time, and still are in some important sectors, such as textiles. Practically nothing has been done to eliminate or reduce harassment of the developing countries through measures disguised as anti-dumping action and as action to establish or maintain conformity with technical standards and to protect the environment. Service sectors of interest to them have not been taken up for serious negotiation, and the labour movement has hitherto been given only scanty attention. The possibility of uni-

lateral trade action by a major developed country is still permitted by its legislation, and the country can continue to use this provision to put pressure on other countries, particularly the developing ones. This provision has not been removed, even though there is a specific commitment in the WTO agreement that the laws of the countries should be made fully compatible with the obligations under the agreements covered by the WTO.

E. *Trends in the dispute settlement process*

Although the new dispute settlement process has brought about some improvement over the past, trends have been developing recently which are contrary to the interests of developing countries. The panels and Appellate Body have often adopted interpretations which constrain the rights of developing countries and enhance their obligations. Four particular cases may be cited:

- First, in the Venezuela gasoline case, the Appellate Body increased national discretion in taking trade restrictive measures for the conservation of non-renewable natural resources. The Appellate Body has said that national discretion in this matter is not limited by the test of necessity, but rather that it is adequate if there is a nexus between the particular trade restrictive measure and the protection of a non-renewable natural resource.

- Second, in the India woollen shirts case the Appellate Body ruled that the onus of justifying the trade restraint in textiles does not lie with the country applying the restrictive measures, but that it is the complaining country which has to demonstrate that the conditions prescribed for the restraint have not been fulfilled.

- Third, in the Indonesia car case the panel has denied developing countries the flexibility to give subsidies for the use of domestic products in preference to imported products, which is allowed by the Agreement on Subsidies. The panel has taken the stand that such a measure would violate the TRIMs Agreement.

- Fourth, in the recent shrimp-turtle case the Appellate Body has given interpretations, at least four of which have adverse implications for developing countries. These are: (i) the Appellate Body has tried to establish the primacy of environmental conservation over the free flow of goods under the normal GATT rules, thereby diluting the disciplines on general exceptions as provided in Article XX of GATT 1994; (ii) it has considered the turtle to be an "exhaustible natural resource" on the grounds that it is covered by multilateral environment agreements for the protection of endangered species; (iii) it has directly implied that a country can take trade restrictive measures for actions and effects outside its jurisdiction, on the grounds that the extraterritorial nature of the action is blurred, as turtles are migratory; (iv) it has approved the filing of briefs and opinions before the panels by persons and organizations not part of the governments involved in the particular case. Serious implications of these interpretations are likely to emerge over the coming years.

F. *Loopholes and traps in the Agreements*

Significant loopholes have been left in some important agreements, to the detriment of developing countries. Three examples will suffice. In the Agreement on Textiles, the developed countries undertook the commitment to bring products accounting for 33 per cent of their imports into the normal WTO discipline, and thus exclude them from the special restrictive regime of the textiles sector by 1 January 1998. The list of the products to be included in the calculation of this percentage is contained in an annex to the Agreement. The loophole is that this annex has been made very large and includes many items which have not been under restraint. The developed countries have taken advantage of this loophole and, for the liberalization process up to 1 January 1998, chosen only such products as are not under restraint. In this manner the obligation is fulfilled, and yet in practice there is no liberalization.

The Agreement on Textiles also contains a barely visible trap: its Article 7.3 includes a requirement of sectoral balance of rights and obligations – a concept alien to the GATT/WTO system, which works on the principle of overall balance. The requirement of sectoral balance could serve as a justification for developed countries not to abolish the special restrictive regime in this sector on 1 January 2005, arguing that developing countries have not adequately liberalized their textile sector.

The special provision for the dispute settlement in the Agreement on Anti-dumping is another example of a major loophole. While this agreement has brought some objectivity to investigations of dumping, the whole subject of anti-dumping has been practically excluded from the normal WTO dispute settlement process. In anti-dumping cases the role of the dispute settlement panels has been severely curtailed, inasmuch as they cannot rule on whether an action or omission by a country violates its obligation – and this role applies almost routinely to the disputes in all other areas.

These specific adverse situations exemplify the weakness of the developing countries in the WTO. There may be many more such examples. Clearly, the developing countries have been on losing ground in the WTO, and more so in recent years. This leads to a discussion of the strategies and role of those countries in that organization.

IV. Strategies of developing countries in the WTO

The strategies of the developing countries and the method of their participation in the WTO are generally of two types. Either they are indifferent and totally silent, or there is rigid opposition, followed by abrupt and total capitulation.

A. *Indifference and silence*

A very large number of developing countries remain silent at WTO meetings and discussions. They attend the meetings, listen to the statements and say nothing. They neither support nor oppose a point. Technically, of course, they do become parties to the decisions taken, even though they have not supported them explicitly.

There are several reasons for their silence. First, they do not feel that the subject under consideration affects their countries directly, and thus they are indifferent. Second, they do not understand the intricacies of the point under consideration, and accordingly prefer to remain quiet, fearing that any statements and opinions might be irrelevant or even betray their ignorance. Third, even if they sometimes feel that a particular proposal has adverse implications, they prefer not to come out openly against it, especially if it involves opposing the major developed countries. They prefer to avoid annoying them, particularly when they have not received any clear instructions from their capitals to oppose or support a given proposal. Fourth, in case of proposals with clearly adverse implications they assume that some other more active and vocal developing countries will speak out against the proposal, thus taking care of their interests.

In the case of numerous developing countries, the Permanent Missions in Geneva do not receive detailed briefs or guidance from their capitals, and thus they do not feel compelled to take a particular line in the meetings. In most cases they do not have full knowledge of the subject and are not confident enough to make any intervention. However, this attitude does not absolve their countries of the obligations imposed by the decisions taken without their actively participating in them – decisions which could prove quite costly in the future.

B. *Stiff opposition and sudden capitulation*

A small group of countries does take an active interest in the meetings and discussions. Most of the time, however, they participate without any detailed examination of the subjects under discussion. Neither their Geneva Missions nor the capitals are equipped with the adequate capacity. Generally speaking, they work on the basis of their quick and instinctive response to the proposals. If they feel that a proposal is not in their country's interest, they will oppose it. Their opposition is quite firm sometimes, and they stick to their line to the bitter end. Finally, when intense pressure has built up in the capitals, or all other countries have acquiesced to the proposal, they also drop their objection, remaining sullen and silent. Decisions are taken to which they become parties, even though they had earlier raised objections, and in this manner their countries become bound by the obligations emanating from the decisions. The immediate political cost of obstructing a consensus appears much more significant than the burden these obligations will mean in the future.

In the course of the long process of determined opposition to sudden capitulation into acquiescence these countries are denied the opportunity of getting anything in return for the concessions they made in the negotiations. Some illustrations will suffice.

In November 1996, when the Uruguay Round was launched at Punta del Este, after stiff opposition the developing countries finally agreed to include services and IPRs in the negotiations, but had the satisfaction of keeping the two subjects totally separate from goods. They also thought that in respect of IPRs the negotiations would be limited to trade-related issues and would not cover IPR standards. In April 1989 they had been persuaded to agree to include those standards in the negotiations. In fact, the negotiations on IPRs practically centred around the standards, and there was hardly anything of the trade-related subjects in either these negotiations or the agreement that emerged. Furthermore, through the cross-retaliation provision in the integrated dispute settlement mechanism, obligations in goods, services and IPRs were linked, and it became possible to take retaliatory action on goods for violation of obligations in services or IPRs, something which the developing countries had persistently opposed in the past.

As mentioned earlier, the very inclusion of the topics of services and IPRs in the framework of the WTO was a major concession by the developing countries. They also agreed to negotiate special agreements in specific services sectors: financial services, telecommunications services and maritime services. The agreements on the first two have been completed, with major gains by the developed countries, the main suppliers of services in these areas.

An unfair basis of reciprocity was also adopted in some of the negotiations. In the financial services, for example, concessions are exchanged in respect of permission to open a specific number of branches of banks. Developing countries have agreed to permit a certain number of bank branches of other countries to be opened in exchange for their being allowed to open certain a number of branches in those countries. The reciprocity in exchange of concession on the basis of the number of branches is not fair and appropriate at all, because the transaction volume of a branch of a bank from a major developed country will be far in excess of the possible transaction volume of a branch of a developing country bank. A better standard of reciprocity would have been based on cross-sectoral concessions or the volume of transaction, rather than the number of branches. The developing countries were not able to present an alternative framework for reciprocity in those negotiations.

C. *Missed opportunities*

There have been several instances in which developing countries neither asked for nor insisted on reciprocal concessions, while making important concessions of their own. For example, they agreed to zero duty on information technology goods at the WTO Ministerial Meeting in Singapore, December 1996, and agreed to provisional zero duty on electronic commerce for 18 months at the WTO Ministerial Meeting in Geneva, May 1998. These two proposals were sponsored by the major developed countries, which were the main beneficiaries. Electronic commerce is an area with very high growth prospects, and duties in this area would be a potentially high source of revenue for the developing countries. In addition, the users will generally be in the high-income group of the population and, as such, even in terms of equity, a tax in this area in the developing countries would be appropriate. Thus, the developing countries have really surrendered a major source of their revenue without any benefit. They were not prepared with any counterdemands for negotiating reciprocal concessions from the sponsors and beneficiaries of these proposals, and therefore could not steer the negotiations in these directions.

In fact, developing countries have repeatedly been missing opportunities for negotiating reciprocal concessions or for limiting their own concessions. For example, during preparations for the Uruguay Round, the major developed countries had insisted on including three new subjects in the negotiations: services, IPRs and investment. All of them were finally included among the subjects to be negotiated, although the developing countries put up stiff resistance right up to the end. With the benefit of hindsight, one can now say that with a proper negotiating strategy the developed countries could have been persuaded at that time to give up at least one of these subjects in return for an agreement to negotiate the other two. Also, permitting the very entry of services and IPRs into the WTO negotiations for trade in goods was a major step; and the developing countries could rightfully have asked for major concessions from the sponsors when that step was taken. As the situation developed, however, they could neither stop their entry nor get anything for it in return.

Such opportunities are likely to come soon. Some major developed countries are strongly insisting that negotiations on investment and the social clause should be started. Some of them have also made their intention clear that they have sponsored negotiations on government procurement with the objective of expanding the market access of their goods. These will be totally new areas to be taken up in the WTO, if they do get taken up. Investment

and the social clause do not have any place in the GATT/WTO forum at present. In respect of government procurement, although the subject relates to trade in goods, the existing framework as enunciated in Articles III and XVII of GATT 1994 prescribes some rights on giving special treatment to domestic products and some discretion on selecting the countries for the supply of these goods. Even the start of negotiations on the disciplines for investment and the social clause and new disciplines on government procurement will be a major concession to the developed countries. The developing countries have been resolutely resisting such moves so far. If, however, they decide at a later date to start negotiations in these areas, they should do so only after obtaining commensurate major concessions from the sponsors, i.e. the major developed countries. Concessions in the areas of interest to the developing countries are necessary, simply by virtue of their having agreed to the inclusion of these topics in the WTO negotiations.

As mentioned above, the approach of developing countries has so far been either to remain silent or to present stiff opposition, followed in the end by sudden capitulation. If they have to concede on a proposal which has been opposed by them earlier, a better strategy will be to have a planned withdrawal, if and when they decide to yield for various reasons. Following this strategy, they can have a chance of getting something in return for the concessions.

D.   *Process of cooperation and coordination*

The weakness of individual developing countries is also reflected in very poor cooperation and coordination among themselves. They have not been able to evolve common positions and common strategies on important issues. In fact, they do not have a proper mechanism for such efforts.

Despite the existence of an informal group of developing countries within the WTO, it is not utilized for identifying common interests and working out common positions. The discussions are more of a general nature, although sometimes countries explain their perceptions and positions and describe their problems with specific issues.

In one sector, textiles, there is an effective coordination among the exporting developing countries. They have formed a formal organization called the International Textiles and Clothing Bureau, which is fully financed by them and which has a functioning secretariat. The member countries meet regularly to discuss the issues in the textiles sector and to formulate a common position. Most of the time they are able to do so, as well as to articulate their common stand and position quite effectively and put forward specific common proposals.

It is difficult to say why the developing countries are not able to articulate a common platform on other important issues when they have succeeded in developing such an effective cohesiveness in the textile sector. Various reasons may be proposed. First, in this specific sector, the problems are well identified and focused, and direct import restraints in the developed country markets have an immediate and visible impact on the production and export prospects of the developing countries. Second, the exporting developing countries have long suffered at the hands of major developed countries, and have practically been pushed into an effective mutual coordination by their long and severe suffering in this sector. Perhaps the interests of developing countries are too dispersed in respect of the WTO issues in general, which is why they cannot identify a cohesive cementing force which would make them overcome the current hesitation emerging from their fear of annoying the major developed countries.

There is generally a strongly discouraging environment for their efforts in this direction, as such efforts are immediately dubbed by major developed countries as politicizing the GATT/WTO system. A general idea is spread by them that every country should be on its own in this system as it has to safeguard its own interests. This, however, has not prevented them from achieving sound coordination among themselves through various formal institutional arrangements, such as the Quad, the G-7 and OECD. It is a very ironical that in the GATT/WTO system major developed countries, which are quite strong even individually, are moving towards closer coordination, whereas the developing countries that are in weak and vulnerable positions are unable to come together and coordinate their interests and efforts.

Some insight into the plight of the developing countries may be had if we examine the WTO environment in which they have to operate. This environment must be understood and kept in mind when considering any change or improvement in the role of those countries in that organization.

V. The WTO decision process

It is a major paradox of international economic relations that the developing countries, numbering about four times the developed countries in the WTO, are not having their way in this forum and have to face adverse situations almost perpetually. Unlike the IMF and the World Bank, there is no weighted voting in the WTO, which works on the principle of one country one vote. And yet the developing countries, which comprise the overwhelming majority of its members, have not had any success in pursuing their objectives. They are always on the defensive and have to strive hard to reduce the hazards and damage to them. It is important to understand how this sad situation has come about.

The highest decision-making body in the WTO is the Ministerial Meeting, which is generally held once every two years. The next highest decision-making body is the General Council, which takes decisions inbetween the Ministerial Meetings. The formal decision-making process in these bodies is by simple majority of the members present, with each member having one vote. However, there is hardly any occasion for formal voting as, in practice, the decisions are taken by consensus, and consensus is held to exist when no member present in the meeting formally opposes a proposal. Then there are specialized bodies, such as the Councils on Goods, Services and TRIPs, the Committee on Trade and Development, and various working groups. Generally, these bodies take decisions based on consensus. The reports of the panels and the Appellate Body are considered by the Dispute Settlement Body, which also works on the basis of consensus.

In this forum of decision-making, a country wishing to oppose a harmful proposal can be effective only if it expresses its formal opposition at the time of decision by consensus. For a positive action, it has to muster the support of the majority of the members present. One would expect that a developing country convinced that a particular proposal is not in its interest would formally present its objection at the time the consensus is being determined. One would also expect the developing countries formally to oppose a proposal in large number if it is not in their interest and to get it rejected by a majority vote, given that they constitute the majority in the WTO. Similarly, one would expect them to sponsor proposals in their interest, with the support of a large number of them. But nothing like this happens. Part of the reason lies in how the WTO process actually operates when considering a proposal.

Generally speaking, important proposals in the GATT/WTO are made by the developed countries. After they have formally made a proposal in a particular WTO body, delegations make preliminary observations in a non-committal manner. Thereafter the action shifts away from the main stage. The main sponsors hold limited consultations with certain delegations, first trying to consolidate support and then involving the others in order to soften their possible opposition. Sometimes, the chairmen of the relevant bodies or even the secretariat organizes these consultations, which are invariably limited to a small number of delegations, chosen either because they have a keen interest in the subject or because they are vocal about their opposition in the open forum. A very large number of developing countries are left out of this process of consultations, which in reality are full-fledged negotiations. If the subject is important, the chairman sometimes makes an interim report in the formal meeting. Such reports are generally very brief, merely stating that the consultations are going on, and often failing to give the details of the main issues at stake or the conflicting positions of various countries.

In the meantime, pressures build up on the developing countries that had been opposing the proposal. Depending on the intensity of the opposition, pressure may be applied to the delegations in Geneva or even bilaterally in the capitals. The technique of winning away the opponents one by one is also applied. Finally, the hard-core opponents are left with the option of either keeping quiet or preventing consensus in the open meeting. Frequently they do not want to face the political cost of formally opposing a decision at the end if they are left alone or are in a very small group. That leaves the decision to be taken in the open meeting by consensus.

In this process, a large number of developing countries do not have the opportunity to participate in the negotiations going on behind the scenes in small groups. They are faced with the final result in the open meeting at the end, and they do not have enough courage or motivation to express clear opposition or to make an effective reservation at that stage, even if the particular decision is not fully in their interest. Sometimes, they mumble a few words of protest but do not come round to formally preventing consensus.

In this manner, even though each country has a vote in the WTO and an equal right to participate in the decision-making process, many developing countries are left out of the actual negotiations. Their lack

of agreement with the decisions is evidenced by the bitter critical statements made by some of them after important WTO meetings, such as the recent Ministerial Meetings in Singapore and Geneva.

In these small group consultations and negotiations off stage, the Quad countries (United States, European Union, Canada, Japan) are almost always present. As the host country, Switzerland is usually invited as well, as is either Australia or New Zealand, or both. Thus the developed countries are almost fully represented. But among the 100 or so developing countries, barely five or ten get a place in these informal discussions and negotiations. The scale is therefore tilted against them not only by economic and political weight, but also, quite ironically, by the weight of numbers.

From the viewpoint of developing countries, the decision-making process is very much untransparent and non-participatory, as an overwhelming number of them are associated only at the beginning, when the proposals are made formally, and at the end, when the conclusions have already been worked out. Nonetheless, as mentioned earlier, they are bound by the obligations imposed by these decisions, even though they have not participated in the actual negotiations. This is no doubt very unsatisfactory for the developing countries.

The consequences have been quite adverse to their interests, as the obligations are heavily tilted against them. If the situation continues in future, they are likely to lose even more. The year 1999 and the next few years are likely to be filled with sensitive and difficult negotiations in the WTO, which may have a significant impact on developing economies. A quick look at the tasks ahead will make clear the potential for damage if they continue to be on the fringe of the WTO process.

VI. A glimpse of the tasks ahead

The work to be undertaken in the next few years may be divided into four categories: implementation of the WTO agreements, review of some of the provisions of the agreements, continuing negotiations in some areas, and work in new areas.

Implementation of the agreements involves formulation of legislation and procedures, establishment of institutions and machineries, removal of certain import control measures and sending notifications to the WTO. Some of these actions will already have been taken by now, while others may have to be taken in the near future. Even in the former case, the work might not be completed, as it is subject to scrutiny by other countries. The country taking the action may have to satisfy the other countries that its implementing action has been correct and adequate. Some more difficult implementing measures are yet to be taken, such as the formulation of enforcing legislation for the IPRs and creation of appropriate machinery for enforcement, introducing a *sui generis* system for the protection of rights on plant varieties, and so forth. One important task for the developing countries in all this is to explore the options for implementation, so that the adverse effects may be minimized and the benefits maximized. This requires a very elaborate exercise. Even the seemingly simple obligation of sending notifications to the WTO may constitute a heavy burden, as arrangements have to be made to maintain the relevant information in appropriate formats, adequate training has to be given to the personnel handling it, and in many cases information may have to be collected and compiled from remote regional areas.

There is yet another aspect to implementation. A country has to keep watch on implementation done by others, so that its own rights and opportunities are fully safeguarded. For example, the textile-exporting developing countries have to watch carefully the process of progressive liberalization in the developed textile-importing countries.

The reviews of some of the agreements' provisions will involve serious negotiations. The more important of such reviews are in the areas of subsidies, TRIPs, TRIMs, anti-dumping and services. In the area of subsidies, the review will cover the provisions relating to non-actionable subsidies, export competitiveness of developing countries and presumption of serious prejudice. In the TRIPs area, the provisions on patenting of plants and animals will be reviewed. In the area of TRIMs, the review will consider whether the agreement should be expanded to cover investment policies and competition policies. In the anti-dumping area, the review will consider whether the restriction on the role of panels should be extended to other areas. In the services area, the review will cover current exemptions from MFN treatment. The provision on the negotiating right of small exporting countries will also be reviewed.

Important new negotiations will take place on agriculture and services. In agriculture, the negotiations will cover the reduction of protection and subsidies. In services, the negotiations will focus on further liberalization of services sectors in terms of market access and national treatment and on the three subjects on which disciplines have not yet been worked out: subsidy, safeguard and government procurement.

These negotiations are likely to be as difficult as they were during the Uruguay Round. The negotiations on services are intensely technical, particularly in respect of the basis for the reciprocity of benefits. The developing countries also have to identify the sectors of interest to them and propose the elements of liberalization to the developed countries in these sectors.

In the agriculture sector, the Uruguay Round resulted in the anomaly of developed countries continuing with their import control measures and subsidies of up to 60 to 80 per cent of the base levels, whereas the developing countries, which had not been applying the general import controls and subsidies earlier, were prohibited from applying them in future. The developing countries will have to negotiate in an effective way to remove this anomaly. They will also need to acquire flexibility in respect of import control and subsidy, in order to encourage food production for domestic consumption and protection of their small and household farmers. In addition, concrete proposals will have to be made for relieving the burden of the net food-importing developing countries.

There are severe deficiencies, imbalances and inequities in the existing agreements, some of which have been illustrated and described above. The developing countries will have to strive very hard to obtain their removal and effect basic improvements in the agreements.

Apart from these exercises in respect of the current agreements, several new areas have been taken up for consideration: environment, investment, competition, government procurement, trade facilitation, and electronic commerce.

In the area of environment, the thrust of the major developed countries is to enhance the scope of trade restrictive measures for environmental protection, following the provisions of the multilateral environment agreements.

In the areas of investment and competition, studies are under way in the WTO, as decided at the

Singapore Ministerial Meeting in December 1996. The pressure from major developed countries is to upgrade the level of consideration in the WTO from studies to negotiations. The fear is that the negotiation on investment, if carried out in the framework of the WTO, will concern the protection of the rights of investors and erosion of the discretion of host governments. Similarly, the proposed negotiation on competition may actually be concerned with reducing the discretion of governments in controlling the adverse effects of the activities of big foreign firms and also in providing support to domestic firms.

In government procurement, the current exercise has to do with working out the elements for an agreement on transparency. The fear is that it may result in placing undue burden on the developing countries and also that the exercise may extend to expanding market access for the developed countries in respect of government procurement in developing countries.

Similarly, in the area of trade facilitation, the developing countries will have to ensure that the elements of facilitation do not actually result in the obstruction of their production and exports.

A further new subject, electronic commerce, suddenly emerged in the negotiations during the Geneva Ministerial Meeting in May 1998. For 18 months there has been a provisional agreement on standstill, i.e. zero duty on electronic commerce, and the proposal is to negotiate the subject further. Since zero duty on electronic commerce mainly benefits the major developed countries, the efforts of developing countries will focus on obtaining adequate reciprocal benefits, if the provisions of the provisional agreement are to be allowed to continue further.

From the list of activities above, it is clear that the developing countries face a difficult task in the years ahead. If past experience is any guide, they are likely to suffer colossal losses unless they improve their approach, strategy and preparation.

VII. The future course

First and foremost, the developing countries have to have the political determination not to be pushed around in the WTO. They should also have a resolute will to utilize that forum to serve their interests and minimize its adverse effects. In this process

they will have to move with a degree of confidence, identify their negotiating strengths, and use them effectively. Efforts have to be mounted at the national, group and multilateral levels.

The biggest strength of a negotiator in a multilateral negotiation is to have the country's full support of the stand being taken. This can happen only if that stand is decided after thorough deliberation. Developing countries need to improve and strengthen their decision-making machinery and institutions. There is also a need to change their negotiating strategy and to prepare thoroughly for a role in the WTO. At the same time they must also work towards a complete change in the WTO negotiating process.

A. *Strengthening national decision-making institutions*

The developing countries must identify their specific interests and objectives with regard to the subjects of the WTO. This can be done through a broad-based, in-depth examination of the issues and implications, and requires some institutional changes in the decision-making process. The subjects are so complex, and their implications so widespread, that no one government ministry will be fully equipped to handle them on its own. Almost every issue being taken up in the WTO involves differing interests of various wings of the government. Each issue also involves a clash of interest among various industry groups and economic operators. The overall interest and stand of the country can be worked out only after balancing and harmonizing all these individual differing and clashing interests.

A simple proposal to reduce the tariff on a particular product, for example, will invite different reactions from different industry sectors and different wings of the government. The producer industry will feel threatened with competition from imports, whereas the consumer industries will feel happy, as they will have the prospect of cheaper supplies of inputs. Likewise, the government branch responsible for the development of the producer industry will tend to oppose the proposal, while the one responsible for the downstream industries will be inclined to support it. This is not a new dilemma. But such dilemmas have now become very numerous, with complex ramifications. A typical example of the emerging complexity is the proposal to liberalize the entry of foreign investment. It may be welcomed by the industry and trade, as it gives them a wider choice of the sources of funds; but it may have adverse implications for the balance-of-payment position over a course of time, and may disturb balanced sectoral and territorial development.

These subjects require a very comprehensive examination of implications and a balancing of differing interests. A government ministry working in the traditional manner is hardly equipped to perform this task. It appears necessary to have a standing expert body of high standing, credibility and objectivity, in the nature of a commission, to supplement the efforts of the current machinery. Such a commission would examine the issues critically, taking into account all the aspects and interests and would hold wide consultations with the affected groups in trade and industry, consumer forums, various government branches and other interested groups and persons. After this exercise, the commission would make recommendations to the decision-making body about specific positions the country should take. If the country's position is adopted after such a detailed examination, in an atmosphere of transparency, it will naturally have a strong political backing, and the negotiators will be able to negotiate with full confidence and strength. In addition, with such a decision-making process in the developing countries, the pressures normally placed on them by the major developed countries in the course of negotiations will be much less strongly felt.

B. Change in strategy and approach

A change in strategy and approach is needed. The current feeling of helplessness among developing countries, that they cannot have their say in the WTO, should be replaced by a new conviction that they can achieve their objectives if a number of them work together and if they prepare well. The developing countries are quite numerous in the WTO and, even if one does not expect all of them to come together on all the issues, one can at least expect a large number of them to have a common perception and stand on a number of subjects.

The current process of being pushed into making one-sided concessions or facing a sudden collapse at the end should be changed to engaging in a meaningful give-and-take-negotiation and insisting on receiving commensurate concession from others before finally agreeing to their own concessions. Opposition and resistance to harmful proposals is all right, but whenever a decision is taken to yield, it

should be done in a proper and planned manner, after negotiating for commensurate concessions from the beneficiaries of the proposal.

C. Preparatory process

All of this, however, needs the support of detailed analytical examination of the issues involved, as well as identification of interests. The developing countries should undertake such an examination, but their capacity is limited. They should build up and strengthen their capacity. They could sponsor such work in national universities and institutions. They should also build up a network of institutions in developing countries for this purpose. But considering their limitation of resources and capacity, it is doubtful they will be able to undertake studies and analysis on their own on a sustained basis. They need assistance.

Earlier, particularly during the Tokyo and Uruguay Rounds of MTNs, UNCTAD undertook a massive technical assistance programme to help the developing countries in the negotiations. It was supported by UNDP financing. UNCTAD is still engaged in studying the subjects and issues relating to the WTO, but its work in this area is mainly centred around the intergovernmental meetings. It also continues with a technical assistance programme in the area of international trade, but assistance in negotiations is not the prime focus at present.

Some other organizations are also engaged in assisting the developing countries. WTO itself has such a programme, which is devoted mainly to assistance in implementing the agreements. It prepares analytical papers at the request of a developing country or group of countries. Quite understandably, one cannot expect the WTO secretariat to provide a critical and analytical evaluation of the various proposals put forward, but such an evaluation is at the very core of the developing countries' preparations for trade negotiations.

The South Centre has started a pilot project with financial assistance from UNDP. It has prepared analytical papers and a discussion paper setting out the current issues in the negotiations and their implications for developing countries. It has suggested preferred alternatives for the developing countries on various issues. But its work is very limited in scope, and in its present form it is unlikely to cater fully to the needs of the developing countries.

The Commonwealth Secretariat has also been running a programme of technical assistance. It is mainly devoted to the preparation of short analytical papers at the request of individual countries or a group. Although useful, this programme is too small at present to satisfy the emerging needs.

The Third World Network, a non-governmental organization, has also undertaken technical assistance for developing countries on WTO issues over the last three or four years. It has concentrated on the topical subjects under consideration and has prepared analytical and briefing papers. It has organized seminars and workshops for an exchange of views and expertise among the developing countries, and it has assisted them in developing cooperation among themselves in the formulation of positions on important areas. It brings out a daily bulletin from Geneva with reports on the negotiations and analyses of issues by experts. This organization, however, has only a small presence in Geneva, and a strong presence in Geneva is important for assistance in the negotiation process.

None of these efforts, on its own and in its present form, can satisfy the emerging needs of the developing countries over the next few years, although each of these efforts is an important contribution in support of the developing countries. There is a need for a comprehensive assistance programme. Preferably, it could be mainly funded by the developing countries themselves, or at least a large number of them. There could be supplemental funding from other benevolent sources. This programme could be located in one of the existing organizations with the appropriate capacity and orientation or could be established as a separate unit. Even if located in an existing organization for administrative and accounting purposes, however, it should work as an independent programme and unit.

The main functions of the programme could be the following:

•   Critical and analytical examination of the current and emerging issues from the perspective of the developing countries and their implications for those countries;

•   Assisting developing countries in preparing their own proposals in various areas of the WTO;

•   Examining the proposals of others with respect to their implications for the developing coun-

tries, and assisting developing countries in preparing their responses;

•   During the intense phase of negotiations, providing quick and prompt assistance in respect of the formulation of, and responses to, the amended proposals, which normally get tabled at that stage.

Such an assistance programme would be supportive of the preparations of developing countries for trade negotiations. In fact, this programme could be constructively linked to, or made complementary with, national, regional and group efforts.

D.   *Regional and group efforts*

The effectiveness of the developing countries will be enhanced if there is better coordination among them. The exercise of coordination should start right from the stage of identification of interests and formulation of positions. Under the overall umbrella of the Informal Group of Developing Countries in the WTO there may be some smaller groups – constituted on the basis of specific issues and interests – which interact in full transparency with other Group members. There may also be burden-sharing in preparations for specific areas and exchange of information, which would avoid duplication of efforts and ensure better use of their scarce resources.

There should also be coordination, linkages and networking among research institutions and universities engaged in analysis of the issues before the WTO. There could also be arrangements for burden-sharing among such institutions. The efforts of these institutions should also be coordinated with the multilateral central assistance programme proposed above.

E.   *Change in the WTO negotiating process*

The developing countries have to endeavour to bring about changes in the negotiating process in the WTO, so that there is greater transparency and wider participation of developing countries in the negotiations. Discussions in small groups for explanations of proposals and persuasion of other countries is a natural process; but for negotiation on the texts of proposals and agreements, there must be much wider direct participation. There may be difficulties in negotiating the texts in very large groups, but a balance has to be worked out between the needs for efficiency and for full direct participation of the countries in the negotiating process. Developing countries may deliberate on this issue and make specific proposals for an improved method of negotiation in the WTO.

The WTO agreements and their operation will have a profound impact on developing economies. Hence, it is imperative that they do not remain indifferent and handicapped, but that they participate actively in the negotiations and other activities in this forum, and make themselves effective in its decision-making and operation.

UNITED NATIONS CONFERENCE ON TRADE AND DEVELOPMENT

Palais des Nations
CH-1211 GENEVE 10
Switzerland
(http://www.unctad.org)

International Monetary and Financial Issues for the 1990s

Other selected UNCTAD publications

Trade and Development Report, 1996   United Nations Publication, Sales No. E.96.II.D.6
ISBN 92-1-112399-2

Part One   Global Trends
　　I   The World Economy: Performance and Prospects
　　II   International Capital Markets and the External Debt of Developing Countries

Part Two   Rethinking Development Strategies: Some Lessons from the East Asian Experience

　　I   Integration and Industrialization in East Asia
　　II   Exports, Capital Formation and Growth
　　III   Responding to the New Global Environment

Annex   Macroeconomic Management, Financial Governance, and Development: Selected Policy Issues

Trade and Development Report, 1997   United Nations Publication, Sales No. E.97.II.D.8
ISBN 92-1-112411-5

Part One   Global Trends

　　I   The World Economy: Performance and Prospects
　　II   International Financial Markets and the External Debt of Developing Countries
　Annex   Issues Involved in Trade Disputes that Have Arisen Concerning the National Treatment Provision of the WTO Agreement

Part Two   Globalization, Distribution and Growth

　　I   The Issues at Stake
　　II   Globalization and Economic Convergence
　　III   Income Inequality and Development
　　　　Annex: Trends in Personal Income Distribution in Selected Developing Countries
　　IV   Liberalization, Integration and Distribution
　　V   Income Distribution, Capital Accumulation and Growth
　　VI   Promoting Investment: Some Lessons from East Asia

Trade and Development Report, 1998　　　　　　United Nations Publication, Sales No. E.98.II.D.6
ISBN 92-1-112427-1

Trade and Development Report, 1999　　　　　　United Nations Publication, Sales No. E.99.II.D.1
ISBN 92-1-112438-7

****

These publications may be obtained from bookstores and distributors throughout the world. Consult your bookstore or write to United Nations Publications/Sales Section, Palais des Nations, CH-1211 Geneva 10, Switzerland, fax: +41-22-917.0027, e-mail: unpubli@un.org, Internet: http://www.un.org/publications; or from United Nations Publications, Two UN Plaza, Room DC2-853, Dept. PERS, New York, N.Y. 10017, U.S.A., telephone: +1-212-963.8302 or +1-800-253.9646; fax: +1-212-963.3489, e-mail: publications@un.org.

African Development in a Comparative Perspective

In September 1996 UNCTAD launched the project *Economic Development and Regional Dynamics in Africa: Lessons from the East Asian Experience.* Building on earlier research on the role of policies in successful economic development in East Asia, the project aimed to identify development strategies for Africa to promote investment and exports, as well as to stimulate regional growth dynamics. It examined selected African development problems, including reasons for poor supply-side response to policy reforms, the lack of export diversification and difficulties in building up domestic capacity in the private and public sectors; it considered the applicability of East Asian type policies to solving these problems. The studies listed below were prepared under the project and provided the background for the International Conference on African Development in a Comparative Perspective, held in Mauritius, 24-25 September 1998:

No. 1   *Capital accumulation and agricultural surplus in sub-Saharan Africa and Asia*
Massoud KARSHENAS (School of Oriental and African Studies, University of London, UK)

No. 2   *Informal economy, wage goods and the changing patterns of accumulation under structural adjustment – Theoretical reflections based on the Tanzanian experience*
Marc WUYTS (Institute for Social Studies, The Hague, Netherlands)

No. 3   *A comparative analysis of the accumulation process and capital mobilization in Mauritius, the United Republic of Tanzania and Zimbabwe*
L. Amedee DARGA (Straconsult, Curepipe, Mauritius)

No. 4   *Africa's export structure in a comparative perspective*
Adrian WOOD and Jörg MAYER (Institute of Development Studies at the University of Sussex, UK; and Macroeconomic and Development Policies, UNCTAD, Geneva)

No. 5   *How African manufacturing industries can break into export markets with lessons from East Asia*
Samuel WANGWE (Economic and Social Research Foundation, Dar es Salaam, Tanzania)

No. 6   *Trade policy reform and supply responses in Africa*
Charles Chukwuma SOLUDO (University of Nigeria, Nsukka, Nigeria)

No. 7   *The role of policy in promoting enterprise learning during early industrialization: Lessons for African countries*
Lynn K. MYTELKA and Taffere TESFACHEW (Division on Investment, Technology and Enterprise Development, UNCTAD, Geneva)

No. 8   *Financing enterprise development and export diversification in sub-Saharan Africa*
Machiko K. NISSANKE (School of Oriental and African Studies, University of London, UK)

No. 9   *Thinking about developmental States in Africa*
Thandika MKANDAWIRE (UN Research Institute for Social Development, Geneva)

No. 10   *The relevance of East Asian institutions designed to support industrial and technological development in Southern African countries*
Martin FRANSMAN (Institute for Japanese-European Technology Studies, University of Edinburgh, Scotland)

No. 11   *Trade in the Southern African Development Community: What is the potential for increasing exports to the Republic of South Africa?*
Friedrich von KIRCHBACH and Hendrik ROELOFSEN (UNCTAD/WTO International Trade Centre, Geneva)

No. 12   *Movements of relative agricultural prices in sub-Saharan Africa*
Korkut BORATAV (University of Ankara, Turkey)

No. 13   *The impact of price policies on the supply of traditional agricultural export crops – Africa vis-à-vis the rest of the developing world*
Alberto GABRIELE (Macroeconomic and Development Policies, UNCTAD, Geneva)

UNCTAD Discussion Papers

No. 124, March 1997	Jörg MAYER	Is having a rich natural-resource endowment detrimental to export diversification?
No. 125, April 1997	Brigitte BOCOUM	The new mining legislation of Côte d'Ivoire: Some comparative features
No. 126, April 1997	Jussi LANKOSKI	Environmental effects of agricultural trade liberalization and domestic agricultural policy reforms
No. 127, May 1997	Raju Jan SINGH	Banks, growth and geography
No. 128, September 1997	Enrique COSIO-PASCAL	Debt sustainability and social and human development: The net transfer approach and a comment on the so-called "net" present value calculation for debt relief
No. 129, September 1997	Andrew J. CORNFORD	Selected features of financial sectors in Asia and their implications for services trade
No. 130, March 1998	Matti VAINIO	The effect of unclear property rights on environmental degradation and increase in poverty
No. 131, Feb./March 1998	Robert ROWTHORN & Richard KOZUL-WRIGHT	Globalization and economic convergence: An assessment
No. 132, March 1998	Martin BROWNBRIDGE	The causes of financial distress in local banks in Africa and implications for prudential policy
No. 133, March 1998	Rubens LOPES BRAGA	Expanding developing countries' exports in a global economy: The need to emulate the strategies used by transnational corporations for international business development
No. 134, April 1998	A.V. GANESAN	Strategic options available to developing countries with regard to a Multilateral Agreement on Investment
No. 135, May 1998	Jene K. KWON	The East Asian model: An explanation of rapid economic growth in the Republic of Korea and Taiwan Province of China
No. 136, June 1998	JOMO K.S. & M. ROCK	Economic diversification and primary commodity processing in the second-tier South-East Asian newly industrializing countries
No. 137, June 1998	Rajah RASIAH	The export manufacturing experience of Indonesia, Malaysia and Thailand: Lessons for Africa
No. 138, October 1998	Z. KOZUL-WRIGHT & Lloyds STANBURY	Becoming a globally competitive player: The case of the music industry in Jamaica
No. 139, December 1998	Mehdi SHAFAEDDIN	How did developed countries industrialize? The history of trade and industrial policy: The cases of Great Britain and the USA
No. 140, February 1999	M. BRANCHI, A. GABRIELE & V. SPIEZIA	Traditional agricultural exports, external dependency and domestic prices policies: African coffee exports in a comparative perspective
No. 141, May 1999	Lorenza JACHIA & Ethél TELJEUR	Free trade between South Africa and the European Union – A quantitative analysis
No. 142, October 1999	J. François OUTREVILLE	Financial development, human capital and political stability
No. 143, November 1999	Yilmaz AKYÜZ & Andrew CORNFORD	Capital flows to developing countries and the reform of the international financial system

****

Copies of the studies on *African Development in a Comparative Perspective* and *UNCTAD Discussion Papers* may be obtained from the Editorial Assistant, Macroeconomic and Development Policies Branch, GDS, UNCTAD, Palais des Nations, CH-1211 Geneva 10, Switzerland (telephone: +41-22-907.5733, fax: +41-22-907.0274, e-mail: nicole.winch@unctad.org).

The Journal of Development Studies, Vol. 34, No. 6, August 1998

Special Issue for UNCTAD on
East Asian Development: New Perspectives

****

This publication may be obtained from Frank Cass Publishers, Newbury House, 900 Eastern Avenue, Ilford, Essex IG2 7HH, UK, Tel: +44 (0)181 599 8866; Fax: +44 (0)181 599 0984; Website: http://www.frankcass.com; e-mail: sales@frankcass.com.